WELFARE REFORM IN AMERICA

WELFARE REFORM IN AMERICA

SHENHAR VENAKHI
EDITOR

Nova Science Publishers, Inc.
New York

Art Director: Maria Ester Hawrys
Assistant Director: Elenor Kallberg
Graphics: Susan A. Boriotti and Frank Grucci
Manuscript Coordinator: Phylis Gaynor
Book Production: Gavin Aghamore, Joanne Bennette,
                Michele Keller, Christine Mathosian
                and Tammy Sauter
Circulation: Iyatunde Abdullah, Cathy DeGregory and
                Annette Hellinger

Library of Congress Cataloging–in–Publication Data
available upon request

ISBN 1-56072-408-0
© *1996 Nova Science Publishers, Inc.*
   6080 Jericho Turnpike, Suite 207
   Commack, New York 11725
   Tele. 516-499-3103 Fax 516-499-3146
   E Mail Novasci1@aol.com

Printed in the United States of America

CONTENTS

STATE WELFARE INITIATIVES[*]

Jennifer A. Neisner

INTRODUCTION

The issue of welfare reform is perennial. Both States and the Federal Government have long struggled to find ways to change the program of cash aid for families with children so as to not encourage dependency, yet provide sufficient benefits for those in need. The 104th Congress is currently considering legislation that would eliminate the Aid to Families with Dependent Children (AFDC) program, replacing it with a block grant to States. The most recent effort of Congress to reform AFDC resulted in the Family Support Act of 1988. That law established the Job Opportunities and Basic Skills (JOBS) program, a new education, training, and employment program designed to help AFDC recipients "avoid long-term welfare dependence." Replacing the Work Incentive (WIN) program, JOBS extended work and training rules to mothers with children as young as 3, increased the role of education, and greatly expanded Federal matching funds for welfare-to-work activities. However, faced with mounting budget pressures and caseloads that have grown over 25% since 1989, States have not provided sufficient matching funds to receive all available Federal JOBS funds.

Established in 1935 under the Social Security Act as a cash grant program for needy children with only one parent, AFDC was originally in-

---

[*] Excerpted from *CRS Report* 94-183 EPW

tended primarily to help widows care for their children at home. It now serves primarily divorced, deserted, and never-married mothers and their children. All States, the District of Columbia, Guam, Puerto Rico, and the Virgin Islands operate an AFDC program. States administer AFDC and set its maximum benefits, which in January 1995 ranged for a three-person family (average size) from $120 per month in Mississippi to $923 per month in Alaska. Federal funds pay at least 50% of each State's benefit and administrative costs, and about 55% of total AFDC benefit costs. In May 1995, 4.8 million families received AFDC, including 9.2 million children. The average benefit per family that month was $378. All AFDC families are also eligible for Medicaid. Almost all are eligible for Food Stamps and free school lunches. Under the Family Support Act, child care is also provided to AFDC families for whom it is deemed necessary for employment or for participation in education or training activities.

During the 1992 Presidential campaign, then-candidate Clinton promised if elected, to "end welfare as we know it." Over 20 major welfare-reform related bills were introduced in the 103rd congress, including the administration's *Work and Responsibility Act.* The issue of welfare reform has been at the forefront of the 104th Congress. The House-passed *Personal Responsibility Act* (H.R. 4), derived from the House Republican Contract with America, would ban AFDC for unwed minor mothers, offer block grants to States for services to these excluded families, require recipients to work after 2 years of benefits, cap spending for AFDC and some other welfare programs, and replace major nutrition programs with a block grant. The Senate is considering several proposals, including those developed by both the Republican and Democratic leadership. Many States, however, have not waited for Congress to act. Using the current AFDC program as a "stepping-off point" and building on the reforms prompted by the Family Support Act, a number of States are experimenting with innovative approaches that seek to increase self-sufficiency and move families off welfare. The Federal Government must approve any State changes that contradict Federal law or regulations. Under section 1115(a) of the Social Security Act, the Secretary of the Department of Health and Human Services (DHHS) is permitted to waive specified Federal AFDC requirements in order to allow States to carry out experimental, pilot, or demonstration projects that the Secretary "deems likely to assist in promoting the objectives of the program." This paper gives an overview of the AFDC waivers requested and granted between Jan. 1, 1992 and Aug. 15, 1995.[1]

In his 1992 State of the Union address, President Bush encouraged States to design and test improvements to the AFDC program, and he said that an interagency review process had been established to coordinate and expedite decisions on waiver requests. The policy of the Bush Administration emphasized two criteria: the demonstration had to be cost neutral to the Federal Government and it had to include provisions for rigorous evaluation. By the end of the Bush Presidency in January 1993, 12 States had been granted waivers under the accelerated approval process: California, Georgia, Illinois, Maryland, Michigan, Minnesota, Missouri, New Jersey, Oregon, Utah, Virginia, and Wisconsin.

Early in his Administration President Clinton signaled his support of the use of waivers. In a speech to the National Governors' Association in February 1993, he stated: "We need to encourage experimentation in the States .... There are many promising initiatives right now at the State and local level, and we will work with you to encourage that kind of experimentation." In August 1992, DHHS Secretary Donna Shalala announced new policies and procedures designed to make the waiver review process both faster and simpler to give States more flexibility.[2] In a speech to the Governors in July 1995, President Clinton announced further changes to the waiver process, promising that the DHHS would cut from 120 days to 30 days the time in which it evaluates requests for waivers in

---

[1] Waivers have been granted to Arizona, Arkansas, California (3), Colorado, Connecticut, Delaware, Florida, Georgia (2), Hawaii, Illinois (2), Indiana, Iowa, Maryland (2), Massachusetts, Michigan (2), Minnesota, Mississippi, Missouri (3), Montana, Nebraska, New Jersey, New York, North Dakota, Ohio, Oklahoma (2), Oregon (2), Pennsylvania, South Carolina, South Dakota, Texas, Utah (2), Vermont, Virginia (3), West Virginia, Wisconsin (6), and Wyoming. The following States have waivers pending: California, Georgia, Hawaii, Illinois, Kansas, Maine, Mississippi, Missouri, New Hampshire, New Mexico, North Dakota, Ohio, Oregon, Pennsylvania, South Carolina, Texas, Washington, and Wisconsin. Ten States have neither applied for nor received approval for waivers since January 1992: Alabama, Alaska, District of Columbia, Idaho, Kentucky, Louisiana, Nevada, North Carolina, Rhode Island, and Tennessee.

[2] The new policy will measure cost-neutrality over the life of the demonstration, as opposed to the year-to-year time frame previously employed.

five areas. Waiver requests eligible for the fast track include those that impose: (1) tougher welfare-to-work requirements and provide child care services; (2) time limits on benefit receipt; (3) tougher child support enforcement programs; (4) requirements that minor parents to live at home and stay in school in order to receive benefits; and (5) requests to divert AFDC and Food Stamp money to subsidize private employers who hire welfare recipients. President Clinton also moved to change Federal regulations governing the Food Stamp program. Under current law, reductions in cash income, including AFDC benefits, are partially offset by an increase in Food Stamp benefits. As of Aug. 15, 1995, the Clinton Administration had approved waivers in 34 States: Arizona, Arkansas, California, Colorado, Connecticut, Delaware, Florida, Georgia, Hawaii, Illinois, Indiana, Iowa, Maryland, Massachusetts, Mississippi, Michigan, Missouri, Montana, Nebraska, New York, North Dakota, Ohio, Oklahoma, Oregon, Pennsylvania, South Carolina, South Dakota, Texas, Utah, Vermont, Virginia, West Virginia, Wisconsin, and Wyoming. Pending were 27 applications from 17 States. Twenty States had received approval to operate some or all demonstration components statewide; the remaining waivers are limited to selected geographic areas within a State (i.e., particular counties or school districts).   In both scope and breadth, the kinds of demonstration projects authorized since Jan. 1, 1992 vary widely. The use of section 1115(a) waiver authority has increased dramatically over the past 3 years. In 1992, States were likely to request waivers from only a few Federal rules. Today, ii is common for a demonstration project to require upwards of 40 waivers from Federal law. Most waivers share the goal of decreasing dependency on welfare, but they adopt different approaches toward accomplishing this goal. Some proposals seek to limit benefits, others to expand them. Some seek to reward productive behavior, others to punish dependency. Some tinker at the edges, others seek a complete overhaul. Most waivers reflect at least one of the following assumptions about AFDC: that program rules serve as a disincentive to work and therefore encourage long-term dependency; that they discourage marriage and encourage out-of-wedlock births; and that welfare dependence is a cycle of hopelessness, passed on from one generation to the next. These assumptions have received greater credence in recent years because of the growing number of families reliant on welfare and the increasing number of births to unwed teen mothers. Accordingly, waivers are being used to test changes in AFDC program terms and rules that are seen to present negative incentives. They can be grouped in three broad areas: (1) restriction benefits by such means as time limits and benefit cuts, (2) making work more rewarding, and (3) efforts to change conduct. Table 1 shows, by State, the major types of State welfare initiatives for which waivers under section 1115(a) of the Social Security Act were granted or pending as of Aug. 1, 1995. Ten waiver types are presented: Time limits -- 26 requests from 25 States, 19 approved, 7 pending; limiting benefits to "migrants" -- 5 State requests, 2 approved, 2 denied, 1 withdrawn; modifying earnings disregards -- 35 requests from 33 States, 29 approved, 7 pending; liberalizing rules for the two-parent program, AFDC for Unemployed Parents (AFDC-UP) -- 31 requests from 29 States, 25 approved, 1 withdrawn, 6 pending; limiting or ending benefits for additional children -- 17 requests from 15 States, 13 approved, 4 pending; Learnfare -- requiring regular school attendance or participation in educational activities -- 30 requests from 28 States, 26 approved, 4 pending; permitting "special" savings accounts -- 14 requests from 12 States, 12 approved, 2 pending; welfare-to-work rules -- 44 requests from 39 States, 35 approved, 9 pending; requiring unwed minor parents to live with a parent or guardian -- 10 State requests, 8 approved, 2 pending; and increasing resource and/or vehicle asset limits -- 34 requests from 33 States, 28 approved, 6 pending. The Clinton administration has denied waiver applications from 3 States: Illinois, Massachusetts, and Wyoming.

TABLE 1. State AFDC Waivers—Major Types, Jan. 1, 1992 - Aug. 15, 1995

State	Time-limits	Limit AFDC benefits for "migrants"	Modify earnings disregards	Liberalize AFDC-UP rules	Limit or end benefit increase for additional children	Learnfare	Allow "special" savings accounts	Welfare-to-work requirements (including JOBS)	Require unwed minor parents to live with parent/guardian	Increase resource/asset limits (including vehicle)
Arizona	Approved		Approved	Approved	Approved	Approved	Approved	Approved	Approved	Approved
Arkansas					Approved	Approved				Approved
California	Pending (2)	Approved	Approved(2)	Approved	Pending		Approved/Pending	Pending		Approved
Colorado	Approved		Approved			Approved		Approved		Approved
Connecticut	Approved		Approved	Approved		Approved	Approved	Approved		Approved
Delaware	Approved			Approved	Approved	Approved	Approved	Approved	Approved	Approved
Florida	Approved		Approved	Approved		Approved	Approved	Approved		Approved
Georgia	Pending		Pending	Pending	Approved			Pending(2)/Approved		Pending
Hawaii				Pending				Approved		
Illinois	Pending	Denied	Approved	Approved	Pending	Pending/Approved		Pending/Approved		
Indiana	Approved			Approved	Approved	Approved		Approved		Approved
Iowa	Approved	Withdrawn	Approved	Approved			Approved	Approved		Approved
Kansas	Pending		Pending	Pending	Pending	Pending		Pending	Pending	Pending
Maine								Pending		
Maryland	Approved		Approved	Approved	Approved	Approved(2)		Approved	Approved	Approved
Massachusetts	Approved		Approved	Approved	Approved	Approved		Approved	Approved	Approved

TABLE 1. State AFDC Waivers--Major Types, Jan. 1, 1992 - Aug. 15, 1995

State	Time-limits	Limit AFDC benefits for "migrants"	Modify earnings disregards	Liberalize AFDC-UP rules	Limit or end benefit increase for additional children	Learnfare	Allow "special" savings accounts	Welfare-to-work requirements (including JOBS)	Require unwed minor parents to live with parent/ guardian	Increase resource/ asset limits (including vehicle)
Michigan			Approved	Approved(2)				Approved		Approved
Minnesota			Approved							Approved
Mississippi			Approved	Approved	Pending	Approved	Approved	Approved		
Missouri	Approved		Approved	Approved		Approved		Approved	Approved	Approved
Montana	Approved		Approved	Approved		Approved		Approved		Approved
Nebraska	Approved		Approved	Approved	Approved	Approved		Approved		Approved
New Hampshire			Pending							
New Jersey			Approved		Approved					
New Mexico			Pending					Approved		
New York				Approved		Approved	Approved	Approved		Approved
North Dakota	Pending		Pending	Pending				Pending/ Approved		Pending
Ohio			Approved	Approved		Approved		Approved		Withdrawn/ Approved
Oklahoma	Approved		Approved	Approved		Approved		Approved		Approved
Oregon	Pending		Approved	Pending		Approved	Approved	Pending/ Approved (2)	Pending	Pending(2)/ Approved
Pennsylvania			Approved	Approved		Pending	Pending/ Approved			Approved
South Carolina	Approved		Approved	Approved		Approved		Approved		Approved

TABLE 1. State AFDC Waivers—Major Types, Jan. 1, 1992 - Aug. 15, 1995

State	Time-limits	Limit AFDC benefits for "migrants"	Modify earnings disregards	Liberalize AFDC-UP rules	Limit or end benefit increase for additional children	Learnfare	Allow "special" savings accounts	Welfare-to-work requirements (including JOBS)	Require unwed minor parents to live with parent/guardian	Increase resource/asset limits (including vehicle)
South Dakota	Approved		Approved					Approved		Approved
Texas				Withdrawn		Pending				
Utah	Approved		Approved					Approved		Approved
Vermont	Approved		Approved	Approved		Approved		Approved	Approved	Approved
Virginia	Approved		Approved		Approved	Approved (2)	Approved (2)	Approved (2)	Approved	Approved (2)
Washington	Pending		Pending	Pending						
West Virginia			Approved					Approved		
Wisconsin	Approved	Approved	Approved (2)	Approved (3)	Approved (3)	Approved	Approved	Pending/ Approved (3)	Approved	Approved
Wyoming		Denied				Approved		Approved		Approved

RESTRICTING AFDC BENEFITS

States administer AFDC, determine "need," and set actual benefit levels. Federal law does not require States to adjust their benefit levels to reflect changes in living costs. Only four jurisdictions, Alaska California, Connecticut, and the District of Columbia have provisions in State law requiring benefits to be adjusted for inflation, but none are currently in effect.[3] Federal law does, however, forbid States to reduce benefits below "payment" levels in effect on May 1, 1988, by prohibiting the Secretary of DHHS from approving a State's Medicaid plan if the State reduces its AFDC payment levels below those used on that date.[4] In 1992, California received approval from the Bush Administration to cut its AFDC below the May 1988 level. In constant dollars the maximum monthly benefit for a four-person family dropped from $852 in 1970 to $450 in 1995 in the median State, a reduction in purchasing power of 47.2%. The annual cost-of-living increase in food stamps partly offset this loss, but even so, the combined AFDC food stamp benefit fell 21% in constant dollars between 1971 and 1995. This erosion of benefits has been further exacerbated in recent years as many States *reduced* AFDC benefit levels. Although reducing real benefit levels has made welfare "less attractive," the rolls have increased over 25% in the past 6 years, growing from 3.8 million to 4.8 million families. Tight budgets have forced States to become more creative and more forceful in the means they employ to restrain welfare outlays. Among the ideas proposed, time limits, the most radical of the reforms now under discussion, and migration restrictions have received limited approval.

---

[3] California's law had been in effect since 1973 and in its last years of operation was based on a California "Necessities Index." The other State laws are more recent and require annual AFDC benefit increases, based on changes in the Consumer Price Index (CPI). Notwithstanding these statutory provisions requiring that AFDC benefits be increased annually, in recent years, all of the States have suspended the benefit increases because of budget shortfalls. California's legislature suspended the AFDC benefit increase for 1990 and 1991, reduced benefits in 1992 and 1993, and retained 1993 benefit levels in 1994 and 1995; Connecticut effectively suspended its benefit increases in 1991; the District of Columbia has increased benefits effective Oct. 1993; and Alaska suspended its automatic cost-of-living increase for FY 1994 and FY 1995 and reduced benefits to 1992 levels.

[4] This prohibition, enacted in P.L. 100-360, is found in section 1902 © of the Social Security Act.

TIME LIMITS ON AFDC RECEIPT

Time limits have become an increasingly popular ingredient of State welfare reform. 25 States have applied for waivers that in some way limit the time recipients may receive public assistance, and other States are engaged in pre-waiver discussions with DHHS. Nineteen States have received approval for variations on the time-limit theme: Arizona, Colorado, Connecticut, Delaware, Florida, Indiana, Iowa, Maryland, Massachusetts, Missouri, Montana, Nebraska, Oklahoma, South Carolina, South Dakota, Utah, Vermont, Virginia, and Wisconsin.

Almost half of the people beginning spells on AFDC leave the program, at least temporarily, within 2 years, but a large proportion have repeat spells, and those who are enrolled for many ears account for most of the program's cost. According to recent studies, fewer than one in five persons entering the system receives assistance for more than 5 *consecutive* years, but it is estimated that almost half of the current caseload has accumulated a total of at least 5 years, counting repeat spells.[5] Much attention has been focused on those with prolonged stays on AFDC. The Family Support Act requires States to spend most of their JOBS funds on target groups considered likely to become "long termers": able-bodies mothers under age 24 without a high school diploma or work history, those enrolled for 36 months (of the prior 60), and those whose youngest child is at least 16 years old (within 2 years of losing AFDC). Though it is believed that many long-term welfare recipients confront significant obstacles to employment, such as physical or mental disabilities, there is concern at both the State and Federal level about the effects of long-term receipt on the motivation of recipients and their prospects for eventual self-sufficiency. Imposing limits on the duration of cash aid, in tandem with increasing the work requirements and the education, job training, child care, and other services provided to recipients, is intended to send the message that welfare is a helping hand, not a "way of life."

---

[5] For further information, see: U.S. Library of Congress. Congressional Research Service. *Welfare: A Review of Studies About Time Spent on Welfare.* CRS Report for Congress No. 94-539 EPW, by Gene Falk. Washington, 1994; and *AFDC Reform: Why Again?.* CRS Report for Congress No. 95-63 EPW, by Vee Burke. Washington, 1995. P.3.

Time limits are among the most complex and far-reaching of changes to the present welfare system. There are three main types of time-limiting waivers: (1) those that make benefit receipt contingent upon the fulfillment of work requirements, requiring nonexempt adults who have received benefits for a specified period of time to participate in work activities and return for cash assistance; (2) those that deny cash assistance to the adult in the family after a specified period of time on the rolls; and (3) those that deny cash assistance to the *entire family* after a stipulated period of time on the rolls. Few States impose lifetime limits on the amount of time recipients may receive benefits, most States allow recipients to become eligible again after a time period. All States with provisions to deny AFDC benefits once a time limit is reached grant extensions to those who cooperate with program requirements and cannot find employment, are deemed to be unemployable, or meet other good cause criteria. Families denied cash aid retain their Food Stamp and Medicaid eligibility. A brief description of some of the approved demonstrations illustrates the myriad of questions the concept raises and the different approaches States are taking to answer them.

The Wisconsin *Work Not Welfare (WNW)* demonstration, approved in November 1993, has received the most attention of the time-limiting waiver applications. Since Jan. 1, 1995 in two pilot counties, WNW has "cashed-out" AFDC and Food Stamp benefits into one consolidated grant, which may be received for up to 24 months within a 4-year period. Participants may receive transitional child care and medical services for up to 12 months, but no cash benefits will be available for 36 months after the last WNW payment is made. After the first month of eligibility, the WNW grant is considered "payment" for activities clients performed the previous month. Clients without a high school diploma re referred to a General Education Development (GED) program. Education and training will commonly occur within the first 12 months of eligibility. For those required to work, hours are determined by dividing the grant by the Federal minimum wage, not to exceed 40 hours per week. Work experience may include unsubsidized or partially subsidized employment, the Community Work Experience Program (CWEP), or an "Independence Job," one developed by the county specifically for WNW participants. DHHS made approval of the waiver contingent upon delineation of several categories of persons to be exempted from participation and upon extension of eligibility in very limited circumstances for certain persons not "self-sufficient" after 24 months of receipt.

The *Colorado Personal Responsibility and Employment Program (CPREP)* is similar to the *Work not Welfare* demonstration in consolidating AFDC, Food Stamp, and child care benefits into a single package and establishing a 2-year time limitation on eligibility for benefits. There are, however, major differences between the two programs. Under CPREP, able-bodied adults (with certain exceptions) are required after 2 years of eligibility to be employed (at least 30 hours per week) and/or participate in training or education under the JOBS program. As is true under current law, failure to actively participate causes a reduction in the AFDC benefit (by removing the adult's share of the grant). However, no sanction will be applied to the family's grant if the adult is unemployed and the State has not provided opportunity to participate in the JOBS activities. A financial incentive of up to $500 is offered to JOBS participants who graduate from high school or obtain a GED. The State has enlisted the support of private sector employers to provide career counseling, on-the-job training opportunities, and employer-sponsored higher education.

Iowa's *Family Investment Program (IFIP)* takes a slightly different tack. IFIP requires eligible adults (with certain exceptions) to enter into a "Family Investment Agreement" (FIA), outlining activities and time frames during which the client is expected to become 'self-sufficient," and after which AFDC will be ended. The outline specifies JOBS program activities for IFIP, including vocational assessment, employability planning, parenting skills training, job search, work experience, and basic education activities such as high school completion, GED, and English as a Second Language (ESL). Under the plan, if a client demonstrates "effort and satisfactory progress" but is unable to achieve self-sufficiency within the stipulated time frame, the period is extended. If the client refuses to participate in FIA activities, benefits are phased out over a 6 month period and the client is ineligible to reapply for benefits for 6 months. Transitional child care services are available for up to 24 months.

Florida's *Family Transition Program (FTP),* approved in late January 1994, limits benefit receipt in two pilot counties to 24 months in any 60-month period, guaranteeing a minimum-wage job in either the private or public sector for recipients unable to find work at the end of 24 months. Exemptions are allowed for parents who are disabled, or caring for a disabled or very young child (aged 6 months old or less). Long-term recipients may be given up to 36 months of benefits. In conjunction with the State, FTP participants are required to develop an "FTP plan" specifying the services that will be provided to and the activities that are expected of the participant. The include: vocational assessment, job search, parenting skills training, work experience, and basic education activities such as high school completion, GED, and ESL. Participants are also eligible for up to 24 months of transitional child care and 12 months of Medicaid. For those completing their FTP plans unable to find employment at the end of the time limit or becoming unemployed after losing eligibility for benefits, the State, in partnership with businesses in the pilot counties, has designed a "transitional employment program" to provide private sector employment. Incentive payments of up to 70% of the recipient's current AFDC benefits for up to 1 year are offered to private employers who hire hard-to-place AFDC recipients. If private sector employment is insufficient to meet the needs of the program, the State will provide public sector opportunities. Failure to participate results in a benefit reduction (by removing the caretaker's share of the grant). The family's full AFDC benefit is ended only if it is determined that this will not cause the child to require emergency shelter or placement in foster care.

Vermont's *Family Independence Program (FIP)* requires nonexempt parents in AFDC and AFDC-UP families to be employed or participate in subsidized community service jobs beginning after the 30th month of receiving AFDC (after the 15th month of receipt for AFDC-UP families). Benefits are replaced by "wages," based on the parent's completion of his/her work requirement. Hours of required work are generally: for AFDC families with children under age 13, the lesser of 20 hours per week or the hours equal to the family's grant amount divided by Vermont's minimum wage; and, for AFDC families with children over 13 years, the lesser of 40 hours per week or the hours equal to the family's grant amount divided by

Vermont's minimum wage. Before beginning community service jobs, nonexempt parents must engage in a minimum of 8 weeks of job search activities. If the eligible parent refuses to participate in FIP, the family's benefit is severely reduced and no longer paid directly to it. Instead, the family's reduced benefits are paid directly to their landlords or to utility companies. Incentive payments are offered to parents who successfully complete parenting education and other approved activities.

MIGRATION RESTRICTIONS

Operating on the assumption that higher welfare benefits induce recipients to move from "low-benefit" to "high-benefit" States, six States, have applied for waivers allowing them to limit the AFDC benefit level of "new arrivals" to the lesser of (1) their own level, or (2) that of the State from which the new arrivals moved. A State AFDC provision rendering families ineligible for assistance until they had resided in the State for a year was ruled unconstitutional by the Supreme Court; the migration restrictions raise similar questions. California and Wisconsin received waiver approval from the Bush Administration, but the Clinton Administration denied similar proposals in Illinois and Wyoming, and Iowa withdrew the migration restriction component of its Family Investment Program (FTP), approved August 1993. The California proposal, the *Welfare Reform Demonstration Project,* was ultimately rejected by voters in a 1992 State referendum and supplanted by the *California Assistance Payments Demonstration Project (APDP),* an initiative that did not include the migration restriction.

MAKING WORK MORE REWARDING

Full-time work at the Federal minimum wage ($4.25 per hour) results in annual gross wages of $8,840. Even after addition of the Earned Income Tax Credit ($1,511 in 1993, $2,528 in 1994, $2,644 in 1995) the cash income of a mother working year round at the minimum wage would be below the 1995 poverty guidelines for a family of three as calculated by the DHHS, $12,590. Food Stamps would increase her purchasing power, but she would have to pay work expenses and would have little time to nurture her children. On the other hand, if she did not work and lived in a high-benefit State such as Connecticut, the mother would be eligible for $8,160 in AFDC benefits and $2,508 in Food Stamp benefits, for combined benefits of $10,668. Further, the family would automatically qualify for Medicaid. In cash and in-kind aid, her family would be better off on welfare than if she worked, and she would be available to give full-time care to her children. From 1967 to 1981 AFDC law provided financial incentives to encourage work. In 1979, the share of AFDC mothers who reported that they worked at paid jobs was 14.1%. By 1990, that number had fallen to 7%. In part this drop may be attributable to the 1981 repeal of a permanent work bonus for AFDC recipients.

MODIFICATION OF EARNINGS DISREGARDS

Federal law requires that all income received by AFDC recipients, with certain exceptions, be counted against their AFDC grant, resulting in a dollar for dollar reduction in benefits. Before the 1981 Omnibus Budget Reconciliation Act (OBRA), Federal law required a work bonus deduction of $30 of monthly earnings plus one-third of the remainder, in addition to deductions for child care and work expenses. The 1981 OBRA amendments limited the time the work bonus deduction could be applied to 4 months and restricted the amount that could be deducted for child care and work expenses (previously, all "reasonable" work expenses were deducted to assure no loss in net earnings). The Family Support Act of 1988 further modified these disregards. Under current rules, deductions for earned income are limited to a monthly disregard of $30 and one-third of remaining earnings for 4 months, a work expense disregard of $90 per month, and up to $175 per month per child (or up to $200 per month for a child under age 2) for child care expenses. After the first 4 months, the standard monthly deduction is $120 ($30 plus $90); after 1 year, it falls to $90. In effect, after 4 months on the rolls, any work effort is "taxed" at a rate of virtually 100% (that is, an extra net $1 of wages causes a cut of $1 in AFDC benefits).

To counter this and other work disincentives, States have sought waivers to do the following: liberalize the treatment of earnings, increase the resource and vehicle asset limits, allow recipients to open special savings accounts for specified purposes, and alter the rules for receipt of AFDC-UP. Waivers have been granted to 27 States allowing them to treat earned income more liberally. These include increasing the initial $30 deduction, adjusting the percentage of remaining earnings recipients are permitted to keep, and in many States, lifting the time limit on these deductions. These modifications allow recipients to keep more of their earned income without a concomitant reduction in benefits. This "make work pay" approach is designed to increase employment rates among AFDC families as well as reduce the poverty of working poor families.

RESOURCE AND ASSET LIMITS

In addition to placing limits on gross income and earnings of AFDC families, Federal law (P.L. 97-35) restricts the resources a family may accumulate to $1,000, excluding the value of a home and one automobile (States may set a lesser amount). Federal regulation limits the value of the car to $1,500. Established in 1981 and 1977, respectively, the total resource rule and the vehicle asset rule have not been increased to allow for inflation, and currently, they effectively deny AFDC eligibility to those with modest savings or cars worth more than the limit. Several States, including Arizona, Hawaii, Maine, Tennessee, and Virginia, have sought to overturn the vehicle asset limit in court, arguing that it impedes recipients' ability to find jobs and leave welfare, particularly in rural areas without mass transportation. Arizona, California, Colorado, Connecticut, Delaware, Florida, Indiana, Iowa, Maryland, Massachusetts, Michigan, Minnesota, Missouri, Montana, Nebraska, New York, Ohio, Oklahoma, Oregon, Pennsylvania, South Carolina, South Dakota, Utah, Vermont, Virginia, Wisconsin, and Wyoming have received waivers allowing them to increase the resource and/or vehicle asset limit. Additionally, as part of integrated efforts to increase self-sufficiency, Arizona, California, Connecticut, Delaware, Iowa, Mississippi, New York, Oregon, Pennsylvania, Virginia, and Wisconsin have received waivers that permit recipients to open "special resource accounts" to accumulate money for specified purposes, such as education and housing.

AFDC-UP RULES

The family Support Act requires all States to offer AFDC benefits to two-parent families needy because of unemployment of the "principal earner" (AFDC-UP). AFDC-UP eligibility is contingent upon the unemployed parent's having a history of work and it is limited by several rules. The "100-hour" rule denies benefits to families whose principal wage earner is employed for *more than* 99 hours per month, regardless of wage paid or family size. To demonstrate a "connection to the workforce" the unemployed parent must either have earned at least $50 in 6 or more of 14 calendar-quarters ending within a year of the application for benefits or have received or been eligible to receive unemployment benefits in the prior year.[6] Modifications to AFDC-UP rules are among the most common waiver requests. Under current law, these rules discourage work effort and are also seen as a potential "marriage penalty." A large family with a principal earner working at minimum wage for 100 hours per month (above the limit) would earn only $425 before taxes ($578 with the Earned Income Tax Credit (EITC); below the amount the family would receive in AFDC in many States if not working.[7] Additionally, many teen parents are unable to fulfill the labor force attachment requirement. By eliminating the 100-hour and work history rules, States hope to increase employment rates among two-parent families and remove a financial disincentive for marriage. Approval for waivers of UP rules has been granted to 22 States (Arizona, California, Connecticut, Delaware, Florida, Illinois, Indiana, Iowa, Maryland, Massachusetts, Michigan, Mississippi, Missouri, Montana, Nebraska, New York, Ohio, Oklahoma, Pennsylvania, South Carolina, Vermont, and Wisconsin), and is pending in 6 Georgia, Hawaii, Kansas, North Dakota, Oregon, Washington, and Wisconsin).

---

[6] Full-time attendance of elementary or secondary school, vocational or technical training, or JTPA training and education may, at State option, be credited for up to 4 calendar quarters under Section 407 (b) (1) (A) (iii) (I) of the Social Security Act.

[7] For further information, see: U. S. Library of Congress. Congressional Research Service. *The Earned Income Tax Credit: A Growing Form of Aid to Low-Income Workers.* CRS Report for Congress No. 95-542 EPW, by James R. Storey. Washington, 1995.

PERSONAL RESPONSIBILITY

A major aim of State reform efforts is to change the perception of welfare from an entitlement program requiring no effort to a reciprocal obligation between recipients and the State. Fiscal incentives and penalties are used to influence conduct and promote personal responsibility. With the goal of promoting self-sufficiency and moving families off welfare, waivers are used to encourage AFDC recipients to attend school, participate in job training, seek appropriate preventive health care, and avoid having additional children.

LEARNFARE

The JOBS component of the Family Support Act requires teen parents age 16 to 19 who have dropped out of school to attend school or participate in another education/employment activity if the program is operating and State resources permit. Teen parents under age 16 as well as those with children under 3 years are exempt from JOBS requirements.

Waivers have been used to expand the education component of JOBS. Collectively known as *Learnfare*, these waivers attempt to tie a family's AFDC benefit to school attendance. AFDC parents and/or children may be required to fulfill specified attendance requirements. Some States provide bonuses to encourage participation. All reduce the family's grant for failure to comply. Learnfare waivers differ from current JOBS law by (often) targeting parents under age 15, removing parental exemptions based on children's age, and focusing on both school drop-outs and current enrollees. An evaluation of Ohio's *Learning, Earning, and Parenting (LEAP)* program shows small but statistically significant increases in school retention (the number of teens remaining in school), school return (the number returning after dropping out), and in school attendance rates of participants, but it is not clear what impact these gains may have on future employment rates of welfare receipt. Learnfare waivers have been approved in 24 States: Arizona, Arkansas, California, Colorado, Connecticut, Delaware, Florida, Illinois, Indiana, Maryland, Massachusetts, Mississippi, Missouri, Montana, Nebraska, New York, Ohio, Oklahoma, Oregon, South

Carolina, Vermont, Virginia, Wisconsin, and Wyoming and are pending in four other States: Illinois, Kansas, Pennsylvania, and Texas.

WELFARE-TO-WORK REQUIREMENTS

The Family Support Act greatly expanded the work effort required of AFDC recipients. Since Oct. 1, 1990, States have been required (to the extent resources are available) to require *nonexempt* recipients of AFDC to participate in education, work, and training activities under the JOBS program. Exempt individuals include the ill, incapacitated, and aged; those caring for an incapacitated family member; the caretaker of a child under age 3 (or less than age 3 but over 1 year at State option); those employed 30 hours a week or more; children under age 16 or between the ages of 16 and 18 (19 at State option) attending school full time; and those living in an area where the program is not yet available. Under JOBS, AFDC recipients with children under age 13 cannot be compelled to enroll in JOBS unless child care is "guaranteed." In FY1995, 20% of all persons *not exempt* from participation in the JOBS program must actually be JOBS program must actually be JOBS participants (up from 15% in FY1994). Additionally, the law imposes special JOBS participation requirements on AFDC-UP families. (Fifty percent must be in a work program in FY1995).

Thirty-one States have applied for and received Federal waivers that allow them to require JOBS participation by some of the persons exempted by Federal law and/or to require recipients to participate in work and education activities beyond the scope of the JOBS program. These waivers include: requiring minor parents under the age of 16 to participate in JOBS activities; designating AFDC recipients between the ages of 14 and 20 as mandatory JOBS participants; offering unemployed noncustodial fathers JOBS program services or requiring their participation; lengthening the required job search period in the JOBS program; using AFDC funds to supplement wages for those employed under certain types of programs; requiring recipients with children aged 1 to 6 to participate full-time (ore than 20 hours per week) in JOBS; eliminating all present JOBS exemptions; increasing the sanction imposed on recipients refusing to participate in JOBS or other work programs; and developing commitments with public and private sector employers to secure employment for program participants.

PREVENTIVE HEALTH PRACTICES

Although Federal AFDC rules do not condition AFDC receipt upon the practice of any specific health behaviors by AFDC family members, several States have sought to tie payment levels to prescribed health practices. Waivers have been granted to Colorado, Delaware, Florida, Georgia, Indiana, Maryland, Michigan, Mississippi, Montana, South Carolina, Texas, and Virginia mandating immunization of preschool children. Maryland also requires AFDC children to receive annual health check-ups and for pregnant women to receive prenatal care. Failure to comply results in a reduction of benefits.

FAMILY CAP[8]

All States are required by Federal law to take account of family size as an element of need in setting benefit levels. States may decide to freeze the maximum level at a particular family size (eight States currently have such ceilings), but generally, families of the same size are required to be treated equally.[9] The average AFDC family now has 1.9 children, and States are exploring ways of discouraging recipients from bearing another child. Arizona, Arkansas, Delaware, Georgia, Indiana, Maryland, Massachusetts, Nebraska, New Jersey, Virginia, and Wisconsin have received waivers permitting them to "freeze" the size of family on which the AFDC grant is

---

[8] For family cap legislative proposals and legal issues, see: U.S. Library of Congress. Congressional Research Service. *Welfare Reform: The Family Cap.* CRS Report for Congress No. 95-503 EPW, by Carmen D. Solomon. Washington, 1995.

[9] As of Jan. 1, 1995, the following States have maximum benefit ceilings: Arkansas, a maximum benefit of $475 to families of 9 or more; California, a maximum benefit of $1,286 to families ofd 10 or more; Georgia, a maximum benefit of $568 to families of 11 or more; Kentucky, a maximum benefit of $419 to families of 7 or more; Oklahoma, a maximum benefit of $723 to families of 9 ore more; Virginia, a maximum benefit of $518 falling between family size of 5 and 6; Washington, a maximum benefit of $1,075 to families of 8 or more; and West Virginia, a maximum benefit of $477 to families of 8 or more.

based to its initial number of children. The needs of any child born, or in certain cases conceived, after this point, are reduced or not considered when determining the family's grant amount. This fiscal disincentive is intended to discourage AFDC mothers from having additional children they cannot support. The *Family Cap* concept has peen proposed and rejected and in many State legislatures over the past 3 years. Waivers are pending in California, Illinois, Kansas, and Mississippi.

OTHER

Other State proposals requiring Federal Waivers include: simplifying the welfare system by "cashing -out" a family's AFDC, Food Stamp, child care, and other benefits into one consolidated benefits package; providing transitional child care and Medicaid, currently available up to 12 months, for up to 24 months; disbursing all current child support payments received on behalf of an AFDC child directly to the family and counting payments in excess of the $50 pass-through as income when calculating benefits; and requiring pregnant or parenting minors to live with their parents or guardians in order to receive AFDC benefits. The last measure, included in House-passed *Personal Responsibility Act*, is designed to eliminate a possible incentive for children under age 18 to become pregnant and move out of their parents' home by depriving them of the resources to establish their own households, and has been included in 10 waiver requests.[10]

Table 2 summarizes the State waivers applied for and granted from Jan. 1, 1992 through Aug. 15, 1995.

---

[10] Section 402(a)(43)(A)(I) of the Social Security Act gives States the option to require an unwed minor with a dependent child (or who is pregnant and is eligible for AFDC under the State plan) to "reside in a place of residence maintained by a parent, legal guardian, or other adult relative ... or reside in a foster home, maternity home, or other adult-supervised supportive living arrangement" in order to receive AFDC. Thus, this component of AFDC law does not require a waiver to be enacted. However, waiver requests from Kansas, Maryland, Massachusetts include this element, and it was a component of approved waiver packages in Arizona, Delaware, Missouri, Vermont, and Virginia.

State AFDC Waivers: Summary of Provisions and August 15, 1995 Status

State/Project	Waiver description	Status
Arizona: Employing and Moving People Off Welfare and Encouraging Responsibility (EMPOWER)	*A statewide component that will:* Eliminate incremental AFDC benefit increases for additional children born more than 10 months after family begins receiving AFDC, but increase the family's earned income disregard by the amount of the withheld benefit; require unwed minor parents to live in an adult-supervised setting: require minor parents and pregnant teens under 16 to attend school; eliminate the 100-hour rule for AFDC-UP families; limit benefits to adults to 24 months in any 60 month period and increase the family's earned income disregard by the amount of the reduced benefit; allow recipients to save up to $12,000 for education/training purposes in Individual Development Accounts (IDAs), of which $9,000 would be disregarded from the resource limit; disregard all interest and 50% of earned income IDA deposits (up to a $200 per month maximum) when determining eligibility and benefits; provide transitional child care and medical assistance for 24 months; impose sanctions for failure to comply with JOBS program requirements.

A one county Full Employment Demonstration Project that will: provide selected JOBS participants with 9 to 12 month private or public On-the-Job training that pays at least the Federal minimum wage (wages will be paid by cashing out and diverting AFDC and Food Stamp benefits to employers); provide monthly supplemental payments to offset any loss in income; require employers to provide mentoring; after 9 months of work provide participants with up to 8 hours of paid time per week to engage in job search; impose sanctions of up to 50% of the family's AFDC grant for unjustified failure to comply with program requirements; disburse all current child support payments directly to the AFDC family and count payments in excess of $50 pass-through as income in calculating benefit. | Application received Aug. 4, 1994. Approved May 23, 1995. Proposed implementation statewide and in selected counties by the end of September 1995. |
| **Arkansas:** Reduction in AFDC Birthrates Project | Two-tiered project: eliminate AFDC benefit increases for additional children born into families already receiving AFDC; provide family planning counseling to teens age 13 to 17; require minor parents under age 16 to participate in the New Hope component of the State JOBS program. | Application received Jan. 14, 1993. Approved Apr. 5, 1994. Implemented statewide in all but 10 counties July 1994. |

State/Project	Waiver description	Status
California: Welfare Reform Demonstration Project	Reduce AFDC payments by 10 percent to all households, by 15% to households headed by nondisabled adults after 6-month transition period; apply the $30 and one-third earned income disregard permanently; eliminate the 100-hour rule for AFDC-UP families; eliminate benefit increase for children conceived after family begins receiving AFDC; require minor AFDC parents to live under adult supervision to be eligible for benefits; provide payment incentive of $50 per month or reduce grant by $50 per month based on school attendance of pregnant or parenting teens on AFDC.	Application received May 20, 1992. Approved July 14, 1992, subject to voter referendum. Referendum failed in November 1992 and waiver request was supplanted by the *Assistance Payments Demonstration Project*, below.
California: Assistance Payments Demonstration Project (APDP)	Reduce benefits levels for all households to 1.3% below May 1988 amounts; limit, for 12 months, grant level of new arrivals to level of State from which they moved if it is lower than California's; apply the $30 and one-third earned income disregard indefinitely; eliminate 100-hour rule for AFDC-UP recipient families.	Application received Sept. 17, 1992. Approved Oct. 29, 1992. Implemented statewide Dec. 1992.
California: California Work Pays Demonstration Project	Implement Cal. Learn, a Learnfare program providing fiscal bonuses and sanctions tied to school attendance and graduation for pregnant and parenting teens; increase resource limit to $2,000; increase vehicle asset limit to $4,500; allow savings up to $5,000 in restricted accounts; create an "Alternative Assistance Program" (CAAP) allowing AFDC applicants and recipients with earned income to choose Medicaid and Child Care Assistance in lieu of a cash grant; streamline eligibility determinations for AFDC and Food Stamps by making eligibility requirements compatible between the two programs.	Application received Sept. 29, 1993. Provisions would be added as amendments to *Assistance Payments Demonstration Project (APDP)*. Approved Mar. 1, 1994. Implemented April 1994.
California: Amendments to the California Work Pays Demonstration Project	Reduce maximum assistance payment (MAP) by 10%; reduce (with certain exemptions) MAP rate by an additional 15% for families with an able-bodied adult who have received AFDC benefits for 6 months; exclude the needs of able-bodied adults who have received AFDC benefits for 24-cumulative months from consideration when determining benefit levels (with certain exemptions); eliminate benefit increases for additional children conceived or born into families already receiving AFDC. Families reapplying for assistance after not receiving AFDC benefits for 24 consecutive months not subject to 6- and 24-month benefit reduction provisions.	Application received Mar. 11, 1994. **Decision pending.**

State/Project	Waiver description	Status
California: Assistance Payments Demonstration Project (APDP) -- Renewed Waiver	Exempt households containing AFDC-eligible children in which the parent receives Supplemental Security Income/State Supplementary Payments (SSI/SSP) or AFDC-eligible children who are living with unaided, non-parent caretaker relative from the State's benefit cuts (benefits will be based on grant levels in effect on Aug. 1, 1992).	Application received Aug. 26, 1994. Decision **pending.**
California: AFDC/Food Stamp Compatibility Project	Statewide, test methods for determining AFDC and Food Stamp eligibility that are designed to simplify the eligibility process and reduce errors by aligning the rules of the two programs. These include: a standard 40% self-employment deduction for the cost of doing business; a maximum $100 exclusion per calendar quarter per household for nonrecurring gifts and irregular/infrequent income; exempting undergraduate student assistance and work study income not already excluded by federal laws if the payments are based on need; establishing categorical eligibility for Food Stamp households in which all members are determined eligible for AFDC Immediate Needs benefits.	Application received May 20, 1994. Approved Apr. 11, 1995. Proposed implementation statewide by end of April 1996.
California: School Attendance Demonstration Project	Require AFDC recipients ages 16 to 18 in San Diego County to attend school or participate in the State's JOBS program.	Application received Dec. 5, 1994. Decision **pending.**
California: Incentive to Self-Sufficiency Demonstration	Statewide, require mandatory JOBS participants who have received AFDC for 22 of the previous 24 months, failed to comply with JOBS without good cause, completed or had an opportunity to complete post-assessment education and training, but are working less than 15 hours per week two years after their JOBS assessment, to become employed a minimum of 100 hours per month by participating in CWEP; provide Transitional Child Care and Medicaid to families who become ineligible due to an increase in earnings, or because of marriage or reconciliation; increase sanctions for fraud.	Application received Dec. 28, 1994. Decision **pending.**

State/Project	Waiver description	Status
Colorado: Colorado Personal Responsibility and Employment Program (CPREP)	Establish a 2-year limitation for AFDC eligibility for employable recipients, if not employed or in training, with JOBS exemptions; "cash out" AFDC, Food Stamps, and child care benefits into a consolidated benefits package; increase earned income disregard to $120 and 58% of the remainder; increase the resource limit to $5,000 for families with a recipient who is employed or has been employed in previous 6 months ($2,000 for others); exempt value of one car from countable resources; provide financial incentives for recipients who graduate from high school or receive GED; require immunization of children under 24 months or reduce AFDC benefits for failure to comply.	Application received June 30, 1993. Approved Jan. 12, 1994. Implemented in selected counties June 1994.
Connecticut: A Fair Chance	A *statewide component* that will: allow children to receive assistance even if they are living with both parents; exclude from consideration children in the filing unit who have other support; increase the asset limit to $3,000; exempt the value of one car from countable resources; change earnings disregards to 33% of gross earnings indefinitely; disburse all current child support payments directly to the AFDC family and count payments in excess of $100 as income; eliminate 100-hour rule and work history requirements for receipt of AFDC-UP; deduct Unemployment Compensation from State's Need Standard rather than Payment Standard; provide savings bonds or other incentives to students for excellence in grades or attendance; disregard such awards from consideration for AFDC and Food Stamps; exclude assets specifically designated for future educational purposes for dependent children; extend transitional child care benefits until family's income is above 75% of State median income; for nonexempt households with weekly earned income equal to at least $85 (20 hours at the Federal minimum wage), sanction benefits for terminating employment without good cause; extend transitional Medicaid benefits to 2 years; modify JOBS program provisions; eliminate the 185% of need test. In addition to changes cited above, *in selected geographic areas*: after 2 years on assistance base AFDC eligibility for nonexempt families on participation in approved work activities; base required hours of work activity on length of time on assistance rather than benefit amount; establish a child support assurance program and allow eligible families to receive the payment for 3 years following the discontinuance of AFDC benefits; eliminate certain JOBS exemptions.	Application received Dec. 30, 1993. Approved Aug. 29, 1994. Implemented statewide and in selected counties September 1994.

State/Project	Waiver description	Status
Delaware: A Better Chance	A two-part demonstration to be implemented statewide. The Welfare Reform Project (WRP) will: require compliance with Contract of Mutual Responsibility, limit cash benefits for households headed by employable adults age 19 over to 24 cumulative months; family eligible for additional 2 years of benefits if participating in State's pay-for-performance workfare program or if adult is working and family income below 75% of the Federal poverty level; time limit disregarded when State unemployment rate exceeds national average or is greater than 7.5%; provide non-time-limited Children's Program benefits to non-employable cases; require participation in self-sufficiency activities such as parenting classes, obtaining appropriate immunizations, and regular school attendance; require minor parents to live in adult-supervised setting (disregard adult's income up to 200% of poverty); eliminate incremental benefit increases for additional children born into families already receiving AFDC; eliminate 100-hour rule and work history requirements for receipt of AFDC-UP; increase vehicle asset limit to $4,500 for AFDC and Food Stamp eligibility; use fill-the-gap budgeting for recipient families; deduct Unemployment Compensation from State's Need Standard rather than Payment Standard; allow savings of up to $5,000 in Educational and Business Investment Accounts ; provide one-time $50 bonus to teens who graduate from high school by age 19; provide transitional child care and Medicaid for 24 months; fiscal sanctions and penalties for non-compliance.	Application received Jan. 30, 1995. Approved May 8, 1995. Proposed implementation on a phased-in basis statewide October 1995.
Florida: Family Transition Program (FTP)	With some exceptions, restrict receipt of AFDC benefits to 24 months in any 60-month period; increase earned income disregard to $200 and one-half of the remainder indefinitely; eliminate the 100-hour rule and work history requirements for AFDC-UP; increase transitional Medicaid and child care benefits; increase asset limit to $5,000 plus the value of one vehicle up to $8,500 used primarily for self-sufficiency; disregard income of stepparent for first 6 months of benefit receipt; require school conferences, regular school attendance, and immunizations; disregard income earned for summer work by teenager or teen parent enrolled in school; lower age of child for JOBS exemption to 6 months; allow noncustodial parents to participate in JOBS employment and training activities; establish a "bootstrap training program" to continue JOBS education and training services for those who lose AFDC benefits; design, in conjunction with businesses, a transitional employment program to provide private sector employment opportunities for program participants unable to find employment at end of AFDC benefit time limit (State will provide public sector employment opportunities if private sector employment is insufficient to meet needs of the program).	Application received Sept. 1, 1993. Approved Jan. 25, 1994. Implemented in selected counties February 1994.
Georgia: Preschool Immunization Project (PIP)	Require immunization of preschool children or reduce AFDC benefits for failure to comply.	Application received Nov. 3, 1992. Approved Nov. 17, 1992. Implemented statewide November 1993.

State/Project	Waiver description	Status
Georgia: Personal Accountability and Responsibility Project (PAR)	Provide family planning advice and parenting skills training for new AFDC parents; eliminate benefit increase for additional children born to families who have received AFDC benefits for 24 months; require all able-bodied, nonexempt AFDC recipients not caring for children under age 14 to accept full-time employment if offered, reduce benefits if offer is refused or employment ended without good cause; provide additional job search assistance; adopt fill-the-gap budgeting.	Application received May 18, 1993. Approved Nov. 1, 1993. Implemented statewide January 1994.
Georgia: Work for Welfare (WFW) Project	*Statewide:* Increase the vehicle asset limit to $4,500, adjusted annually based on the new car component of the Consumer Price Index; disregard earned income of children up to age 19 who are full-time students when determining 185 percent of need. *In 10 volunteer pilot counties:* Require every nonexempt recipient and non-supporting parent to work up to 20 hours per month in a State, local, government, Federal agency or nonprofit organization; require job search of participants for whom job placements are unavailable; increase sanctions for non-compliance.	Application received July 6, 1994. **Decision pending.**
Georgia: JOBS First Program	In ten pilot counties, eliminate 100 hour-rule for receipt of AFDC-UP; replace AFDC payment with paid employment; extend transitional Medicaid to 24 months.	Application received July 5, 1995. **Decision pending.**
Hawaii: Creating Work Opportunities for JOBS Families	Place individuals on waiting lists on JOBS services into temporary employment.	Application received Nov. 1, 1993. Approved June 24, 1994. Implemented in Oahu January 1995.
Hawaii: Families Are Better Tomorrow	Eliminate the 100-hour rule and work history requirements for receipt of AFDC-UP; redefine eligibility for intact families to include those in which one parent is employed less than 40 hours per week (if all other requirements are met); implement JOBS Works to place individuals on waiting lists for JOBS services into temporary employment.	Application received May 18, 1995. **Decision pending.**
Illinois: Fresh Start Initiative (originally entitled Multi-Pronged Welfare Reform Demonstration)	A demonstration consisting of five parts designed to contribute to eventual self-sufficiency, these waivers allow the State to: require AFDC recipients age 14 to 20 to participate in JOBS; eliminate the 100-hour rule and work history requirement for receipt of AFDC-UP; provide extensive support services to homeless AFDC families, including extended child care benefits and additional earned income allowances; offer noncustodial fathers JOBS program services and additional support services to increase their emotional and financial support of their AFDC recipient children.	Application received Oct. 7, 1992. Approved Jan. 15, 1993, then tabled by the State. The Work Pays Project (application received Aug. 2, 1993) is now part of the revised demonstration retitled *Project Fresh Start*. **Approved** Nov. 23, 1993. Implemented in selected counties (varies by project) November 1993.
Work Pays Project	Change earnings disregards and increase gross income test for both applicants and recipients.	

State/Project	Waiver description	Status
Illinois: One Step at a Time and Relocation to Illinois	Require recipients with children under the age of 3 to participate in a mandatory employment transition program for long-term recipient families; limit, for 12 months, the grant level of new arrivals to the level of the State from which they moved if it is lower than Illinois'.	Application received Oct. 7, 1992. *Relocation to Illinois* component denied Aug. 3, 1993; *One Step at a Time* component **withdrawn.**
Illinois: Six Month Paternity Establishment Demonstration	In 20 counties, require the establishment of paternity, unless good cause exists, within 6 months of application or redetermination as a condition of AFDC and Medicaid eligibility for both mother and child; when custodial parent has not cooperated in establishing paternity. deny Medicaid to children age 7 and under, exclude children from filing rules, and exempt Department from making protective payments to eligible children.	Application received July 18, 1995. **Decision pending.**
Illinois: School Attendance Demonstration	Statewide, require elementary school age AFDC children to comply with plan for regular school attendance; sanctions for poor attendance include the establishment a protective payee, progressing to the removal of the caretaker's portion of the AFDC grant.	Application received July 18, 1995. **Decision pending.**
Illinois: Work and Responsibility Demonstration	A six component demonstration, five of which will be implemented statewide, that will: require all applicants and recipients to complete a self-sufficiency plan as a condition of eligibility; limit receipt of AFDC benefits to a total of 24 months for households who have no earned income and whose youngest child is at least 13 years of age; any month with income due to employment will not be counted toward the 24 month time limit; require job ready applicants whose children are between 5 and 12 to participate in job search for up to 6 months; eliminate incremental benefit increase for children born to families already receiving AFDC; eliminate exemptions for JOBS volunteers; limit participation in basic education or GED programs to 2 years unless the individual is working or participating in an approved work activity.	Application received July 18, 1995. **Decision pending.**

State/Project	Waiver description	Status
Indiana: Indiana Manpower Placement and Comprehensive Training Program (IMPACT)	Condition program eligibility on the development of a personal responsibility agreement and self-sufficiency plan; limit taking into account the needs of job-ready adults on the placement track to 24 months; eliminate incremental benefit increases for additional children; eliminate the 100-hour rule for AFDC-UP; increase the resource limit to $1,500; require children to attend school and to be immunized; participants securing a "Work Supplementation" job may have part or all of their AFDC benefits diverted to subsidize wages, residual AFDC benefits will be frozen at initial payment levels until the time limit ends; Food Stamp benefits will continue at unreduced levels for 6 months after initial employment; extend grant diversion to 24 months; eliminate JOBS exemptions for those living in rural or hard-to-access areas, and those employed more than 30 hours per week; impose sanctions for failure to comply; establish Food Stamp eligibility policies that are compatible with AFDC.	Application received June 21, 1994. **Approved** Dec. 15, 1994. Implemented statewide May 1995.
Iowa: Family Investment Program (IFIP)	Require all parents (with limited exceptions) to sign a Family Investment Agreement (FIA) that outlines activities and time frames for achieving self-sufficiency; disregard as income interest and deposits into Individual Development Accounts (IDAs); allow IDA withdrawals for certain purposes (i.e., education); replace current $90 work expense disregard with a 20% work expense deduction; replace current $30 and one-third earned income disregard with permanent disregard of 50% of all earned income remaining after other deductions; increase resource limit to $2,000 for applicants and $5,000 for recipients; increase vehicle asset limit to $3,000; eliminate 100-hour rule and work history requirement for receipt of AFDC-UP; limit, for 12 months, the grant level of new arrivals to the level of the State from which they moved if it is lower than Iowa's; extend transitional child care from 12 to 24 months.	Application received Apr. 29, 1993. **Approved** Aug. 13, 1993. Migration restriction withdrawn. Implemented statewide October 1993.

State/Project	Waiver description	Status
Kansas: Actively Creating Tomorrow for Families Demonstration	After 30 months of JOBS participation, make adults ineligible for AFDC for 3 years (with exceptions); expand the work experiences allowable under the CWEP program; sanction adults who refuse job offers, quit without good cause, or are fired for misconduct, or for non-compliance with work program requirements; standardize employment requirements and penalties, standardize work-program requirements, remove nonexempt parents or spouses not meeting work-requirements, and parents not cooperating with child support enforcement, from the budget group for up to 3 months (after which the case will be closed if non-compliance continues); replace current earned income disregards with permanent disregard of 40% of all earned income after other deductions; for AFDC and Food Stamps: exclude the value of one vehicle from the resource requirements, disregard the income of children up to age 19 who are in school when determining benefits, limit the incremental AFDC benefit increase for additional children to 1/2 the normal for a child conceived into a family with at least two children already receiving assistance, and deny increases for subsequent children; give full incremental benefit increase to child born into family with one child at the time of application, pay 1/2 the normal increase for a second additional child, and no further increase for subsequent children (limitations do not apply if one parent is working); require unwed minor parents to live with a parent or guardian, or in a supervised setting; exempt up to $50 in interest income, deny assistance to fugitive felons, standardize the treatment of sponsor's income and resources in determining eligibility for a sponsored alien, and penalize households that don't submit monthly reports in a timely manner; eliminate 100-hour rule and work history requirements for AFDC-UP receipt; increase transitional Medicaid for up to 24 months (with a co-pay for the second 12 months); implement KanLearn, a program that provides financial incentives to teens to attend school and requires all pregnant and parenting teens to participate in the JOBS education component if they do not have a high school diploma or GED in three counties; eliminate the SSI income disregard in determining AFDC and Medicaid eligibility.	Application received July 22, 1994. **Decision pending.**
Maine: Project Opportunity	A six county demonstration designed to: increase the time allowed for Work Supplementation positions to 18 months; use diverted grant funds to pay for education, training, or support services in addition to wages; allow Work Supplementation participants to receive JOBS support services, transitional child care, and Medicaid; extend transitional child care and Medicaid benefits up to 24 months (with a co-pay for the second 12 months).	Application received Aug. 1, 1994. **Decision pending.**
Maryland: Primary Prevention Initiative	Require children in AFDC families to receive immunizations and annual preventive health check-ups, and to attend school regularly; require pregnant women to receive prenatal care. Reduce benefits for failure to comply.	Application received May 22, 1992. Approved June 30, 1992. Implemented statewide July 1992.

State/Project	Waiver description	Status
Maryland: Welfare Reform Project	*Statewide*, require minor custodial parents to live under adult supervision to be eligible for AFDC benefits (unless it is determined not to be in the best interest of the minor parent); eliminate benefit increases for additional children born to families already receiving AFDC (with exceptions). *In selected counties*, offer applicants judged to need only short-term assistance a single payment (up to an amount equal to three times the monthly grant for the household size); require all able-bodied recipients to participate in job search activities; require nonexempt custodial parents to participate in JOBS or face sanctions; after 18 months of receipt, require able-bodied recipients not employed at least 30 hours to participate in community service jobs; eliminate work history and 100-hour rule for AFDC-UP eligibility; increase resource limit and vehicle asset limit to $5,000; disregard earned income of dependent children; require custodial teen parents to attend family health and parenting classes; provide JOBS services to noncustodial parents unable to pay child support.	Application received Feb. 25, 1994. **Approved** Aug. 14, 1995.
Massachusetts: Welfare Reform '95 (amendments to Employment Support Program)	Require all recipients to reapply for AFDC within 90 days of notification; non-exempt families are limited to 24 months of AFDC assistance within a 60 month period (extensions available); increase earned income disregard to $30 and one-half without time limit for nonexempt recipients, reducing benefits by 2.75%; require teen parents to live in supervised setting; require children under age 14 to attend school; eliminate incremental benefit increase for children born to families already receiving AFDC; increase resource limit to $2,500 and vehicle asset limit to $5,000; disregard the first $600 of lump sum income; eliminate the 100-hour rule for receipt of AFDC-UP; exclude caretaker from grant if children are not immunized; after 60 days of AFDC receipt, require nonexempt recipients not working at least 20 hours per week in paid employment to participate in the Work Program, consisting of community service and job search activities; establish an Employment Development Plan (EDP) for nonexempt participants not required to participate in the Work Program; sanctions for non-participation; create a grant diversion program based on the value of AFDC and Food Stamp benefits to provide subsidized employment for up to 12 months for a limited number of volunteer recipients; disregard grandparent income up to 200% of Federal poverty level.	Application received Apr. 4, 1995. **Approved** August 1995. Implementation on hold.
Michigan: To Strengthen Michigan Families	Eliminate 100-hour rule and work history requirement for AFDC-UP; replace current earned income disregard with single disregard of $200 plus 20% of the remainder with no time limit; exclude for AFDC purposes income of dependent children who are in school; facilitate participation in JOBS; make improvements in child support enforcement and Medicaid programs.	Application received July 31, 1992. **Approved** Aug. 25, 1992. Implemented statewide October 1992.

State/Project	Waiver description	Status
Michigan: Addendum to Strengthen Michigan Families	Consolidate AFDC and Food Stamp benefits into a single cash benefit for households with gross earnings of $350 or more per month; exempt one vehicle of any value for AFDC and Food Stamps; require AFDC applicants to participate in job search activities regardless of the time-limit or face delay in assistance; eliminate deprivation as an eligibility factor in AFDC; require children under age 6 to be immunized or reduce benefits for failure to comply; eliminate all JOBS exemptions except those for VISTA volunteers and dependent children under age 16.	Application received Mar. 8, 1994. Approved Oct. 5, 1994. Implemented statewide October 1994.
Minnesota: New Vistas School Demonstration	Expand apprenticeship project between Honeywell Corporation and Minneapolis public schools by disregarding for AFDC purposes income earned by project participants; allow participants to qualify for $30 and one-third earned income disregard after completing the program.	Application received Dec. 14, 1992. Approved Jan. 15, 1993. State chose not to implement.
Mississippi: A New Direction Demonstration Program (MNDDP)	A demonstration consisting of three components:

Statewide: require parenting teens receiving AFDC who have not completed high school to attend school or have benefits reduced; eliminate 100-hour rule and work history requirements for receipt of AFDC-UP; require children in AFDC families to attend school regularly and receive immunizations and preventive health check-ups or reduce benefits $25. | Application received Dec. 10, 1993. Approved Dec. 22, 1994. Proposed implementation statewide and in selected counties by end of 1995. |
The Work First Demonstration Component (WF)	*In six counties:* require nonexempt recipients to participate in Work Supplementation program (positions limited to 6 months, with up to 3 month extension if job is expected to become permanent); divert AFDC benefits to supplement private sector wages; use 130% of Federal poverty guideline to determine income eligibility for participants; disburse all current child support payments directly to the family; allow "Individual Development" savings accounts up to $1,000 for education or retirement purposes; require unemployed, noncustodial fathers to participate in JOBS.	
The Work Encouragement Demonstration Component (WE)	*In two counties:* eliminate time limits on earnings disregards; calculate grant amount without the ratable reduction (deduct countable income from 100 percent of the need standard instead of 60% of the need standard); to facilitate child support payment, require unemployed, noncustodial fathers to participate in JOBS; provide volunteer "work component" with fiscal bonus for regular attendance.	
Mississippi: A New Direction Demonstration Program -- Amendment	Eliminate incremental benefit increases for additional children born into families already receiving AFDC.	Application received Feb. 17, 1995. Decision pending.

State/Project	Waiver description	Status
Missouri: People Attaining Self-Sufficiency (PASS)	In selected school districts, require regular school attendance from 7th grade through completion of high school/GED for AFDC children and teen parents, reduce benefits for noncompliance; provide support services through JOBS program.	Application received Aug. 4, 1992. **Approved** Oct. 26, 1992. State chose not to implement.
Missouri: 21st Century Communities Demonstration Project	As part of community-level projects addressing economic and job development, learning readiness and education, expanded housing opportunities, and integrated family support services, these waivers will allow the State to: use AFDC funds to supplement wages of individuals volunteering for employment under this component of JOBS program for up to 48 months; disregard child support payments paid directly to the family that exceed AFDC grant amount when determining eligibility and benefit amount; increase resource allowance up to $10,000 for participants; eliminate AFDC-UP 100-hour rule for participants.	Application received Jan. 8, 1993. **Approved** Jan. 15, 1993.
Missouri: Missouri Families Mutual Responsibility Plan	A statewide demonstration that would: require unwed minor parents, with exceptions, to live with a parent or other supervised setting and disregard earned income up to 100% of the Federal poverty guideline for such households; allow AFDC families to establish a separate assistance group consisting of a minor parent and her child within the adult parent's household; disregard the earned income of minor parents who are students; eliminate the 100-hour rule and work history requirements for receipt of AFDC-UP for parents under age 21; exclude the full value of one vehicle and up to $1,500 of a second; increase resource limit to $5,000 for those with self-sufficiency agreements; require JOBS mandatory applicants and recipients to enter into a self-sufficiency agreement establishing a 24 month time limit for receipt of AFDC (extensions available up to 48 months); deny AFDC to individual reapplying for benefits after completing self-sufficiency agreement and having received benefits for at least 36 months (with exceptions).	Application received Aug. 15; re-submitted Jan. 30, 1995. **Approved** Apr. 18, 1995. Proposed implementation Statewide by the end of June 1996.

State/Project	Waiver description	Status
Montana: Achieving Independence for Montanans (AIM)	A comprehensive welfare reform demonstration consisting of three new programs: the Job Supplementation Program (JSP), a set of AFDC-related benefits (maximum cash amount equal to three times the AFDC grant amount to which the family would be entitled) to assist and divert individuals at risk of becoming dependent on welfare; the time-limited (with certain exceptions) AFDC Pathways Program (APP), requiring families to enter into a "Family Investment Contract" and providing employment, training, and education opportunities; and the Community Services Program (CSP) a work program requiring participation for 20 hours per week for those who reach the APP time limit but have not yet achieved self-sufficiency. AIM also includes the following provisions: limit adult eligibility to 24 months (18 months for two-parent families), after which time adult must participate in CSP for 20 hours per week to receive benefits; establish the child care disregard at $200; allow $200 work expense disregard ($100 for CSP participants) and 25% disregard of remaining earned income for demonstration participants; eliminate JOBS exemptions for minor parents under age 16; disburse all current child support payments directly to the family; require children to be immunizedand enrolled in EPSDT; provide Transitional Child Care and up to 12 months of Transitional Medicaid to families who leave JSP, APP, or CSP because of increased income; eliminate the work history requirement and 100-hour rule for receipt of AFDC-UP; increase resource limit to $3,000 and eliminate the vehicle asset limit for AFDC, Food Stamps, and Medicaid; exclude the cash value of life insurance policies when calculating resources; cash-out Food Stamp benefits.	Application received Apr. 18, 1994. Approved Apr. 18, 1995. Proposed implementation statewide between February 1996 and February 1997.

State/Project	Waiver description	Status
Nebraska: Welfare Reform Waiver Demonstration	The demonstration will establish three programs: the Time-Limited, High Disregards Program; the Time-Limited, Alternative Benefit Program; and the Non-Time-Limited Program, limited to those for whom self-sufficiency is not possible because of mental, emotional, or physical conditions, and for certain others. All three programs will: require recipient to develop a self-sufficiency contract; limit incremental benefit increase for additional children born into families already receiving AFDC; raise resource limit for applicants and recipients to $5,000; exclude the value of one car; reduce benefits by $50 for each minor child not attending school; if a minor parent lives with her parents, income which is in excess of 300% of the Federal poverty level will be deemed to the family; if a minor parent lives independently, support will be secured from her parent (s) to the extent that it exceeds 300% of the Federal poverty level; eliminate the 100-hour rule and work history requirement for AFDC-UP. The Time-Limited, High Disregards Program will: time-limit cash assistance, with some exceptions, to a total of 24 months in a 48 month period; cash out Food Stamps; replace current earned income disregard with a non-time-limited disregard of 60%; reduce AFDC payment schedule; extend 24 month period of benefits under specified conditions; require adult wage earners to participate in educational job skills training, work experience, intensive job search, or employment activities; eliminate most JOBS exemptions (require parents with children age 12 weeks to 6 months to participate part-time); sanction recipients for failure to comply; provide transitional Medicaid and child care for up to 24 months to families terminated from AFDC because of employment or because of the time-limit. The provisions of the Time-Limited, Alternative Benefit Program are the same as those above, except with slightly higher benefits and with current earned income disregards.	Application received Oct. 4, 1994. Approved Apr. 18, 1995. Proposed implementation in selected counties October 1995.
New Hampshire: Earned Income Disregard Demonstration	Replace current earned income disregard with permanent $200 and one-half disregard for both AFDC recipients and applicants.	Application received Sept. 13, 1993. **Decision pending.**
New Jersey: Family Development Program	Eliminate benefit increases for additional children born to women already receiving AFDC; require vocational assessment for cases otherwise exempt with children under age 2; provide AFDC benefits to married families in which the husband is not the father of the children receiving AFDC benefits as long as family income is no more than 150% of the poverty level or the State need standard for the family size; increase earnings disregards for JOBS participants; provide 24 months of transitional Medicaid coverage for families made ineligible for AFDC due to increased earnings or hours of work.	Application received June 8, 1992. Approved July 20, 1992. Implemented statewide October 1992.

State/Project	Waiver description	Status
New Mexico: Untitled Project	In order to increase the consistency between AFDC and Food Stamps, increase the vehicle asset limit to $4,500; disregard earned income of a dependent child who is a student for the entire year; for Food Stamp purposes disregard all loans and grants used for education; allow the AFDC applicant to sign the declaration of citizenship on behalf of the family; implement an AFDC Intentional Program Violation procedure identical to the Food Stamp program's.	Application received July 7, 1994. **Decision pending.**
New York: Jobs First Demonstration	A six site demonstration that will: provide child care and/or cash payment for one-time related expenses to help applicant retain or regain employment; require immediate job search and participation in other "job readiness" not allowed under current law, or refer job-ready applicants to transitional/permanent employment; allow applicants the option of receiving child care and/or JOBS services in lieu of AFDC; provide incentives for children to remain in school; allow transitional child care to AFDC cases closed because of child support, provided they are otherwise eligible; change income reporting guidelines; eliminate deprivation (the 100-hour rule, the work history requirement, and the 30-day unemployment requirement) as a basis for AFDC-UP eligibility; allow certain disregards of cash and assets for future business and entrepreneurial ventures (up to $10,000 allowed for reinvestment purposes); raise AFDC vehicle asset and resources limits to food stamp program levels ($2,000 asset limit, $4,500 vehicle asset limit); remove the assets test for recipients who are employed at least 30 hours per week on average; apply the $50 child support pass-through to Food Stamp budgeting.	Application received June 7, 1994. **Approved Oct. 19, 1994.** Implementation on hold by State.
North Dakota: Early Intervention Program (EIP)	Expand AFDC eligibility to include women in their first and second trimesters of pregnancy (if they are single and have no other children); requiring immediate participation in JOBS through end of second trimester, resuming participation four months post-partem (with exemptions).	Application received Aug. 31, 1993. **Approved Apr. 11, 1994.** Implemented statewide October 1994.
North Dakota: Training, Education, Employment and Management (TEEM) Project	Combine AFDC, Food Stamps, and Low-Income Home Energy Assistance (LIHEAP) into a single cash grant with uniform income and resource exclusions; require recipients to develop a social contract outlining the expected time limit for achieving self-sufficiency; failure to develop such a contract within two months of TEEM eligibility will result in case termination; failure to comply with terms of the agreement will result in a sanction of the recipient's benefit; set the gross income test at 50% of the base year poverty level; redefine countable income; increase and graduate earned income disregards; exempt one vehicle; eliminate the 100-hour rule for AFDC-UP receipt; increase resource limit and include burial plots, funeral agreements, and per capita funds to Indians within the limit; require EPSDT screenings; exempt stepparent income for 6 months in when determining grant; eliminate the $50 child support pass through.	Application received Sept. 6, 1994. **Decision pending.**

State/Project	Waiver description	Status
Ohio: Automobile Resource Limit Demonstration	Increase vehicle asset limit to $6,000.	Application received Sept. 13, 1993. Application **withdrawn** Apr. 18, 1994.
Ohio: "A State of Opportunity"	A demonstration consisting of three separate components: In up to five sites *Communities of Opportunity* will: eliminate the 100-hour rule for AFDC-UP applicants and recipients; freeze benefits on entry into the program and divert all AFDC and Food Stamp benefits for up to 24 months to a wage pool to supplement wages to at least $8 per hour; allow Work Supplementation placements in established unfilled positions. In 10 sites *Families of Opportunity* will: eliminate the 100-hour rule and work history requirements for AFDC-UP receipt; increase the child support pass-through to $75; provide a one-time $150 bonus for paternity establishment; increase the vehicle asset limit to $4,500; provide fill-the-gap budgeting for 12 months from month of employment; provide 18 months of transitional child care; apply fill-the-gap budgeting using 50% of the State's Need Standard. In two sites *Children of Opportunity* will: sanction all recipients aged six to 19 who do not meet school attendance requirements; disregard JTPA earnings of dependent children and teen parents without time limit.	Application received May 28, 1994. **Approved** Mar. 7, 1995. Proposed implementation in selected sites July 1995.
Oklahoma: Learnfare Program	Require AFDC children and parents, aged 13 to 18, to graduate from high school/obtain GED. Reduce benefits for noncompliance.	Application received Dec. 28, 1992. **Approved** Jan. 24, 1994. Implemented in selected school districts February 1994.
Oklahoma: Mutual Agreement, A Plan for Success (MAAPS)	Eliminate 100-hour rule for AFDC-UP; increase vehicle asset limit to $5,000; require mandatory JOBS participants who have received AFDC benefits for 36 cumulative months out of 60 consecutive months to become employed a minimum of 24 hours per week by participating in a community work experience program (CWEP); allow time limit extensions for recipients expected to complete a JOBS plan potentially leading directly to employment within one semester, including post-secondary education if combined with part-time employment; provide case management for teen custodial parents, long-term AFDC recipients, and AFDC recipients with a history of repeated receipt; apply fill-the-gap budgeting for earned income only, raising the earnings cap to the need standard instead of the payment standard (which is 63% of the need standard).	Application received Feb. 18, 1994. **Approved** Mar. 14, 1995. Proposed implementation in selected counties by end of 1995.

State/Project	Waiver description	Status
Oregon: JOBS Waiver Project	Expand participation requirements in JOBS program, i.e., require recipients with children age 1 to 6 to participate full-time (more than 20 hours per week) in JOBS; eliminate time limit on jobs search; require pregnant and parenting teens under 16 to participate in educational activities; require participation in mental health or substance abuse treatment if deemed necessary; allow pregnant women with no dependent children who are Medicaid eligible and at risk of going on AFDC to participate in JOBS activities.	Application received Apr. 10, 1992. Approved July 15, 1992. Implemented statewide February 1993.
Oregon: Increased AFDC Motor Vehicle Limit Demonstration	Increase vehicle asset limit to $9,000 for applicants and recipients.	Application received Nov. 12, 1993. **Decision pending.**
Oregon: JOBS Plus Program	In six counties, convert AFDC and Food Stamp benefits into a single cash benefit to subsidize short-term public or private jobs paying the State minimum wage and ensure no loss of income; disburse all current child support payments directly to the family; allow "individual education accounts" to which employers contribute $1 per hour; after 6 months of work, allow participants 8 hours of paid time per week for job search purposes; disregard JOBS Plus wages and supplemental payments as income for program participants; increase asset limit to $10,000; use 130% of Federal poverty guideline to determine eligibility.	Application received Oct. 28, 1993. Approved Sept. 19, 1994. Implemented in selected counties January 1995.
Oregon: Expansion of the Transitional Child Care Program	Provide transitional child care benefits for up to 24 months; eliminate prior 3 of 6 months requirement.	Application received Aug. 8, 1994. **Decision pending.**
Oregon: Oregon Option	A statewide project incorporating waivers already approved in 1992 for JOBS Welfare Program and in 1994 for the JOBS Plus Demonstration with previously pending waiver requests to increase vehicle asset limit and extend transitional child care, that will: request guaranteed level of federal funding, with funds not used for benefits to be used for other community support or prevention; limit receipt of AFDC benefits to no more than 24 out of 84 months for families with employable parents; allow case manager to determine JOBS exemptions on an individual basis; eliminate the time restrictions on job search; impose progressive sanctions, leading to full-family ineligibility, for noncompliance with JOBS; require ineligible alien parents of AFDC children to participate in JOBS; require counseling for recipients with substance abuse problems; require teen parents to live in an adult-supervised setting; discontinue the AFDC-UP program from June through September each year and eliminate the 100-hour rule and work history requirements; increase asset limit to $2,500 for non-JOBS participants and $10,000 for JOBS participants, and treat lump-sum payments as an asset, require annual AFDC eligibility redetermination; modify the rules for potential liability under EBT.	Application received July 10, 1995. **Decision pending.**

State/Project	Waiver description	Status
Pennsylvania: Pathways to Independence	Require demonstration participants to enter into a written "Plan for Independence," including an "Agreement of Mutual Responsibility" designed to move participants to employment; in the third month of employment, combine AFDC and Food Stamp benefits into a single cash grant; eliminate 100-hour rule and work history requirement for of AFDC-UP; provide AFDC to full-time students through age 20; revise treatment of stepparent income; increase earned income disregard to $200 plus one-third for recipients with earnings for two consecutive months; exclude income tax refunds when determining eligibility and grant amount; pay cost of child care directly to provider (less a family fee); revise gross income tests when determining eligibility; increase vehicle asset limit to $7,500; revise resource limit up to $5,000 for families with earnings; exclude as resources up to $10,000 deposited into retirement accounts and funds deposited into savings accounts for educational purposes; provide case management, Transitional Child Care and Medicaid up to 12 months to families who lose eligibility because of earnings (as long as gross income receipt does not exceed 235% of poverty).	Application received Feb. 23, 1994. **Approved Nov. 3, 1994.** Proposed implementation in a selected county by end of April 1996.
Pennsylvania: School Attendance Improvement Program (SAIP)	In seven sites: sanction all recipients aged eight to 18 who do not meet school attendance requirements; require parents to consent to the release of school attendance records to the IV-A agency of face sanction of benefits.	Application received Sept. 12, 1994. **Decision pending.**
Pennsylvania: Savings for Education Program	Allow savings accounts for children's educational expenses established at or after reaching 8th grade.	Application received Dec. 29, 1994. **Decision pending.**
South Carolina: Private/For Profit Work Experience Project	Allow work experience assignments at for-profit sites; require participation of those deemed "eligible" as condition of AFDC eligibility; disregard earnings of project participants for AFDC and Food Stamps purposes for 12 months.	Application received Dec. 9, 1992. **Application withdrawn.**
South Carolina: Self-Sufficiency and Parental Responsibility Program	A four county demonstration that will: limit, with some exceptions, AFDC benefit receipt to the time it takes to complete an Individualized Self-Sufficiency Plan (ISSP) which will identify and remove barriers to employment and self-sufficiency; sanction those who refuse to comply; require adult recipient not securing unsubsidized employment within the time frame stipulated by the ISSP to participate in a full-time public service job and to continue job search activities in order to receive benefits; disregard 50% of gross earned income of adults, including stepparents; disregard the earned income of minors and interest and dividend income when determining eligibility and benefit amount; reduce age of child exemption for JOBS to 6 months; increase vehicle asset limit; increase resource limit to $3,000; eliminate the 100-hour rule and work history requirements for AFDC-UP receipt; require school attendance and immunization; continue to pay AFDC benefits and transitional Medicaid to families no longer eligible because of employment for 12 months (as long as income is below 185% of Federal poverty level), gradually phasing them out.	Application received June 13, 1994. **Approved Mar. 14, 1995.** State chose not to implement.

State/Project	Waiver description	Status
South Dakota: Strengthening of South Dakota Families Initiative	A voluntary social contract with the State under which adult AFDC recipients pledge to develop a plan for self-sufficiency, participant subject to the following provisions: time-limit cash benefits to 24 months for those assigned to employment-readiness track and to 60 months for those in training track, followed by required employment or volunteer service; make total family ineligible for benefits for 3 months for voluntarily quitting jobs of at least 20 hours per week without good cause; provide 1-month transitional employment allowance after case closes due to earnings; disregard earned income and other assets of full-time students; exempt up to $2,500 of a second vehicle under certain circumstances; allow children up to $1,000 in exempt savings accounts if they are employed students and the funds are partly from earnings.	Application received Aug. 6, 1993. Approved Mar. 14, 1994. Implemented statewide June 1994.
Texas: Two-Parent Families Demonstration	Eliminate the 100-rule and labor force attachment rule for AFDC-UP recipients and applicants.	Application received Sept. 29, 1993. Review terminated Apr. 18, 1994.
Texas: Promoting Child Health in Texas	Require preschool age children to be immunized; $25 per child per month sanction for failure to comply.	Application received Apr. 11, 1995. Approved July 31, 1995. To be implemented statewide.
Texas: Service Management and Resources for Teens (SMART)	In pilot site, require non-parenting AFDC children age 10 and over to participate in selected communities in schools programs.	Application received July 1995. Decision pending.
Utah: Single Parent Employment Demonstration (SPED)	Multi-pronged demonstration seeking to change AFDC from an income maintenance program to an employment program. Subject all new AFDC applicants to "self-sufficiency planning"; offer a one-time "AFDC diversion payment" (up to an amount equal to three times monthly grant for the household size) to help applicants who are not likely to warrant ongoing assistance and have agreed to have their application for AFDC denied; eliminate all JOBS exemptions except for children under age 16; increase current resource limit to $2,000 and vehicle asset limit to $8,000; replace current earned income and work incentive disregards with single $100 disregard plus 45% without time limit; expand eligibility for transitional Medicaid and child care services; provide extra $40 per month to those with high level of SPED participation and to those with earnings of at least $500 per month; focus child support enforcement on participant self-sufficiency, including: coordinating with AFDC and JOBS, fast-tracking certain populations.	Application received June 29, 1992. Approved Oct. 5, 1992. Implemented in selected counties January 1993.
Utah: Single Parent Employment Demonstration (SPED) – Amendments	Amend SPED by applying full-family sanction for repeated non-participation in JOBS; provide JOBS support services for 2 years after family leaves rolls; expand income disregards and auto equity limits for Food Stamps.	Application received May 17, 1995. Approved July 31, 1995. To be implemented in selected counties.

State/Project	Waiver description	Status
Vermont: Family Independence Project (FIP)	Provide permanent earned income disregard of $150 (includes current $90 work expense disregard) plus one-fourth; eliminate 100-hour rule, work history requirement, and unemployment rule for AFDC-UP eligibility; require parents in AFDC and AFDC-UP cases who have not obtained unsubsidized employment to participate in subsidized community service jobs, beginning after 30th month of receipt for AFDC-Basic cases and 15th month for AFDC-UP cases; require pregnant and parenting minors to attend school or other education or training activity; require minor AFDC parents to live under adult supervision to be eligible for benefits; disregard value of cash assets from earnings previously counted as income, the value of one automobile, and Job Training Partnership Act (JTPA) stipends when determining AFDC eligibility; exclude grandparent income in determining eligibility and benefit level for minor parent and her children; provide AFDC benefits to families in which the dependent child is unrelated to the caretaker; disburse all current child support payments directly to the AFDC family and count payments in excess of $50 pass-through as income in calculating benefit; extend transitional Medicaid coverage for 36 months.	Application received Oct. 27, 1992. **Approved** Apr. 12, 1993. Implemented statewide July 1994.
Virginia: Incentives to Advance Learning (VITAL)	A pilot program in three schools designed to: require AFDC children in grades six through eight to attend school regularly, using an increase in AFDC payments from 90 to 100% of need standard and student rewards as incentives; provide drop-out prevention counseling; remove caretaker needs from the AFDC assistance unit for certain cases in which children remain truant.	Application received June 1, 1992. **Approved** Sept. 8, 1992. Implemented in selected sites September 1992.
Virginia: Welfare Reform Demonstration	For recipients who have been on AFDC for at least 2 years continuously, completed high school or GED, and have no children under age 5: freeze AFDC/food stamp benefits and pay a training stipends (at least equal in value to the welfare benefits), followed by jobs expected to pay $15,000-18,000/year for up to 600 job-ready voluntary participants; provide recipients employed at least 30 hours per week with transitional child care and Medicaid benefits for up to 36 months (or until income exceeds 150% of Federal poverty level); establish child support insurance program for those leaving AFDC because of earnings; increase resource limit to $5,000 for education and housing purposes; extend AFDC eligibility to full-time students to age 21; disregard stepparent income for AFDC children when a recipient marries, unless/until family's total income exceeds 150% of poverty; pass-through all child support payments directly to the family.	Application received Aug. 6, 1993. **Approved** Nov. 23, 1993. Implemented in selected sites July 1994.

State/Project	Waiver description	Status
Virginia: Virginia Independence Program	Statewide: provide one-time grant diversion payment equal to 3 months of benefits to qualified applicants in lieu of AFDC; require minor parents to live in supervised setting; eliminate incremental benefit increases for additional children born into families already receiving AFDC; require children to be immunized; exempt up to $5,000 in savings for starting a business; require AFDC parents age 24 and younger without highschool diploma, and children age 18 and younger, to attend school; require cooperation with paternity establishment procedures. Over 4 years, phase in the Virginia Initiative for Employment Not Welfare (VIEW) work component statewide. VIEW will: modify current JOBS exemption criterion; require signing of an Agreement of Personal Responsibility; eliminate 185% needs test for eligibility (determine eligibility by subtracting earnings and benefits from Federal poverty guidelines); increase vehicle asset limit to $7,500; limit AFDC benefit receipt to 24 cumulative months for nonexempt participant (exemptions granted to: those under 16, those under 19 enrolled in school full-time, those incapacitated with a medically documented condition, and others); time-limit extensions available if case satisfies hardship exemption criterion; require both parents in AFDC-UP cases to participate unless exemption criterion are met; require non-exempt caseheads to participate in employment related activities, including education and training; require job search without time limit; may place participants age 19 to 24 immediately into CWEP for up to 32 hours per week; for those unable to find unsubsidized employment, implement the grant diversion Full Employment Program (FEP) using frozen AFDC and Food Stamp benefits to subsidize private sector employment for up to 6 months.	Application received Mar. 8, 1995. Approved July 1, 1995. Implemented statewide and in selected sites July 1995.
Washington: Success Through Employment Program (STEP)	Eliminate the 100-hour rule for AFDC-UP recipients; subtract earnings from 55% of the State need standard rather than the State payment standard (fill-the-gap budgeting).	Application received Nov. 8, 1993. **Decision pending.**
Washington: Success Through Employment Program	Eliminate 100-hour rule for receipt of AFDC-UP; impose 10% AFDC grant reduction for adults receiving benefits for 48 out of 60 months (with exceptions); reduce grant by additional 10% for every 12 months thereafter, with no concomitant increase in Food Stamp benefits; budget earnings against original AFDC Payment Standard.	Application received Feb. 1, 1995. **Decision pending.**
West Virginia: Joint Opportunities for Independence (JOIN)	Require 32 hours of CWEP participation and 6 hours of job search activities per week for AFDC-UP cases unless one parent is employed such that the number of hours would be infeasible; sanction family for noncompliance; deny Medicaid to sanctioned adults; no Food Stamp benefit increase for sanctioned families.	Application received Apr. 11, 1995. Approved July 31, 1995. To be implemented statewide.

State/Project	Waiver description	Status
Wisconsin: Parental and Family Responsibility Demonstration	A pilot program designed to provide a comprehensive package of education and employment services to teens who are pregnant or have their first child and apply for AFDC. Limit AFDC benefit increases to one-half the normal increase for second child born to families in the demonstration, pay no additional increase for subsequent children; eliminate work history requirement and 100-hour rule for AFDC-UP eligibility; increase earned income disregard to first $200 plus one-half; require unemployed, noncustodial fathers to participate in the JOBS program; eliminate most JOBS exemptions.	Application received Mar. 19, 1992. **Approved** Apr. 10, 1992. Implemented in selected counties July 1994.
Wisconsin: Two-Tier AFDC Benefit Demonstration	Limit, for 6 months, grant level of new arrivals to level of State from which they moved if it is lower than Wisconsin's.	Application received June 30, 1992. **Approved** July 27, 1992. Implemented in selected counties July 1994.
Wisconsin: Vehicle Asset Waiver Demonstration	Increase vehicle asset limit to $2,500 for purposes of AFDC eligibility; equity value over that amount would be counted as available asset and applied against limit.	Application received Oct. 29, 1992. **Approved** Jan. 19, 1993. Implemented statewide July 1994.
Wisconsin: AFDC Special Resource Account Demonstration	Allow AFDC recipients to open a special resource account of up to $10,000; allow withdrawals for training or education of parent or child, or to improve employability as defined by State policies, or for approved emergency expenses of no more than $200 per 12 month period.	Application received Oct. 29, 1992. **Approved** Jan. 19, 1993. Implemented statewide July 1994.
Wisconsin: Work Not Welfare (WNW) Demonstration	Cash out Food Stamps; provide a maximum of 24 months of cash benefits within a 4-year eligibility window; provide 12 months of transitional child care and medical benefits within that 4-year period; pay no cash benefits for period of 36 months following last month in which a demonstration benefit was paid; require participants to take part in education, training, or work activities (WNW grant is to be considered "payment" for such activities); provide education and training services; provide CWEP placements or "Independence Jobs" (developed specifically for WNW participants) for those required to work not finding private employment; disburse all current child support payments directly to the family and count payments in excess of $50 pass-through as income; eliminate benefit increases for additional children born into families already receiving AFDC; non-time-limited earnings disregard of $30 and one-sixth; eliminate 100-hour rule for AFDC-UP recipients; provide up to 12 months of transitional child care and Medicaid during the 48 month period.	Application received July 14, 1993. **Approved** Nov. 1, 1993. Implemented in selected counties January 1995.

State/Project	Waiver description	Status
Wisconsin: AFDC Benefit Cap (ABC) Demonstration Project	For "ongoing" cases (one that has been closed less than 6 contiguous months within the last 16 months), eliminate benefit increases for additional children born more than 10 months after family has initially applied for benefits (except for verified cases of rape or incest, or if the child has been placed in the care of a non-legally responsible relative); increase awareness and availability of family planning resources among AFDC applicants and recipients.	Application received Feb. 9, 1994. Approved June 24, 1994. Proposed implementation statewide January 1996.
Wisconsin: Pay for Performance (PFP)	A 5-year statewide demonstration that would: eliminate 100-hour rule for AFDC-UP recipients (but not applicants); eliminate JOBS exemptions except for exemption for age of child under 1; require up to 40 hours per week of JOBS participation; determine required number of CWEP hours by dividing AFDC grant by Federal minimum wage; for each hour of non-participation reduce grant by Federal minimum hourly wage, with no concomitant adjustment in Food Stamp benefits; no limit on Work Supplementation activities.	Application received Apr. 17, 1995. Approved Aug. 14, 1995.
Wisconsin: Self Sufficiency First (SSF)	A 5-year statewide demonstration that would, in conjunction with the PFP demonstration: require new AFDC applicants to meet with a financial resource specialist; require all nonexempt JOBS individuals to participate in 60 hours of JOBS program activities within a 30 day application period; failure to participate would result in benefit denial for entire family.	Application received Apr. 17, 1995. **Decision pending.**
Wyoming: Welfare Reform: New Opportunities and New Responsibilities	Require all able-bodied AFDC recipients in pilot counties to work or perform community service unless specifically exempted; reduce monthly benefit to families with children age 16 or over who have not graduated from high school, refuse to attend school, or accept suitable employment; increase resource limit to $2,500 while a recipient is employed; limit, for 12 months, grant level of new arrivals to level of State from which they moved if it is lower than Wyoming's; disallow AFDC benefits for households where "primary recipient" is pursuing a second bachelor's degree, in B.A. program of 6 years or more, or in an associate degree program of 4 or more years; allow court-ordered support obligers to participate in the State's JOBS program, Wyoming Opportunities for Work (WOW).	Application received May 20, 1993. Approved Sept. 1, 1993. Migration restriction denied. Implemented in selected counties September 1993.

JOBS FOR WELFARE RECIPIENTS[*]

Linda Levine

Some policymakers are proposing time-limited receipt of income support provided by the Aid to Families with Dependent Children (AFDC) program, the major cash welfare program to assist predominantly single-parent, mother-only families. Welfare dependence would become a temporary condition by ending eligibility for cash benefits after some period of time.[1]

According to economic theory, the provision of an income guarantee discourages work effort. The subsidy enables individuals to substitute time spent in leisure and home production (e.g., child care) for work time, and raises their reservation wage (i.e., the wage at which they would be willing to enter the workforce). Restriction eligibility for income support can be expected to motivate AFDC beneficiaries to increase their supply of labor.[2]

One of the key rationales underlying this proposed policy is that it is now commonplace for mothers -- even those with young children -- to work outside the home. On equity grounds, many expect AFDC mothers to

---

[*] Excerpted from *CRS Report* 94-457 E

[1] For more information on specific proposals, see: U. S. Library of Congress. Congressional Research Service. *Welfare Reform: A Comparison of H.R. 3500 and S. 1795 with Current Policy,* by Carmen D. Solomon. CRS Report No. 94-176 EPW. Wash., Feb. 23, 1994. 41 p.; and, *Time-Limited Welfare Proposals,* by Vee Burke. Issue Brief 93034. Updated periodically. 15p.

[2] See, for example: Hoynes, Hilary Williamson. *Welfare Transfers in Two-Parent Families: Labor Supply and Welfare Participation Under AFDC-UP.* Cambridge, Mass., National Bureau of Economic Research, July 1993. P.30.

behave like most other mothers, that is, to contribute through their own earnings to the financial support of their children. In 1960, fewer than one-fifth of married mothers with children under 6 years old were in the labor force; by the mid-1980s, their labor force participation rate had climbed to over 50 percent; and, in 1993, it reached 60 percent.[3] In contrast, the presence in the workforce of never-married mothers with young children has remained more-or-less unchanged, hovering around 45 percent.[4] More particularly, among all AFDC mothers regardless of the age of their dependent children, employment rates actually have fallen from a high of 18 percent during the early-to-mid 1970s to single digit rates since the early 1980s.[5]

To make the proposed policy feasible, namely, to get recipients off the welfare rolls and onto payrolls, there need to be jobs available. This report identifies the kinds of jobs that most adults receiving AFDC would be qualified to hold based on their typical level of educational attainment. Whether these low-skilled jobs would be available in numbers sufficient to match an influx of employable welfare recipients is analyzed as well. Given the dominance of mother-only families in the AFDC program, the usual earnings of working women in low-skilled occupations also are examined. And lastly, this report explores potential effects of "making work pay" by means of guaranteeing education and training assistance to AFDC parents.

THE KIND OF JOBS

Presumably, adult AFDC recipients would be qualified to fill those jobs typically held by workers with similar levels of educational attainment.

---

[3] U.S. Bureau of Labor Statistics' data.

[4] Over half of mother-only AFDC families in 1991 were headed by a never-married women; and, this family type has increased more rapidly than other mother-only AFDC families. See: U.S. Library of Congress. Congressional Research Service. *Demographic Trends Affecting Aid to Families With Dependent Children (AFDC) Caseload Growth.* CRS Report no. 93-7 EPW, by Thomas Gabe. Washington, Dec. 9, 1992. P. 18 and 22.

[5] Moffitt, Robert. Incentive Effects of the U.S. Welfare System: A Review. *Journal of Economic Literature,* vol. XXX, March 1992. Table 4, p. 12.

This does not imply, however, that welfare recipients would compete for these jobs on equal footing with other low-productivity workers. AFDC mothers might have less work experience or have experienced deterioration of their skills due to lengthy or frequent absences from the labor market.[6] In addition, were potential employers to learn of the welfare status of applicants, it might have a negative influence on hiring decisions.

EDUCATIONAL ATTAINMENT OF AFDC RECIPIENTS

Until the mid-1980s, more than half of the unmarried mothers receiving AFDC payments were high school dropouts. Reflecting the general increase in educational attainment over the years, high school dropouts have accounted for a decreasing share of welfare recipients. But, in 1990, they still comprised between 43 percent and 47 percent of AFDC single mothers. (See table 1.) In contrast, under 14 percent of all employed workers in 1992 had fewer than 12 years of formal education -- about one-third the rate among AFDC recipients.[7]

---

[6] According to results from the National Longitudinal Survey of Youth, the average number of weeks worked between 1983 and 1987 by 22-30 year old mothers who were receiving AFDC payments in 1987 was 59 out of a possible 260 weeks. In contrast, poor non-AFDC mothers of the same age averaged 99 weeks of work in the 5-year period, and non-poor non-AFDC mothers averaged 155 weeks. See: Zill, Nicholas with Kristin A. Moore, Christine Windquist Nord, and Thomas Stief. *Welfare Mothers as Potential Employees: A Statistical Profile Based On National Survey Data. Washington, Child Trends Inc., 1991. Table 8.*

[7] U.S. Bureau of Labor Statistics' unpublished data.

Table 1. Estimates from Seven Sources of Data on High School Dropout Rates among Single Mothers Receiving Welfare

Year	Data Source					
	Current Population Survey	Decennial Census	Survey of Income & Program Participation (SIPP)	National Longitudinal Survey of Youth (NLSY)	Panel Study of Income Dynamics (PSID)	Ways & Means Committee's *Green Book*
1969	73%	NA	NA	NA	NA	77%
1970						
Blacks	78	74	NA	NA	68	NA
Whites	70	64	NA	NA	66	NA
1975	59	NA	NA	NA	60	63
1979	56	NA	NA	55	55	58
1980						
Blacks	53	53	NA	60	47	NA
Whites	55	47	NA	46	63	NA
1985	49	NA	48	56	49	NA
1986	45	NA	53	47	46	47
1987	46	NA	49	48	50	NA
1988	46	NA	48	50	52	48
1990	46	43	--	45	NA	47

Notes: NA = not applicable/not available. -- = not computed. When one figure is shown for a year it includes both blacks and whites; Hispanics are excluded from the analyses. Generally, the data relate to unmarried mothers, 18-64 years old, who reported receipt of AFDC. Data after 1983 from the House Ways and Means Committee's *Green Book* refer to all adult AFDC recipients. In the SIPP, NLSY, and PSID surveys, results are not inflated by GED attainment; in the *Green Book* data, GED attainment is not known and the educational attainment of about one-half of recipients is unknown as well.

Source: Brandon, Peter D. *Trends Over Time in the Educational Attainments of Single Mothers*, Discussion Paper 1023-93. Madison, Wisconsin, Institute for Research on Poverty, October 1993. p. 22-23.

Since about the mid-1980s, slightly over 40 percent of adults receiving welfare payments have completed high school.[8]

Moreover, based on their performance on standardized ability tests, AFDC mothers' years of schooling might overstate their actual capabilities. Results from a representative national sample of young women who took the Armed Forces Qualification Test (AFQT)[9] in 1980 showed that nearly three-fourths of 25-year -old women who received AFDC benefits for 12 months scored in the bottom quartile of all test-takers. Even among women who were somewhat less dependent on welfare benefits, scores were well below the norm.[10]

EDUCATIONAL ATTAINMENT OF WORKERS BY OCCUPATION

Workers with 12 or fewer years of education usually hold jobs in one of six major occupational groups. (See chart 1.) However, these workers are most often employed in three occupational groups: almost 7 out of 10 low-skilled jobs are in the service; operators, fabricators, and laborers; and, administrative support occupational groups.

Of the 17.4 million jobs in low-skilled service occupations, most are concentrated in food service and preparation (7.7 million). This group includes waiters and waitresses; cooks; and food counter, fountain, and related workers. Another 3.3 million jobs are in cleaning and building service occupations (predominantly janitors and cleaners), and 2.0 million are in health-related occupations (predominantly nursing aides and psychiatric

---

[8] This figure is based upon the number of adult AFDC recipients who reported their level of educational attainment. For roughly half of all adult recipients, the number of years of school completed is unknown. See: U.S. Congress. House. Committee on Ways and Means. *Overview of Entitlement Programs: 1993 Green Book, Committee Print 103-18. 103d Cong., 1ˢᵗ Sess. Washington, U.S. Govt. Print. Off., July 7, 1993. P. 696.*

[9] The composite score on the AFQT reflects the test taker's problem-solving ability with regard to arithmetic reasoning, numerical operations, work knowledge, and paragraph comprehension.

[10] Burtless, Gary. *The Employment Prospects of Welfare Recipients.* First draft of paper presented at the Urban Institute conference, Self-Sufficiency and the Low-Wage Labor Market: A Reality Check for Welfare Reform, April 12-14, 1994. P. 8 and Table 2. [Hereinafter referred to as the Urban Institute conference]

aides). (Employment data on low-skilled jobs by detailed occupation are shown in Appendix Table 1.)

Chart 1. The Employment Distribution of Low-skilled Jobs

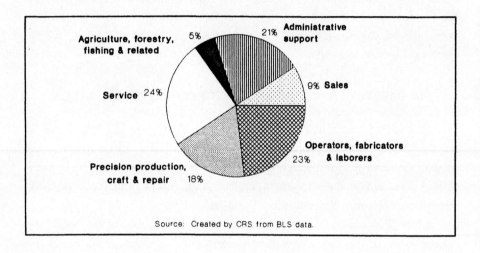

Source: Created by CRS from BLS data.

Some 16.3 million jobs as operators, fabricators, and laborers are largely held by workers with limited formal education. This less skilled blue-collar group includes such jobs as sewing, pressing, and laundering machine operators; hand packers and packagers; and, bus, taxicab, and truck drivers.

Another 15.0 million low-skilled jobs can be found in the administrative support group. These occupations include general office clerks (2.7 million); bookkeeping, accounting, and auditing clerks (2.1 million); and stock clerks (1.8 million).

The sales occupational group contains relatively fewer low-skilled jobs. However, two sales occupations -- retail salespersons (3.7 million jobs) and cashiers (2.7 million jobs) -- provide numerous low-skilled employment opportunities.

Two of the three largest low -skilled occupational groups predominantly employ women. In 1993, on average, women composed almost two-thirds of workers in service occupations (except private household and protective service occupations), and over three- fourths of workers in administrative support occupations.[11]

AFDC mothers more likely would seek jobs in these and other female-dominated fields (e.g., retail salespersons and cashiers) than in nontraditional blue-collar occupations, such as operators, fabricators, and laborers. Data from the 1988 National Health Interview Survey of Child Health confirm this supposition. AFDC mothers with work experience have been employed in the following occupational groups in descending order of frequency: service; sales; administrative support; machine operator and assembler; professional and technical; helper and laborer; administrative and managerial; private household service; precision production, craft, and repair; transportation and material moving; farming, forestry, and fishing; and, protective service.[12]

JOB AVAILABILITY

It is unlikely that anyone can accurately predict whether or not there would be enough unsubsidized jobs available to make feasible a mandatory work requirement. There are too many uncertainties, including the number of AFDC recipients who would be employable immediately, or would be employable eventually were education/training, child and health care, or transportation assistance to be legislated by Congress; the number of welfare recipients who actually would enter the labor market in a given year; and, the condition of the local economies in which recipients reside.

---

[11] U.S. Bureau of Labor Statistics. *Employment and Earnings,* January 1994. Table 22, p. 206 and 207.

[12] Zill, *Welfare Mothers as Potential Employees,* Table 10.

A RELATIVELY HIGH UNEMPLOYMENT RATE

The unemployment rate can be viewed as a measure of the degree to which the supply of labor exceeds the demand for labor at given wage levels.[13] Over the years, the supply of low-productivity workers has exceeded employers' demand for their services to a greater extent than it has for more productive workers. In March 1993, for example, the inverse relationship between educational attainment and the unemployment rate meant that 16.0 percent of workers with fewer than 12 years of schooling were unemployed -- more than four times the rate among college graduates (3.7 percent) and about twice that of high school graduates (8.1 percent).[14]

Changes in the labor market beginning in the 1980s have caused concern that deteriorating job options among low-skilled workers have worsened their comparative labor surplus. These changes commonly are ascribed to technological innovation and international trade which, it is argued, have shifted the demand for labor in favor of more highly educated workers. However, the unemployment rates of less compared to more educated workers have moved roughly in tandem during the last decade. This trend has caused one analyst to conclude that the relative availability of jobs for less skilled workers has not decreased, which "suggests that the changes in the U.S. labor market are not leading to the elimination of jobs for less skilled workers."[15] (It also suggests that the labor market difficulties of less educated workers might be operating more through wage than

---

[13] The unemployment rate reflects the extent of frictional, cyclical, and structural unemployment in the labor market. Frictional unemployment, thought to range between 1 percent and 3 percent, arises as workers (re)enter the labor force and look for employment of (in)voluntarily leave one job and search for another; it is of short duration and reflects the efficiency of the job search process. The extent of cyclical or demand-deficient unemployment varies depending upon economic conditions; its contribution to the jobless rate falls when the economy expands and rises when it contracts. Structural unemployment arises from changes in the industrial, occupational, and demographic makeup of the economy which cause a mismatch between the composition of labor supplied and demanded; it is of longer duration because of the costs associated with switching from one industry, occupation, or location to another. Only the latter two components of unemployment might be said to reflect the presence of surplus labor.

[14] U.S. Bureau of Labor Statistics' unpublished data.

[15] Blank, Rebecca M. *Outlook for the U.S. Labor Market and Prospects for Low-Wage Entry Jobs.* Preliminary draft presented at the Urban Institute conference, p. 34.

employment opportunities. More particularly, it appears that the wages of low-skilled men have deteriorated while those of low-skilled women have stagnated.)[16]

Because the unemployment rate relates only to those in the labor market, the above-described trend does not fully capture changes in job availability. If, for example, less skilled men perceive that demand for their services has diminished, they might withdraw from or not enter the labor force. Such an increase in worker discouragement and decrease in labor force participation would not be picked up by the unemployment rate, which covers those with jobs and those actively seeking jobs. Indeed, employment rates among low-wage men have fallen considerably over the years.[17]

Regardless of whether employment opportunities of low-skilled workers have worsened since 1979, a sudden influx of millions of job-seeking AFDC recipients certainly would intensify competition for the available openings. An increase over a couple of years in the supply of low-skilled workers might, in the short run, raise the group's unemployment rate, result in the displacement of some low-skilled working mothers, and depress the already low wages of less skilled workers.[18] These adverse consequences could be minimized if welfare recipients were to *gradually* enter the labor force and if, over a longer period, employers adjusted their ways of doing business to make greater use of the more abundant low-skilled labor.

Just as the rate at which welfare recipients might enter the labor market is unknown, so too is the total size of the *employable* AFDC pool. In fiscal year 1993, there were 4.6 million adults receiving AFDC payments.[19] Some members of the adult AFDC population would be unable to move from the welfare rolls onto payrolls because of seemingly unsolvable, work-limiting problems. One analyst has developed the following estimate

[16] Ibid., p. 6-10.

[17] Juhn, Chinhui and Kevin M. Murphy. Wage Inequality and Family Labor Supply. *Proceedings of the Forty-Fourth Annual Meeting of the Industrial Relations Research Association,* January 3-5, 1992. P. 207-208.7

[18] Burtless, *The Employment Prospects of Welfare Recipients,* p. 17-19.

[19] Administration for Children and Families, U.S. Department of Health and Human Services.

of the proportion of welfare recipients who might be permanently exempt from a work requirement:[20]

Grounds for Exemption:	Percent Qualifying	Cumulative Percentage
Very low functional literacy level	18	18
Physical disability	17	28
Mental or emotional disorder	3-15	35
Alcohol dependence or abuse	4-8	38
Drug dependence or abuse	1-4	39
Severe disability of child	1-2	40

Other AFDC adults have temporary work limitations (e.g., pregnancy or the presence of a very young child; problems with day care, housing, or transportation arrangements). These individuals could eventually fulfill a work requirement. But, their ability to enter and remain in the workforce might depend upon the short- or long-term provision of services by the government (e.g., day care). Whether, when, or in what numbers this potentially employable group might enter the workforce is another unknown.

From a labor supply perspective, then, the answer to the question of whether sufficient unsubsidized employment opportunities would be available for job-seeking AFDC recipients depends upon at least two unknowns, namely, the phase-in rate and the size of the employable AFDC population.

GROWTH IN LOW-SKILLED OCCUPATIONS

From the demand side of the job availability questions, the U.S. Bureau of Labor Statistics (BLS) has projected that there will be substantial employment growth through the early part of the next decade in less skilled

---

[20] Zill, Nicholas, *Characteristics of AFDC Recipients that Bear on Their Employability under Welfare Reform.* Exhibits for presentation at briefing on Characteristics of Welfare Families, Senate Finance Committee, Feb. 11, 1994.

occupations. Between 1992 and 2005, occupations that largely employ workers with relatively little schooling could increase by 12.8 million, or 49 percent of total projected job growth.

Many of the occupations projected to experience the largest *absolute* growth require fairly few years of education. (See chart 2.) The low-skilled jobs expected to expand considerably fall mainly in the service, administrative support, and sales occupational groups -- where many women traditionally have found employment. In contrast, only two blue-collar occupations requiring comparatively limited schooling are expected to be among the high-growth occupations (i.e., truck drivers and general utility maintenance repairers).

Chart 2. Occupations Requiring 12 or Less Years of Education with the Largest Projected Job Growth, 1992-2005 (numbers in thousands)

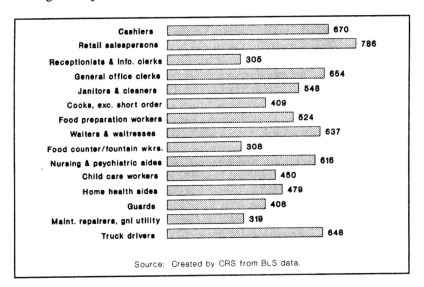

Cashiers	670
Retail salespersons	786
Receptionists & info. clerks	305
General office clerks	654
Janitors & cleaners	548
Cooks, exc. short order	409
Food preparation workers	524
Waiters & waitresses	637
Food counter/fountain wkrs.	308
Nursing & psychiatric aides	616
Child care workers	450
Home health aides	479
Guards	408
Maint. repairers, gnl utility	319
Truck drivers	648

Source: Created by CRS from BLS data.

When the data are examined according to the rate of job growth, many low-skilled occupations are projected to experience well-above-average increases. Across all occupations, the BLS expects that employment could rise by 22 percent between 1992 and 2005. In contrast, the low-skilled occupations shown in chart 3 are projected to grow at two to six times this rate. Service occupations appear more frequently than others among the fast-growing, low-skilled jobs.

A caveat to keep in mind when using this database to assess job availability is that it is national in scope. The projections cannot be used to gauge how many (if any) or which jobs would be available where welfare recipients reside. The projections are based upon an assumed rate of economic growth, which affects the unemployment rate. The accuracy of the anticipated jobless rate is important because the willingness of employers to hire welfare recipients can be expected to increase the tighter the labor market.[21] Even if the actual jobless rate at the national level were to come close to the anticipated rate, there still could be considerable deviation at the State and local levels.

Chart 3. Occupations Requiring 12 or Less Years of Education with the Fastest Projected Job Growth, 1992-2005 (in percent)

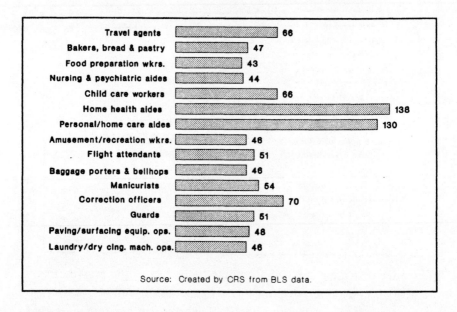

Source: Created by CRS from BLS data.

---

[21] According to the queue theory of labor economics, employers rank potential employees on the basis of their perceived marginal productivity. When the economy is expanding rapidly and the job market is tight, employers will reach farther into the hiring queue to fill vacancies and thereby provide more opportunities for less productive workers.

PAY LEVELS

Some observers argue that welfare recipients should be required to accept any job, regardless of its pay level. They believe that work should be the norm whether or not it immediately makes people self-sufficient and moves them from poverty. They contend that welfare recipients' initial acceptance of any job, even a low-paid entry-level job, would provide them with work experience which they then could use to their advantage when seeking subsequent employment.[22] In contrast, others assert that the nature of the job is important -- that it should not only get families off welfare but also out of poverty. Those who would require that recipients' first jobs be "financially viable" are in effect saying that they must be "good" jobs. The quality of a job often is measured in terms of how much it pays (including fringe benefits, such as health insurance), if it is secure (e.g., full-time), or whether it provides opportunity for advancement.

WAGES FROM LOW-SKILLED EMPLOYMENT

Because earnings are positively associated with a worker's skill level, it should not be surprising that occupations requiring limited schooling pay fairly low wages. All women in wage and salary jobs had median earnings of $295 a week in 1992, according to data from the March supplement of the Current Population Survey. The paychecks of women employed in numerous low-skilled occupations were well below this amount.

---

[22] Mead, Lawrence. The Hidden Jobs Debate. *The Public Interest*, Spring 1988, no. 91. P. 48-49

Chart 4. Median Weekly Earnings of Female Wage and Salary Workers in
Selected Low-Skilled Occupations, 1992

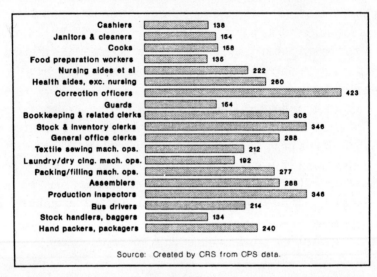

Cashiers	138
Janitors & cleaners	154
Cooks	158
Food preparation workers	135
Nursing aides et al	222
Health aides, exc. nursing	260
Correction officers	423
Guards	154
Bookkeeping & related clerks	308
Stock & inventory clerks	346
General office clerks	288
Textile sewing mach. ops.	212
Laundry/dry clng. mach. ops.	192
Packing/filling mach. ops.	277
Assemblers	288
Production inspectors	346
Bus drivers	214
Stock handlers, baggers	134
Hand packers, packagers	240

Source: Created by CRS from CPS data.

As shown in chart 4, the median weekly earnings of cashiers were
$138; janitors and cleaners, $154; food preparation workers, $135; health
aids (except nursing aides, orderlies, and attendants). $260. In contrast,
correctional institution officers (at $423 a week) and clerical occupations
(e.g., bookkeeping, accounting, and auditing clerks at $308 a week; and ,
stock and inventory clerks, $346) provide higher median wages. Although
blue-collar jobs often are thought of as being high-paid, there are numerous exceptions: the median earnings of women employed as textile sewing
machine operators were $212 a week in 1992; assemblers, $288; bus drivers, $214; and, stock handlers and baggers, $134.

The size of one's paycheck is determined not only by the wage rate but
also by the time spent at work. Although a "good" job usually is thought of
as full-year bull-time employment, some mothers prefer part-time arrangements in order to have more time to care for and spend with their
children. In 1992, according to BLS data, almost 3 of every 10 employed
mothers in married-couple families with dependent children held part-time
jobs (i.e., fewer than 35 hours per week). Should AFDC mothers be ex-

pected to work more hours and have less time to spend with their children than a sizable minority of married mothers?

For other workers, part-time employment increasingly has become less of a matter of choice. Part-time jobholding among workers who would have preferred full-time employment has been expanding relatively rapidly for many years. In light of the increased prevalence of involuntary part-time employment particularly among women,[23] is it reasonable to expect AFDC mothers will be able to obtain full-time jobs? Can part-time jobs serve as stepping stones to full-time employment?[24]

If AFDC mothers work less than full-year full-time,[25] however, their annual earnings would be extremely low. As shown in chart 5 (and in more detain in Appendix Table 2), the number of weeks or hours of work can have a pronounced effect on earnings. While all women employed as general office clerks had median earnings of $13,000 in 1992, those who worked full-year full-time earned $20,000 and those who worked part-year part-time earned $1,900. Falling within the range were the median earnings of women who worked full-year part-time ($7,345) and part-year full time ($6,025). As can be seen, considerable income is foregone by working fewer than 35 hours a week or fewer than 50 weeks a year.

Thus, the potential to work one's way out of dependency and into self-sufficiency is more than a matter of just getting any job. While the Earned Income Tax Credit is intended to supplement the earnings of low-income working families, some AFDC recipients who are able to find employment -- especially those who work less than full-year full-time -- might remain in poverty and still rely on the Government for means-tested assistance (e.g., Food Stamps). One outcome of turning AFDC into a temporary in-

---

[23] Blank, Rebecca M. *Are Part-Time Jobs Bad Jobs?* In Burtless, Gary (ed.) *A Future of Lousy Jobs?* Wash., The Brookings Institution, 1990. P. 125.

[24] Jacobs, Jerry A. *Trends in Wages, Underemployment, and Mobility Among Part-Time Workers,* Discussion Paper 1021-93. Madison, Wisconsin, Institute for Research on Poverty, September 1993. P. 17-44.

[25] Full-year full-time employment means working 50 or more weeks at a full-time job. A full-time job involves working 35 or more hours per week during a majority of weeks worked. Conversely, a part-time job involves working less than 35 hours per week in a majority of the weeks worked during a year. These definitions were developed by the U.S. Bureau of the Census.

come-maintenance program could be to transform the dependent, non-working poor into the working but still partially dependent poor.

Chart 5. Women's Median Annual Earnings by Length of Time Worked

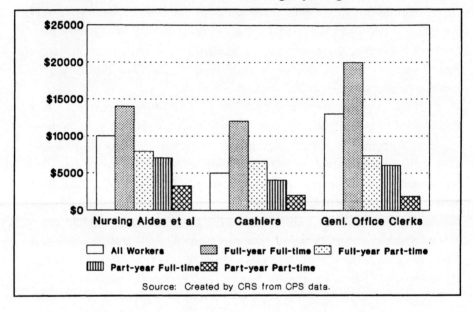

MAKING WORK PAY

To increase the likelihood of AFDC families becoming self-sufficient through the parents' own earnings, their productivity would have to be raised to make them eligible to compete for higher-paying jobs. Under an "accept-any-job" scenario, the government would likely provide job search assistance. Under a "good-jobs" scenario, the cost of attempting to enable people to move from welfare into better-than-entry-level work would be much greater because of the added education and training component.

The cost of an education/training guarantee to the AFDC population could be higher than anticipated because of the entitlement's potential caseload-increasing effect. Although time-limited receipt of welfare benefits is intended to reduce the size of the AFDC population, the availability of education/training services could prompt

(1) some current recipients who otherwise would have exited the rolls to remain in order to use these service;

(2) AFDC-eligibles who do not currently participate in the program to decide to enroll;[26] and,

(3) currently ineligible, low-wage working mothers to quit their jobs in order to become AFDC-eligibles.

Thus, enrichment of the AFDC program through guaranteed access to education and training benefits might somewhat reduce the supply of labor among women with dependent children. "Making work pay" through education/training has the potential to raise welfare costs by providing additional services and by increasing the size of the caseload.[27]

If low-paid working women value education/training assistance,[28] they presumably would be interested in obtaining guaranteed access to such services. How many might be interested? Although adult employed woman earned $9.09 an hour on average in 1993, 6.0 million adult never-married, separated, divorced or widowed women earned below this amount. Within this group, almost 370,000 adult never-married, separated, divorced, or widowed women earned $4.25 an hour; and, nearly 300,000 earned below the Federal minimum wage (due to exemptions from the Fair Labor Stan-

---

[26] The take-up or participation rate among AFDC-eligibles ranges from 62 percent to 72 percent. Blank, Rebecca M. *When Do Women Use AFDC & Food Stamps? The Dynamics of Eligibility vs. Participation,* Working Paper No. 4429. Cambridge, Mass., National Bureau of Economic Research, August 1993. P. 13.

[27] The provision of child care or transportation assistance and continuation of health benefits has similar potential.

[28] The value of training to current or potential AFDC recipients, and hence its caseload-increasing effect, would depend upon "(i) the degree of forward-looking behavior--that is, the individual's discount rate; (ii) the magnitude of the earnings payoff to the program; and (iii) the time and hassle requirements of the program." Moffitt, Robert A. *The Effect of Work and Training Programs on Entry and Exit from the Welfare Caseload.* Discussion Paper 1025-93. Madison, Wisconsin, Institute for Research on Poverty, November 1993. P. 5.

dards Act.)[29] Using another benchmark, the Census Bureau's poverty threshold in 1993 for a 3-person family was $11,521, or $5.54 an hour if it is assumed that the household head was the only earner and she was employed full-year full-time. More than 2.2 million adult never-married, separated, divorced, or widowed women earned below this amount.

For at least two reasons these figures overstate the number of adult women who might join the AFDC rolls if they thought that the training guarantee could lead to higher-paying jobs. First, the data relate to all employed never-married, separated, divorced, or widowed working women, not just those caring for dependent children. And second, the stigma or distaste that a person might associate with receiving public assistance would deter some from entering the AFDC program.[30] Nonetheless, according to one simulation, if AFDC-eligibles with very low earnings capacities eventually recognize the wage growth potential that could be derived from enrollment in a stable welfare-to-work program, and the time and participation requirements of the program are not onerous, the caseload-increasing effect might be substantial.[31]

Alternatively, the provision of training assistance could reduce the size of the AFDC caseload in two ways, First, some AFDC-eligibles who might have joined the caseload before imposition of a training/work requirement would chose not to do so. In their estimation, the burden of the requirement would outweigh the earnings payoff from program participation. These women likely have higher earnings capacities than those who would opt to join the caseload were a training/work requirement imposed. They might already be able to get jobs that pay at least as much as the AFDC benefit.[32] Second, after participating in the training program, the increased earnings capacity of AFDC recipients might enable them to exit from the

---

[29] U.S. Bureau of Labor Statistics' unpublished data. The database covers employed wage and salary workers paid hourly rates.

[30] A portion of the 28-38 percent non-participation rate among AFDC-eligibles could be related to stigma, among other nonmonetary costs (e.g., time). Blank, *When Do Women Use AFDC & Food Stamps? The Dynamics of Eligibility vs. Participation, p. 39.*

[31] Moffitt, *The Effect of Work and Training Programs on Entry and exit from the Welfare Caseload,* p. 16-19.

[32] Ibid., p. 18.

welfare rolls. The likelihood of their rejoin the caseload could lessen as well. According to one simulation, however, it appears that the exit effect due to heightened earnings could be small compared to the caseload-reducing effect of those who would decide to forego AFDC entry and the caseload-increasing effect of those who would decide to enter the AFDC program.[33]

The possibility of increased entry into the AFDC program could be averted were the entire economically disadvantaged population give access to education/training services.[34] The question then becomes whether the market systematically underinvests in the educational/skill development of the whole economically disadvantaged group. If there were such an inefficient allocation of resources, it arguably could justify a universal program. On equity rather than efficiency grounds, another justification for a universal program might be a desire to treat all low-wage workers alike by giving each the same opportunity to enhance her/his human capital and to raise earnings at the low-skilled end of the income distribution.

Were training to become an entitlement for all low-skilled individuals, AFDC entry still would be more financially attractive than solely participating employment programs offered through the Job Training Partnership Act (JTPA). Income support is generally meager and not readily available to JTPA participants.

Currently, AFDC recipients as well as other economically disadvantaged youth and adults are eligible for training and other employment services through Title II-A of the Job Training Partnership Act (JTPA). Since the mid-1980s, more than 120,000 AFDC mothers have participated annually in JTPA'S Title II-A programs; they have accounted for roughly one-third of all female participants in these programs.[35] However, JTPA is a discretionary program; it is not an entitlement. It also is a voluntary program; not a mandatory one.

---

[33] Ibid., p. 23.

[34] Moffitt, *Incentive Effects of the U.S. Welfare System, p. 43-44.*

[35] Romero, Carol J. *JTPA Programs and Adult Women on Welfare: Using Training to Raise AFDC Recipients Above Poverty.* Research Report No. 93-01. Wash., National Commission for Employment Policy, June 1994. P. 1.

Because it is a voluntary program, the results presented below likely overstate the benefits of JTPA participation were enrollment to be required of all AFDC recipients. Although the AFDC/JTPA program participants had labor market problems in the sense that they had not been employed in the year before program enrollment, they still might have been more capable and motivated than those welfare recipients who elected not to enter training.[36] Under a mandatory program, then, with all AFDC adults being served, the *proportion* of participants who would become self-sufficient might be smaller and their progress toward that goal might be slower than is currently the case.

Among this possible more capable/motivated group, participation in JTPA Title II-A programs does *not* appear to make most AFDC mother-headed families financially self-sufficient -- depending upon one's definition.[37] Among the AFDC mothers who had not worked for at least one year before enrolling in JTPA and *who were employed in all four quarters following job placement:*

- 91.3 percent earned more than the maximum AFDC benefit level for a 3-person family in their State (which ranged from $2,388 to $5,904 across the 11 States included in the study);

- 38.7 percent earned enough to completely disqualify a 3-person family from AFDC eligibility in their State (this "gross income limit" ranged from $6,328 to $17,760); and,

- 31.4 percent were paid more than the Census Bureau's poverty level for a 3-person family in 1990 (9,885).

[36] For example, a larger proportion of the AFDC/JTPA participants had graduated high school than was true for the entire female AFDC population who had not been employed in the prior year. Similarly, a larger proportion of AFDC/JTPA participants reported being without jobs but actively looking for work in the prior year. In contrast, relatively more female AFDC recipients who had not worked in the prior year reported themselves as being out of the labor force. Romero, *JTPA Programs and Adult Women on Welfare*, p. 20.

[37] The three measures of self-sufficiency discussed above do not take into account non-cash benefits (e.g., subsidized child care and Medicaid) and do not adjust for taxes.

Because of higher hourly earnings or increases in time worked in the second year of employment, these percentages rose for each measure of self sufficiency:

- 94.2 percent earned more than the maximum AFDC benefit payment;

- 71.2 percent earned more than the AFDC income cutoff; and,

- 44.4 percent earned more than the poverty level.[38]

The year-to-year improvement was quite modest in terms of the proportion of AFDC/JTPA participants whose earnings exceeded the poverty threshold. Somewhat more than half of employed AFDC/JTPA mothers were unable to earn their way out of poverty within two years of job placement. According to the National Commission for Employment Policy,

[f]or a "two years and out" program, much more would be required. A higher percentage would need to be raised above poverty, and at a faster post-program pace ... This would necessitate training activities that are of sufficiently high quality to compensate for the women's lack of recent work experience, and prior education and training.

It is reasonable to believe that positive outcomes for both AFDC recipients and others would be obtained if modest increases in the number of AFDC women in JTPA were phased in over time and in a systematic manner. It seems less reasonable to believe that similar, or better, results would be obtained if there were massive and abrupt increases.[39]

---

[38] Romero, *JTPA Programs and Adult Women on Welfare,* p. 34.

[39] Ibid., p. 36 and 69.

Some JTPA services appear to be more beneficial than others in terms of moving AFDC mothers out of poverty and increasing their employment rate. AFDC/JTPA participants placed into jobs after undertaking either on -the-job training (OJT), occupational classroom training (OCT), or basic/remedial education (B/R Ed) were more likely to have earnings that exceeded the 1990 poverty threshold for a 3-person family in both the first and second post-program years than were participants placed into jobs after receiving job search assistance and/or support services (JSSA/SS), e.g., transportation and child care.[40] And, those AFDC/JTPA participants who were placed following completion of either OJT or OCT were more likely to be employed for the next 2 years than were those placed following receipt of JSSA/SS. The results of the three education/training interventions varied, however, depending upon the AFDC/JTPA participants' demographic characteristics (e.g., age, race/ethnicity, and education).[41]

In Conclusion

If income support through the AFDC program becomes time-limited and recipients are required to move from welfare to work, most recipients' educational attainment would qualify them for low-skilled, low-paying jobs. Depending upon the size of the employable AFDC population and the rate at which AFDC recipients would enter the labor market, there could be sufficient low-skilled jobs available to them. However, these jobs might not be located in close proximity to welfare recipients' homes. And, if there were a sudden, large influx of jobseeking AFDC recipients, it could not only make competition for the available jobs more intense but it could also depress the already low wages afforded by less skilled employment.

Given the low wages associated with less skilled jobs, some AFDC recipients who are able to find employment -- especially those who work less than full-year full-time -- might remain in poverty and still rely on the Government for means-tested assistance. In order for welfare recipients to

---

[40] Ibid., p. 46-49.

[41] Ibid., p. 58-59

be able to compete for higher-paying jobs, their skill levels would have to be raised. There is evidence to suggest, however, that within two years of completing and being placed from a JTPA Title II-A training program, somewhat over half of employed AFDC mothers earned below the poverty level for a 3-person family. While education/training assistance could raise the earnings potential of AFDC mothers, it might not -- on its own -- be up to the task of turning the majority of those on AFDC into economically self-sufficient families within 2-years time.

Although the intent behind time-limited receipt of income support is to reduce the number of AFDC recipients, the caseload might increase if education/training assistance were to become an entitlement for welfare recipients alone. If access to education/training were guaranteed to the entire economically disadvantaged population, however, this outcome might be avoided. But, AFDC recipiency still would likely be more financially attractive than just enrollment in JTPA Title II-A program because of the generally meager income support available through the Job Training Partnership Act.

APPENDIX TABLE 1. Selected Occupations Typically Requiring a High School Education or Less			
	Employment		
Occupations	1992 (000)	Absolute Change, 1992-2005 (000)	Percent Change, 1992-2005
SALES OCCUPATIONS			
Cashiers	6,764	1,620	37
Sales counter clerks	2,747	670	24
Salespersons, retail	242	88	36
Travel agents	3,660	786	21
	115	76	66
ADMINISTRATIVE SUPPORT OCCUPATIONS	15,042	1,852	14
Adjustment clerks	352	93	26
Bill and account collectors	235	94	40
Insurance claims clerks	116	43	37
Insurance policy processing clerks	172	34	20
Telephone operators (e.g., switchboard)	314	-89	-28
Receptionists and information clerks	904	305	34
Mail clerks and messengers	271	26	10
Material recording, scheduling, dispatching and distributing occupations	3,588	455	13
Stock clerks	1,782	158	9
Traffic, shipping, and receiving clerks	824	147	18

APPENDIX TABLE 1. Selected Occupations Typically Requiring a High School Education or Less

Occupations	1992 (000)	Employment Absolute Change, 1992-2005 (000)	Percent Change, 1992-2005
Records processing occupations	3,621	213	6
Bookkeeping, accounting, and auditing clerks	2,112	73	3
Billing, cost, and rate clerks	315	39	12
File clerks	257	48	19
Typists and word processors	789	-125	-16
General office clerks	2,688	654	24
Data entry keyers (except composing)	432	83	19
Bank tellers	525	-24	-4
Duplicating, mail & other office machine operators	162	21	13
Credit authorizers, credit checkers, & loan and credit clerks	218	53	24
Miscellaneous administrative support occupations	655	16	2
SERVICE OCCUPATIONS	17,371	5,906	32
Cleaning and building service occupations (excluding private household)	3,284	629	19
Janitors and cleaners (including maids and housekeeping cleaners)	2,862	548	19
Food preparation and service occupations	7,669	2,391	31
Cooks and other kitchen workers	3,092	1,190	38
Cooks, except shorter order	1,155	409	35

APPENDIX TABLE 1. Selected Occupations Typically Requiring a High School Education or Less

Occupations	Employment		
	1992 (000)	Absolute Change, 1992-2005 (000)	Percent Change, 1992-2005
Cooks, short order and fast food	714	257	36
Food preparation workers	1,223	524	43
Food and beverage service occupations	4,365	1,124	26
Waiters and waitresses	1,756	637	36
Food counter, fountain, & related workers	1,564	308	20
Bartenders	382	-32	-8
Diningroom & cafeteria attendants; bar helpers	441	131	30
All other food preparation & service workers	212	77	36
Health service occupations	2,041	1,032	51
Nursing aides and psychiatric aides	1,389	616	44
Personal service occupations	1,595	1,292	65
Child care workers	684	450	66
Home health aides	347	479	138
Personal and home care aides	127	166	130
Amusement and recreation attendants	207	96	46
Flight attendants	93	47	51
Ushers, lobby attendants, & ticket takers	56	16	29

APPENDIX TABLE 1. Selected Occupations Typically Requiring a High School Education or Less

Occupations	Employment		
	1992 (000)	Absolute Change, 1992-2005 (000)	Percent Change, 1992-2005
Baggage porters and bellhops	34	16	46
Manicurists	35	19	54
Shampooers	12	3	24
Private household workers (including cleaners, child care workers, and housekeepers)	869	-286	-33
Protective service occupations	1,034	495	48
Correction officers	282	197	70
Guards	803	408	51
Miscellaneous protective service workers	115	34	30
All other service workers	879	353	40
AGRICULTURE, FORESTRY, FISHING, & RELATED OCCUPATIONS (including farmers, farmworkers, gardeners & groundskeepers)	3,530	120	3
PRECISION PRODUCTION, CRAFT AND REPAIR OCCUPATIONS	12,618	1,754	10
Blue-collar worker supervisors	1,757	217	12
Construction trades	3,510	786	22
Carpenters	978	198	20
Electricians	518	100	19

APPENDIX TABLE 1. Selected Occupations Typically Requiring a High School Education or Less

Occupations	Employment		
	1992 (000)	Absolute Change, 1992-2005 (000)	Percent Change, 1992-2005
Painters and paperhangers	440	128	29
Plumbers, pipefitters, and steamfitters	351	27	8
Extractive occupations (including roustabouts, mining machine operators)	231	-6	-2
Mechanics, installers, and repairers	4,164	748	8
Machinery & related mechanics, installers, & repairers	1,696	310	18
Maintenance repairers, general utility	1,145	319	28
Vehicle & mobile equipment mechanics & repairers, except aircraft	1,393	309	22
Automotive mechanics	739	168	23
Automotive body & related repairers	202	61	30
Bus & truck mechanics	263	64	24
Telephone & cable tv line installers & repairers	165	-40	-24
Misc. electric/electronic equip. mechanics, installers and repairers	42	1	3
Other mechanics, installers, and repairers	868	168	19
Precision production occupations (including machinists & sheetmetal workers; inspectors, testers & graders; meatcutters; custom tailors and sewers; & cabinetmakers)	2,956	9	0
OPERATORS, FABRICATORS, AND LABORERS	16,349	1,553	10

APPENDIX TABLE 1. Selected Occupations Typically Requiring a High School Education or Less

Occupations	Employment		
	1992 (000)	Absolute Change, 1992-2005 (000)	Percent Change, 1992-2005
Textile, apparel & related machine operators	1,041	-212	-20
Laundry & drycleaning machine operators & tenders (excluding pressing)	162	75	46
Truck drivers, light & heavy	2,391	648	27
Hand packers & packagers	685	85	12

Source: Derived by CRS from unpublished BLS data on workers' educational distribution by detailed occupation and on occupations grouped by usual type of training; and, Silvestri, George. Occupational Employment: Wide Variations in Growth. *Monthly Labor Review*, November 1993. p. 61-73.

APPENDIX TABLE 2. Median Annual Earnings of Female Wage and Salary Workers in Selected Low-Skilled Occupations by Hours and Weeks Worked, 1992

Occupation	All Workers	Full-Year Full-Time	Full-Year Part-Time	Part-Year Full-Time	Part-Year Part-Time
SALES OCCUPATIONS					
Cashiers	$5,000	$12,000	$6,547	$4,040	$2,000
ADMINISTRATIVE SUPPORT OCCUPATIONS					
Information clerks (including receptionists)	$12,160	$17,524	$7,000	$8,000	$2,639
Records processing occupations	$15,000	$19,000	$7,500	$8,800	$2,600
Bookkeeping, accounting, & auditing clerks	$15,325	$19,000	$8,200	$10,102	$4,060
Billing, cost, & rate clerks	$16,500	$21,000	$10,200	$14,400	$3,054
File clerks	$8,000	$16,429	–	–	$2,000
Material recording, scheduling, dispatching & distributing occupations	$15,000	$21,000	$7,800	$9,500	$2,800
Stock & inventory clerks	$15,550	$20,000	–	–	–
Traffic, shipping, & receiving clerks	$12,500	$18,000	–	–	–
Typists	$12,800	$19,000	$8,000	$9,200	–
General office clerks	$13,000	20,000	$7,345	$6,025	$1,900
Data entry keyers (except composing)	$15,000	$17,754	–	$7,975	–
Bank tellers	$12,000	$14,000	$8,260	–	–
SERVICE OCCUPATIONS					
Janitors & cleaners	$5,642	$13,000	$5,000	$3,900	$1,350
Nursing aides, orderlies, & attendants	$10,000	$14,000	$7,900	$7,000	$3,259

APPENDIX TABLE 2. Median Annual Earnings of Female Wage and Salary Workers in Selected Low-Skilled Occupations by Hours and Weeks Worked, 1992

Occupation	All Workers	Full-Year Full-Time	Full-Year Part-Time	Part-Year Full-Time	Part-Year Part-Time
Food preparation & service workers	$5,000	$11,700	$6,000	$5,000	$2,000
Cooks	$7,000	$12,000	$7,000	$7,099	$2,477
Food preparation workers	$4,862	-	-	-	$2,160
Waiters & waitresses	$5,000	$11,000	$6,000	$5,000	$2,500
Food counter, fountain, & related workers	$2,028	-	$4,800	-	$1,500
Bartenders	$9,000	$12,000	-	-	-
Child care providers	$2,500	-	-	-	$1,200
Private household workers	$2,237	$9,200	$4,000	$2,300	$500
Guards	$3,400	-	-	$2,600	$2,000
FARMING, FORESTRY, & FISHING OCCUPATIONS	$3,500	$10,000	-	$4,000	$830
PRECISION PRODUCTION, CRAFT, & REPAIR OCCUPATIONS					
Precision production occupations	$14,560	$18,000	-	$7,800	$2,700
OPERATORS, FABRICATORS, & LABORERS					
Textile sewing machine operators	$10,000	$12,483	-	$6,480	-
Packaging & filling machine operators	$13,000	$15,000	-	$7,000	-
Assemblers	$14,000	$17,000	-	$7,989	-
Production inspectors, checkers, & examiners	$16,276	$19,700	-	$10,000	-

APPENDIX TABLE 2. Median Annual Earnings of Female Wage and Salary Workers in Selected Low-Skilled Occupations by Hours and Weeks Worked, 1992

Occupation	All Workers	Full-Year Full-Time	Full-Year Part-Time	Part-Year Full-Time	Part-Year Part-Time
Bus drivers	$9,235	--	--	--	$7,000
Stock handlers & baggers	$6,000	$12,000	$6,060	--	$1,200
Hand packers & packagers	$10,320	$15,000	--	$4,671	--
Laborers (except construction)	$9,000	$15,500	--	--	--

-- reflects insufficient sample size.
Source: Created by CRS from the March supplement to the Current Population Survey.

TAX INCENTIVES TO TRAIN OR RETRAIN THE WORK FORCE*

Nonna A. Noto
and
Louis Alan Talley

This report explains the provisions contained in the Internal Revenue Code related to training and retraining of workers, in the context of current labor market concerns. In addition, it describes two proposals included in the *Small Business Job Protection Act* (H.R. 3448) and two proposals advanced in President Clinton's FY1997 Budget.

On May 22, 1996, the House of Representatives approved the *Small Business Job Protection Act* (H.R. 3448), which contains provisions that would extend two expired tax provisions related to labor force training.[1] The bill would extend retroactively the expired employer educational assistance provision of prior law. It also would institute a new work opportunity credit designed to replace the expired targeted jobs tax credit (TJTC).

H.R. 3448 was attached to legislation that would increase the minimum wage (H.R. 1227), passed by the House on May 23, 1996. Ways and Means Committee Chairman Archer had expressed concern over the proposed minimum wage hike. He hoped to mitigate entry-level job losses by providing small businesses with tax incentives aimed at increasing training

---

* Excerpted from *CRS Report* 96-439E

and productivity for workers. Senate Finance Committee Chairman Roth announced that the Senate Finance Committee would mark up the legislation following the Memorial Day recess.

In general, the provisions in the current tax code and the expired provisions proposed for extension favor the financing of education and training by employers rather than individuals themselves. The deduction that is available to individuals favors training for a person's current employment rather than retraining for another line of work.

LABOR MARKET CONTEXT[2]

The skills that individuals possess are important to their success in the labor market, and this has become increasingly so in recent decades. For example, many traditionally coveted blue-collar jobs that require relatively little education but provide fairly high wages have in large part been foreclosed to new entrants to the labor force. Employers have been responding to foreign competition by restructuring their operations

> by moving assembly operations overseas or by introducing more productive equipment...[M]any workers who received high wages to repeat simple tasks required by the mass production techniques employed throughout the U.S. economy lost their jobs or moved to other, less well-paying jobs. In some cases, their jobs were reorganized to require an ability to monitor a machine or to work as part of a team; either responsibility makes demands on reading, mathematical, communication, and other skills that operator, fabricator, and laborer jobs typically do not require. [3]

---

[1] U.S. Library of Congress. Congressional Research Service. *Expiring tax Provisions.* Issue Brief No. IB95064, by Sylvia Morrison, (continually updated). Washington, 1996. 8 p.

[2] The authors gratefully acknowledge the writing of Linda Levine, Section Head of the Labor and Industries Section of the Economics Division, in this section on the labor market.

[3] Eck, Alan. Job-Related Education and Training: Their Impact on Earnings. *Monthly Labor Review, October 1993. P. 36.*

In contrast with the downward trend since 1979 in the number of less skilled blue-collar jobs, much of the job growth in occupations that typically require that workers have no more than a high school degree has occurred in relatively low-paying jobs -- such as cleaning, food, and health service jobs.

Job growth has been most rapid among occupations that typically require the highest levels of educational attainment. About 63% of workers between 25 and 64 years old who held managerial and professional jobs in 1195 were at least college graduates, according to data from the U.S. Bureau of Labor Statistics. Employment in this occupational group grew by 66% (or 14 million jobs) between 1979 and 1994.[4] During these years, job growth across all occupational groups averaged 26.4% (or 26.1 million jobs). Thus, the increased demand for workers in the highest skilled group accounted from somewhat more than half of total job growth in the 16-year period.

Moreover, less educated workers have borne the brunt of the decline in real earnings that has been going on since the med-1970s. The most striking trend has been the poor performance among men who have not graduated from high school: the real weekly earnings of all men aged 25-64 with 11 or fewer years of education fell by about 26% between 1979 and 1993.[5] Although real earnings also declined among men who were high school graduates (by 18%) and among men with some post-secondary education (by 12%), the falloff was not nearly as steep. Among women, only those who did not graduate high school experienced a drop (by 9%) in real weekly earnings over the period.

As a consequence, the wage gap between more and less educated workers has widened considerably. Changes in employer demand for occupational groups might account for roughly one-third of the increase in the education-earnings differential during the 1980s. The demand for skills typically possessed by more educated workers actually began to rise dur-

---

[4] U.S. Library of Congress . Congressional research Service. *Employment Trends: A Fact Sheet.* Report no. 95-763 by Linda Levine. Washington, Updated April 17, 1996. 2 p.

[5] U.S. Bureau of Labor Statistics. *Report on the American Workforce.* Wash., 1994. P. 70. For more information on this issue, see: U.S. Library of Congress. Congressional Research Service. *Real Wage Trends: An Overview.* Report no. 95-537 E., by Gail McCallion. Washington, April 27, 1995. 20 p.

ing the 1970s. In that decade, there was less of a supply-demand mismatch because many highly educated baby-boomers were entering the labor force, which helped to fill the increased demand for skilled workers. In contrast, during the 1980s, college graduates entered the labor force at a decelerating rate. Steady increases in the relative demand for skilled workers seemingly outpaced increases in supply, so that the wage premium for college-educated workers rose during the decade. Moreover, there may have been

> an increase in the return to the general skills possessed by college graduates (for example, the analytical and cognitive skills that are not specific to a particular job), and not just to the more specialized skills demanded in the types of occupations college graduates tend to fill.[6]

Thus, it appears that to succeed in the current labor market, skill acquisition matters even more than it did in the not-so-distant past. This is true not only for workers newly entering the labor force, but also for experienced workers striving to improve their skills while remaining in the same field as well as those seeking better opportunities in other fields. In the latter case, some experienced workers may voluntarily by trying to change occupations; others may feel compelled to do so because, as noted above, demand for their occupational "skill bundle" has diminished.[7] Consequently, both training *and* retraining would seem to be important elements in the development of a workforce capable of adapting to ongoing economic change.

Various legislative proposals have been suggested in recent Congresses to help train prospective employees for jobs or retrain current employees for more skilled jobs. The proposals are based upon the belief that human resources are no less important to the economy and welfare of the Nation

---

[6] Gittleman, Maury. Earnings in the 1980's: An Occupation Perspective. *Monthly Labor Review*, July 1994. P. 25.

[7] For more information on the incidence and job and wage prospects of dislocated workers, see: U.S. Library of Congress. Congressional Research Service. *Dislocated Workers: Characteristics and Experiences, 1979-1992.* Report no. 92-813 E, by Linda Levine. Washington, Nov. 16, 1992. 26 p.

than the updating of business plant and equipment. Programs that provide training are seen as one method to help solve unemployment problems.

CURRENT TAX LAW

TRADE OR BUSINESS EXPENSES (SECTION 162)[8]

Under current tax law, qualified educational expenses may be deducted by an individual taxpayer or by a business firm.

EXPENDITURES BY INDIVIDUALS

Under the individual income tax, expenses for training made by the employee (himself or herself) may be deductible if they qualify under the provisions for employee educational expenses. The educational expenses deduction for the individual is <u>not</u> geared toward retraining and has limits that make it unusable for many taxpayers.

Your Federal Income Tax, Publication 17 of the Internal Revenue Service, states:

"Requirements. The education must:

(1)   Be required by your employer or the law to keep your present salary, status, or job (and serve a business purpose of your employer), or

(2)   Maintain or improve skills needed in your present work."[9]

---

[8] *Internal Revenue Code* (I.R.C.) section numbers are provided (in parentheses) from the I.R.C. of 1986.

[9] U.S. Department of the Treasury, Internal Revenue Service. *Your Federal Income Tax: for Individuals, For Use in Preparing 1995 Returns. Tax Guide 1995.* Publication 17. Washington, U.S. Govt. Print. Off., 1994. P. 218.

There are two conditions under which a taxpayer may not claim a deduction for such educational expenses:

"**Exception.** Even if your education meets one of the requirements above, it is not qualifying education if it:

1)   Is needed to meet the minimum educational requirements of your present trade or business, or

(2)   Is part of a program of study that can qualify you for a new trade or business, even if you have no plans to enter that trade or business.

Present work. Your education must relate to your present work. Education that will relate to work you may enter in the future is not qualifying education. Education that prepares you for a future occupation includes any education that keeps you up-to-date for a return to work or that qualifies you to reenter a job you had in the past."[10]

Furthermore, the educational expense deduction may only be claimed by taxpayers who itemize their deductions. Such taxpayers tend to be higher income taxpayers. With the passage of the *Tax Reform Act of 1986* (P.L. 99-514), educational expenses must now be added together with other miscellaneous deductions, and then subject to a floor of 2% of adjusted gross income. Simply stated, only when educational expenses combined with other deductible miscellaneous deductions exceed 2% of adjusted gross income may the portion that exceeds the 2% floor be deducted. The floor negates the benefit of the deduction for many taxpayers who otherwise itemize.

---

[10] *Ibid.*

In addition to the 2% floor on miscellaneous deduction, high income taxpayers are subject to a limitation on certain itemized deductions.[11] Itemized deductions are reduced by 3% of the amount by which the taxpayer's adjusted gross income exceeds a threshold (indexed for inflation). For 1996, the phaseout threshold is $117,950. The law does not allow the affected subgroup of itemized deductions to be reduced by more than 80% in the aggregate.

The *Tax Reform Act of 1986* also provided that educational travel was no longer to be allowable as a deduction. The conference Report states: "No deduction is allowed for costs of travel that would be deductible only on the grounds that the travel itself constitutes a form of education (e.g., where a teacher of French travels to France to maintain general familiarity with the French language and culture, or where a social studies teacher travels to another state to learn about or photograph its people, customs, geography, etc.)."[12]

EXPENDITURES BY BUSINESSES

For a business, training and retraining expenses may be deductible as either in-house training or outside educational assistance. On a business tax return, in-house training expenses could be subsumed under salaries and equipment expenses or could be accounted for as payments to contractors. Outside educational assistance is likely to be accounted for under employee benefits expenses.

DEFINITION OF GROSS INCOME (SECTION 61)

Benefit payments to participants in certain training and retraining programs and work-training programs are not included in the gross income of

---

[11] Itemized deductions of high-income taxpayers subject to the limitation include deductions for mortgage interest, state and local taxes, and charitable contributions. The limitation does not apply to deductions for medical expenses, casualty and theft losses, and investment interest expenses.

[12] U.S. Congress. Conference Committees, 1986. *Tax Reform Act of 1986. Conference Report to Accompany H.R. 3838.* Washington, U.S. Govt. Print. Off., 1986. P. 30 (House, 99th Congress, 2nd session, House Report No 99-841)

recipients, as defined for tax purposes. Simply stated, these payments are exempt from the individual income tax. Under generally accepted principles of taxation, such benefit payments would be treated as income and taxable to the recipient. Thus, the exclusion of these benefit payments from individual income taxation provides a tax incentive effect for individuals to participate in these training, retraining, and work-training programs. The programs are all publicly sponsored--by federal, state, or local government.

PROPOSALS TO EXTEND EXPIRED TAX PROVISIONS

TARGETED JOBS TAX CREDIT (TJTC) (SECTION 51)[13]

Special Note: *This provision expired as of December 31, 1994.*

The targeted jobs tax credit was intended to promote private sector hiring of members of specifically designated, hard-to-employ groups. The tax credit was available to employers who hired members of nine targeted groups. Members of these groups were also considered likely to have educational deficiencies that hampered their employment prospects and to require more than the average amount of training once employed. *However, for an employer to receive the tax credit, the employer needed only to hire the worker; the provision of training was not required.* The nine targeted groups were: vocational rehabilitation referrals, economically disadvantaged youth (18-22) years old), economically disadvantaged Vietnam-era veterans, SSI recipients, AFDC recipients or WIN registrants, general assistance recipients, economically disadvantaged students (16-19) years old) participating in cooperative education programs, economically

---

[13] U.S. Library of Congress. Congressional Research Service. *Targeted Jobs Tax Credit: Prospects in the 104th Congress.* Issue Brief No. IB95005, by Linda Levine, (continually updated). Washington, 1996. 14 p. See also: *The Targeted Jobs Tax Credit, 1978-1994.*CRS Report no. 95-981 E, by Linda Levine. Washington, September 19, 1995. 21 p.

disadvantaged ex-offenders,[14] and economically disadvantaged youth (18-22 years old) hired for summer jobs.

The credit was equal to 40% of the first $6,000 of qualified first-year wages for all target group members except summer youth, for whom it was 40% of up to $3,000. The amount of the company's deduction for wages was reduced dollar-for-dollar by the amount of the credit. To qualify for the credit the employer must have retained these employees for a minimum of 90 days or 120 hours of service, except for summer youth hires whose minimum retention period was 14 days or 20 hours.

PROPOSAL FOR A WORK OPPORTUNITY CREDIT

On May 14, 1996, the House Ways and Means Committee approved as part of the *Small Business Job Protection Act* (H.R. 3448) a jobs credit that is substantially revised and even renamed. While the former TJTC is not included in H.R. 3448, the committee did pass a provision for a new tax credit called the *Work Opportunity Tax Credit*.[15] This proposed credit was previously included in *Budget Reconciliation Act of 1995* (H.R. 2415) vetoed by President Clinton on December 5, 1995. The House of Representatives passed H.R. 3448 on May 22, 1996. The following day, the House passed a bill increasing the minimum wage (H.R. 1227). The minimum wage bill was incorporated into the *Small Business Job Protection Act* (H.R. 3448) before being sent to the Senate for action. The Senate Finance Committee has indicated its desire to mark-up the bill before action by the full Senate in early June.

The proposed new *Work Opportunity Tax Credit* would be available to employers for newly hired employees who begin work after July 1, 1996, and before June 30, 1997. The credit rate of 35% (5% less than the TJTC) is applied to the first $6,000 of wages. Qualified first -year wages are $3,000 for summer youth employees. No credit is allowed unless the

---

[14] *The Revenue Reconciliation Act of 1990* clarified that an individual is to be treated as convicted if a State court places him or her on probation without making a finding of guilty.

[15] U.S. Library of Congress. Congressional Research Service. *The Work Opportunities Tax Credit: A Fact Sheet.* Report no. 96-356 E, by Linda Levine. Washington, May 8, 1996. 2 p.

worker is employed by the employer for at least 180 days or 500 hours (20 days or 120 hours in the case of summer youth employees).

The number of targeted groups would be reduced from nine to six. In some cases, the description of members included within the group is modified. The six groups would include: individuals in families receiving assistance under a IV-A (AFDC) program for at least a nine-month period ending on the hiring date, certain veterans in families receiving assistance under a IV-A (AFDC) program or food stamp benefits and veterans discharged for a service-connected disability, qualified ex-felons, high-risk youth (ages 18 to 25) who reside in empowerment zones or enterprise communities, vocational rehabilitation referrals, and summer youth employees (over age 16 but under age 18) who reside in empowerment zones or enterprise communities. While the tax credit mechanism may provide an indirect incentive for employers to undertake the expense of providing jobs and training to economically disadvantaged individuals, many of whom are underskilled and/or undereducated, the proposal contains no requirement for employer-provided training.

LEGISLATIVE HISTORY OF THE TJTC

The targeted jobs tax credit was first created with the passage of the *Revenue Act of 1978* (P.L. 95-600), effective through the end of 1981. The provision was both amended and extended for one year by the *Economic Recovery Tax Act of 1981* (P.L. 97-34). An extension for two additional years (through 1984) and the establishment of a special credit for creation of summer jobs for economically disadvantaged 16- and 17-year olds was provided under provisions of the *Tax Equity and Fiscal Responsibility Act of 1982* (P.L. 97-248). A one-year extension was provided by the *Deficit Reduction Act of 1984* (P.L. 98-369). The *Tax Reform Act of 1986* (P.L. 99-514) reauthorized the credit retroactively to December 31, 1985, and extended it for 3 years (through December 31, 1988). The act reduced the credit rate, eliminated the second-year credit, and added a retention requirement.

Again, with passage of the *Technical and Miscellaneous Revenue Act of 1988* (P.L. 100-647), the credit was amended and extended, this time for a one-year period that expired on December 31, 1989. With the passage of the *Revenue Reconciliation Act of 1989* (P.L. 101-239), the provision was extended through September 30, 1990. Once again the program was extended retroactively, this time through December 31, 1991, by the passage of the *Omnibus Budget Reconciliation Act of 1990* (P.L. 101-508).

To prevent the program from expiring, the Congress passed the *Tax Extension Act of 1991* (P.L. 102-227), which continued this and a number of other expiring provisions until June 30, 1992. The Congress provided for further extension of the provision in H.R. 4210, the *Tax Fairness and Economic Growth Act of 1992*, but the legislation was vetoed by President Bush. The credit was reauthorized and made retroactive to July 1, 1992, with an extension through December 31, 1994, by the *Omnibus Budget Reconciliation Act of 1993* (P.L. 103-66).

In September 1995 the House Ways and Means Committee approved a *Work Opportunity Tax Credit* available to employers that hire members of five targeted groups. The 35% credit would be applied to a portion of first-year wages. The provision was retained in the proposed *Seven-Year Balanced Budget Reconciliation Act of 1995* (H.R. 2491), approved by the Congress but vetoed by President Clinton on December 5, 1995. The provision was not an issue in the veto. Thus, the TJTC has expired and been reauthorized retroactively three times. While the proposal for a *Work Opportunity Tax Credit* has been previously approved by Congress, it has never been enacted into law. Federal budgetary constraints and negative research findings contributed to the TJTC remaining a temporary measure.

EMPLOYER EDUCATIONAL ASSISTANCE (SECTION 127)[16]

Special Note: This provision expired after December 31, 1994.

Under a comprehensive income tax, employer payments for educational assistance would be treated as income and taxable to the recipient. Thus, like the excluded benefit payments from gross income discussed earlier

---

[16] U.S. Library of Congress. Congressional Research Service, *Employer Education Assistance: Overview of tax Status and Legislation in the 104ᵗʰ Congress.* Report 94-761 EPW, by Bob Lyke. Washington, Updated May 15, 1996. 2 p.

under I.R.C. Section 61, the exclusion of educational payments made by an employer from individual income taxation provides a tax incentive effect for employees to participate in employer-paid educational assistance programs.

Under the expired law, individual taxpayers were able to exclude from gross income employer payments for educational assistance that encompassed tuition, fees, books, supplies, etc. The annual limit for excluded employer payments was $5,250 per employee.

The exclusion was not limited to education that was needed for one's current trade or business, as is the case with educational expense deductions permitted under Section 162 (discussed previously). Consequently, it could have applied to training for a new job or career. Nor was it subject to the requirement that the individual itemize, or to a floor or phaseout related to the individual's adjusted gross income, as is the educational expense deduction for individuals. Thus through the employer educational assistance exclusion the tax code favored training and retraining financed by employers over that financed by individuals.

Beginning in 1991, the exclusion amount applied to employer payment for graduate-level courses taken by an individual pursuing a program leading to a law, business, medical, or similar advanced academic or profession degree. However, this rule did not apply to graduate teaching or research assistants receiving tuition reduction under Internal Revenue Code Section 117(d). Courses involving sport, games, or hobbies were covered only if they involved the employer's business or were part of a degree program.[17]

PROPOSAL FOR EXTENSION AND MODIFICATION

The *Small Business Job Protection Act* (H.R. 3448) passed by the House of Representatives on May 22, 1996, includes an extension of the exclusion for employer provided educational assistance (Section 127) with a modification. The House version would restore the provision retroactive to

---

[17] Commerce Clearing House, Inc. *1995 United States Master Tax Guide.* Chicago, Commerce Clearing House, 1994. P. 240.

its expiration on December 31, 1994, and extend it through December 31, 1997. The House maintained the exclusion for graduate-level courses for tax year 1995, since the past practice of reauthorizing the provision after expiration may have led both employers and employees to assume such courses would remain covered. The House Ways and Means Committee indicated that it is because of budgetary constraints and a desire to target the benefit to those most in need of educational opportunities that, beginning after December 31, 1995, the exclusion would not apply to graduate-level courses.

LEGISLATIVE HISTORY OF SECTION 127

Section 127 was first added to the Internal Revenue Code with the passage of the *Revenue Act of 1978* (P.L. 95-600), effective through the end of 1983. The provision was extended from the end of 1983 through 1985 by *Education Assistance Programs* (P.L. 98-611), which also established a $5,000 annual limit on the exclusion. The *Tax Reform Act of 1986* (P.L. 99-514) raised the maximum excludable assistance from $5,000 to the current level of $5,250 and extended it through 1987. *The Technical and Miscellaneous Revenue Act of 1988* P.L. 100-647) reauthorized the exclusion retroactively to January 1, 1988, and extended it until December 31, 1988. *The Revenue Reconciliation Act of 1989* (P.L. 101-239) again reauthorized the provision retroactively to January 1, 1989, and extended it through September 30, 1990. With the passage of the *Revenue Reconciliation act of 1990* (P.L. 101-239), the provision was extended through December 31, 1991.

The provision was further extended for six month (through June 30, 1992) by the *Tax Extension Act of 1991* (P.L. 102-227). The six-month extension was provided while Congress tried to fashion a longer term solution to the continual reauthorization of the provision. Congress passed legislation in the 102nd Congress to extend the provision (H.R. 4210, *Tax Fairness and Economic Growth Act of 1992)*, but the bill was vetoed by President Bush. During the first session of the 103d Congress, this provision, along with a number of others (see targeted jobs tax credit), was retroactively extended from July 1, 1992, through December 31, 1994, under provisions of the *Omnibus Budget Reconciliation Act of 1993* (P.L. 103-66). Budget constraints have been a principal factor in preventing the Congress from making the provision a permanent one.

The 104th Congress has previously sent to President Clinton an extension of this provision with the modification to exclude graduate-level courses after December 31, 1995 (the restriction retained in the proposed *Small Business Job Protection Act.* (H.R. 3448)). That proposed extension was part of the *Seven-Year Balanced Budget Reconciliation Act of 1995* (H.R. 2491), a bill vetoed by President Clinton on December 5, 1995. The employer educational assistance provision was not an issue in the veto.

CLINTON ADMINISTRATION'S FY1997 BUDGET PROPOSALS

The Clinton Administration's budget for fiscal year 1997 contains two tax proposals that would subsidize expenditures by individuals (rather than employers) for higher education and job training.[18]

A *Tuition Tax Deduction*[19] would permit a deduction of up to $5,000 a year for qualifying education and training expenses in 1996, 1997, and 1998; it would rise to $10,000 in tax years 1999 and 2000. The deduction would sunset after that final year.[20] Under the proposal, the deduction would be phased out for returns with modified AGI[21] of $100,000 to $120,000. The phase-out range would be $70,000 to $90,000 for other taxpayers. Qualifying education expenses would be those related to post-

---

[18] U.S. Executive Office of the President. Office of Management and Budget. *Budget of the United States Government, Fiscal Year 1997.* Washington, U.S. Govt. Print. Off., February 5, 1996 (released March 18, 1996). *Budget Supplement, p. 111-113. Analytical Perspectives,* p. 36-37.

[19] For more information on this proposal, see U.S. Congress. Congressional Research Service. *Tuition Tax Deduction: Issues Raised by the President's Proposal.* Report no. 95-186 EPW, by Bob Lyke. Washington, updated March 1, 1996. 6 p.

[20] The President's original tuition tax deduction proposal was subsequently modified to sunset in 2000.

[21] Modified AGI)adjusted gross income) includes taxable Social Security benefits and certain income earned abroad.

secondary education and paid to institutions and programs eligible for federal assistance. Qualifying expenses would include tuition and fees directly related to a student's enrollment in degree programs and courses to improve or acquire new job skills; they would not include meals, lodging, books, or transportation. The deduction would be available for the education of a taxpayer, his or her spouse, or dependents and would be available whether or not a taxpayer itemizes deductions. When fully implemented, the deduction could cut the federal income taxes of eligible families by up to $2, 800 in a given year.

President Clinton's proposal for *Expanded Individual Retirement Accounts*[22] (IRAs) would permit contributors to withdraw from their account (either the traditional or proposed new Special IRA account), at any time, without the 10% penalty for early withdrawal, to pay for post-secondary education, as well as first-time home purchases, expenses during a period of unemployment, or catastrophic medical expenses (including payments for qualified long-term care services for an incapacitated parent or grandparent).

Under the proposal, qualified educational expenses include directly related expenses such as tuition and fees. Amounts withdrawn may be used to pay the expenses of not only the taxpayer but also the taxpayer's dependents and spouse. Withdrawals may also be made for educational expenses of a child or grandchild even if they no longer qualify as taxpayer's dependent. The proposal also provides that monies from IRAs may be use d to invest in state prepaid tuition programs. Qualified state prepaid tuition programs are defined as those plans established or maintained by states that provide conversion into a percentage of tuition expenses for an individual when funds are used to pay tuition expenses, or may be redeemed if the funds are not used for education (provided that the amount of redemption not be less than the purchase price less administrative expenses).

Currently, for taxpayers who participate in employer-sponsored retirement plans, the tax code phases out the availability of deductible IRAs

---

[22] The President's proposal was introduced May23, 1996, by the Senate and House Democratic leaders. This proposal is called the *Retirement Savings and Security Act*.

(where the amount the taxpayer contributes in a give year can be deducted from taxable income) for AGI from $40,000 to $50,000 for joint returns (and $25,000 to $35,000 for single returns). The President's plan would double this range, in two stages. First, beginning in 1996 the phase-out would range between $70,000 and $90,000 for joint returns (and $45,000 to $65,000 for single returns). Then, beginning in 1999, the phase-out would increase to $86,000 to $100,000 for joint returns (and $50,000 to $70,000 for single returns). The President's plan also would index for inflation these phase-out ranges and the current annual maximum contribution limit of $1,000 per year per individual (or $2,250 for a married couple filing jointly with one wage earner).

The Administration's expanded IRA proposal would also permit eligible taxpayers to contribute to a "Special IRA" as an alternative to a deductible IRA. Amounts contributed to Special IRAs (sometimes referred to as back-loaded IRAs) would not be tax deductible, but distributions of the contributions would be tax-free and, if contributors kept their funds in the account for at least 5 years, earnings on the contributions would be distributed tax-free as well.

WELFARE: WORK (DIS)INCENTIVES IN THE WELFARE SYSTEM[*]

Thomas Gabe
and
Gene Falk

"Welfare" usually refers to the Aid to Families with Dependent Children (AFDC) program, which provides benefits to families with children headed by a single parent (two parents if one is incapacitated or unemployed) and with incomes below State-determined limits. AFDC is jointly financed by the Federal Government and the States, but States administer the program. States define "need," which determines eligibility, and States set benefit levels.

Most AFDC adult recipients are not working or looking for work in months during which they received aid, according to survey data. Income eligibility thresholds in many States are so low that even meager earnings make a family ineligible for AFDC. Research has provided evidence that there is much movement between work and welfare.[1] Though some mothers "cycle" between work and welfare, relatively few simultaneously receive AFDC and work. Need-tested programs other than AFDC provide assistance to low-income families when they have a working member. Such families are much more likely to receive food stamps than AFDC.

---

[*] Excerpted from *CRS Report* 95-105 EPW

[1] For a discussion of research about time on welfare and movements from welfare to work, see: U.S. Library of Congress. Congressional Research Service. *Welfare: A Review of Studies About Time Spent on Welfare*. CRS Report for Congress No. 94-539 EPW, by Gene Falk. (Updated) Dec. 16, 1994. 22 p.

The Earned Income Tax Credit (EITC) provides income supplements only to lower-income workers.

Much has been said about the "work disincentives" of the welfare system. Those on welfare who go to work see their income rise substantially less than the amount of their earnings, because need-tested benefits are reduced as earned income rises. This report illustrates some of the work incentives and disincentives associated with the current welfare system.[2] It provides a State-by-State summary of income levels of women who are not working and women who earn the Federal minimum wage ($4.25 an hour in 1994) at selected levels of work.[3] It also provides a summary of how mothers' net incomes change as they work their way off welfare.

INCOME AND BENEFITS

Mothers receiving AFDC face varying financial incentives to work, depending on States' combined AFDC and food stamp benefit levels, the methods by which these benefits phase out as earnings increase, and the expenses a mother may incur (such as child care) if she decides to go to work. The relative rewards of work compared to welfare also depend on the hourly wage she is able to command in the labor market, the number of hours she is willing to work, and other benefits associated with a job, such as health insurance.

NONWORKING MOTHERS

Most women on AFDC do not work while they are on the program's benefit rolls. A 1992 survey of AFDC cases found that 6.4% of AFDC female adults reported being employed, 12.0% were on layoff or actively looking

---

[2] The illustrations in the report were generated by a computer simulation of the benefits a mother would be eligible to receive at various levels of work effort. See appendix A for details on the methods used to create these illustrations.

[3] The illustrations shown in this report hold the wage rate constant at $4.25 an hour and permit hours of work per week to vary. This greatly simplifies the analysis. Additionally, economic theory generally assumes that, in the short-run, a person with a given set of characteristics (e.g., education, skills, and work experience) has little control over the wage rate offered by, at a given wage rate, has some control over the number of hours of labor she wishes to supply.

for work, and 16.1% were at school or in training. The majority of women on AFDC -- 65.1% -- had no contact with the labor force nor were they engaged in training for future work activity. AFDC recipients also typically report no other form of income. In 1992, 79% said they had no cash income other than AFDC.[4]

The income level that Federal/State governments provide to a woman without any other income varies from State-to-State; that level, the income *guarantee,* depends primarily on State maximum AFDC benefits. State maximum AFDC benefits also vary by family size.

Figure 1 shows combined AFDC benefits (shares paid by State and Federal funds) and food stamp benefits by State, ranked by AFDC benefit, for a nonworking mother with two children.[5] The figure shows that AFDC benefits for a nonworking mother vary markedly among States. Mississippi's annual AFDC benefit for a family of three in January 1994 was $1,440, whereas New York's (Suffolk County) annual AFDC benefit was $8,436, nearly six times that of Mississippi.[6]

---

[4] See: U.S. Congress. House. Committee on Ways and Means. *Overview of Entitlement Programs, 1994 Green Book. Background Materials and Data on Programs Within the Jurisdiction of the Committee on Ways and Means.* WMCP 103-27. Washington, GPO, July 15, 1994. P. 401-404.

[5] In addition to AFDC and food stamps, families on AFDC are automatically eligible for Medicaid. However, because the methods for valuing noncash medical benefits are controversial, the "value" of Medicaid to these families is not shown. In addition, some AFDC families might also be receiving other forms of aid, such as public housing, special supplemental feeding for women, infants, and children (WIC), or free school lunches, which are also not included in this report.

[6] Appendix B provides tables for the data displayed in figure 1 and all the figures shown in this report.

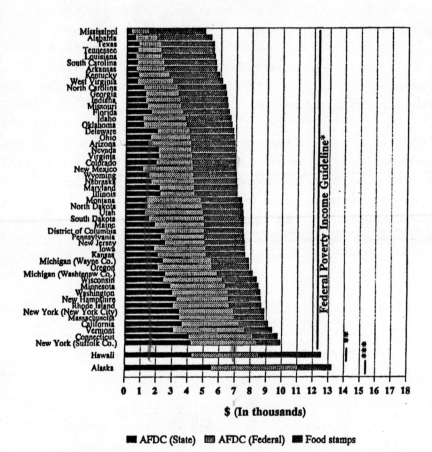

Figure 1. Sources of Income for a Single Mother with 2 Children and Not Working--1994

*   Federal Poverty Income Guideline for a family of 3 (1994): $12,320.
**   In Hawaii: $14,170.
*** In Alaska: $15,400.

Source: CRS.

Under the AFDC Federal matching formula (which relates the Federal funding share inversely to State per capita income), the Federal Government reimburses New York 50 cents for every AFDC dollar it spends, whereas Mississippi is reimbursed nearly 79 cents for every AFDC dollar it spends. Consequently, the Federal Government paid nearly four times as much for an AFDC family in Suffolk County, New York ($4,218) as for one in Mississippi (1,135). New York (Suffolk County) pays nearly 14 times what Mississippi pays out of State funds toward the basic AFDC grant for a family of three.

Federal food stamp benefits lessen State differences in the total income nonworking mothers on AFDC receive. Because the Food Stamp program counts AFDC as income, Federal food stamp benefits are higher in States with low AFDC benefit levels than in States with high benefit levels. In Mississippi, a nonworking mother with two children who received AFDC in January 1994 was eligible for $3, 540 in Federal food stamps, whereas in New York (Suffolk County) she was eligible for $1,476 in food stamps.

In all States, a nonworking mother's combined AFDC and food stamp benefits fall short of the Federal poverty income level. In Mississippi, combined AFDC and food stamp benefits amounted to $4,980, only 40% of the 1994 Federal poverty income guideline for a 3-person family. In New York (Suffolk County), combined benefits were $9,876 (about twice those of Mississippi) and about 80% of the poverty line.

WORKING MOTHERS

Figures 2a through 5b provide State-by-State summaries of "take home" income a mother would receive as she works her way off welfare. The "a-series" figures assume the mother has no child care expenses, whereas the "b-series" figures assume the mother incurs child care expenses.[7] The figures show how a mother's annual income and benefits would change if she worked at a minimum wage job ($4.25 per hour): one-fourth time (10 hours per week), one-half time (20 hours per week), three-fourths time (30

---

[7] Child care expenses are assumed to be equal to the maximum AFDC child care expense disregard ($175 per month per child). Child care expenses are reduced pro-rata for mothers working less than full-time.

hours per week), and full-time (40 hours per week).[8] Each figure shows the share of AFDC (State and Federal) benefits, Federal food stamp benefits, the Federal EITC and earnings (net of taxes, in the "series-a" figures, and net of taxes and child care expenses in the "series-b figures). The figures are based on January 1994 AFDC and food stamp benefit levels but use 1996 EITC provisions (because recent EITC expansions are to take full effect in 1996). The 1996 EITC provisions have been adjusted to 1994 dollars. The figures assume AFDC program rules that apply after having worked 4 months while on AFDC. Under these rules, AFDC benefits are reduced by $1 for every $1 in earnings, after standard earnings disregards(and if applicable, child care expense disregards) have been applied.

MOTHER WITHOUT CHILD CARE EXPENSES

The figures show the effects on AFDC eligibility and total income as a mother capable of earning the minimum wage increases her hours of work. Figure 2a shows that mothers who work one-fourth time at the minimum wage would retain AFDC eligibility in all States, and except in Hawaii, all would have incomes below the Federal poverty line. Figure 3a shows that mothers in six States (Alabama, Texas, Louisiana, South Carolina, Arkansas, and West Virginia would no longer be eligible for AFDC if they were to work one-half time at the minimum wage. In four States, Alaska, Hawaii, New York (Suffolk County) and Connecticut, the mother's net income (after taxes) would be above the poverty line. Mothers who work three-fourths time at the minimum wage (figure 4a) would no longer be eligible for AFDC in most States. They all would continue to received food stamps, and in most (all but eight) States would have net (after-tax incomes) below the poverty line. Mothers working full-time at the minimum wage (figure 5a) would retain AFDC eligibility in only a handful of States (Vermont, Connecticut, New York (Suffolk County), Hawaii and Alaska). In all States, full-time work at the minimum would guarantee net income above the poverty "goal" line. The expanded EITC makes a large

---

[8] For information on the pay level of jobs by hours worked that AFDC mothers might qualify for, see: U.S. Library of Congress. Congressional Research Service. *Jobs for Welfare Recipients.* CRS Report for Congress No. 94-457 E, by Linda Levine. Washington, May 13, 1994.

contribution toward the anti-poverty objective, equaling about one-fourth of full-time working mothers' total after-tax income. The figures also show that State differences in "take-home" income decline with increased hours worked.

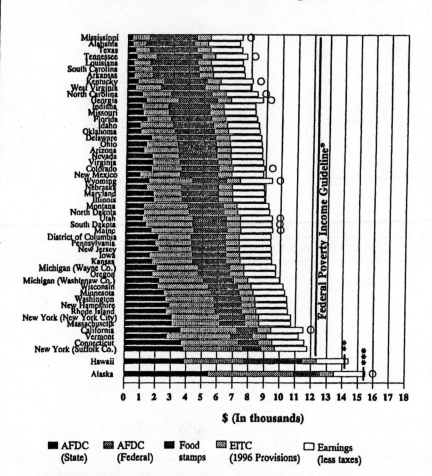

Figure 2a. Sources of Income for a Single Mother with 2 Children Working 1/4-time at the Minimum Wage--1994

■ AFDC   ▨ AFDC   ■ Food   ▨ EITC   □ Earnings
(State)   (Federal)   stamps   (1996 Provisions)   (less taxes)

O   States with AFDC "Fill-the-Gap" Policies.

*   Federal Poverty Income Guideline for a family of 3 (1994): $12,320.
**   In Hawaii: $14,170.
***   In Alaska: $15,400.

Source: CRS.

**Figure 3a. Sources of Income for a Single Mother with 2 Children
Working 1/2-time at the Minimum Wage--1994**

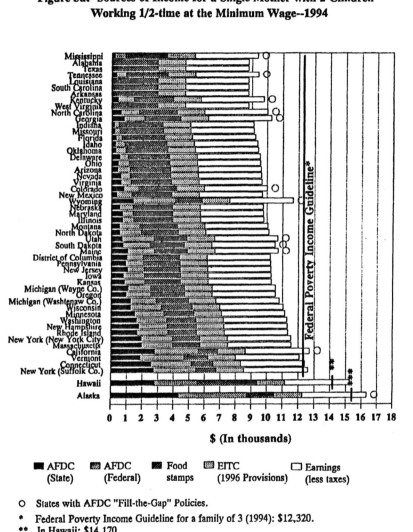

$ (In thousands)

■ AFDC	▨ AFDC	▨ Food	▨ EITC	☐ Earnings
(State)	(Federal)	stamps	(1996 Provisions)	(less taxes)

O States with AFDC "Fill-the-Gap" Policies.

* Federal Poverty Income Guideline for a family of 3 (1994): $12,320.

** In Hawaii: $14,170.

*** In Alaska: $15,400.

Source: CRS.

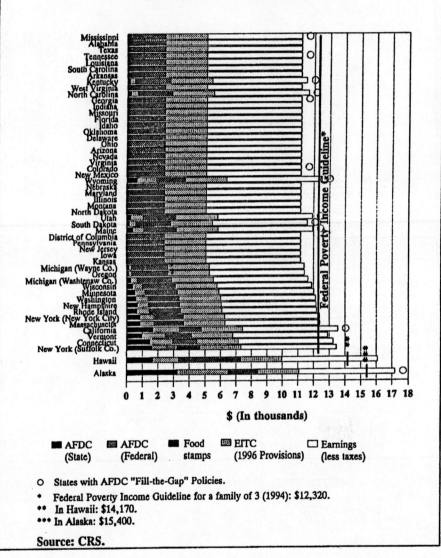

Figure 4a. Sources of Income for a Single Mother with 2 Children Working 3/4-time at the Minimum Wage--1994

$ (In thousands)

| ■ AFDC (State) | ▦ AFDC (Federal) | ■ Food stamps | ▨ EITC (1996 Provisions) | ☐ Earnings (less taxes) |

○ States with AFDC "Fill-the-Gap" Policies.

* Federal Poverty Income Guideline for a family of 3 (1994): $12,320.

** In Hawaii: $14,170.

*** In Alaska: $15,400.

Source: CRS.

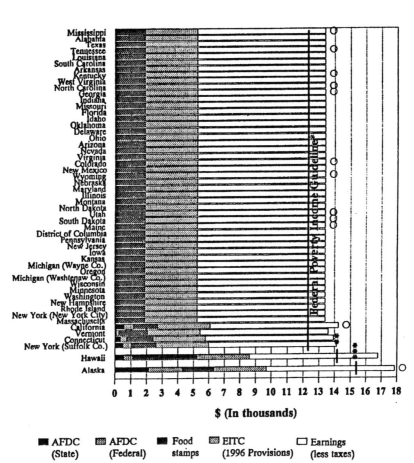

Figure 5a. Sources of Income for a Single Mother with 2 Children Working Full Time at the Minimum Wage--1994

$ (In thousands)

■ AFDC (State)	▓ AFDC (Federal)
■ Food stamps	▓ EITC (1996 Provisions)
☐ Earnings (less taxes)	

O   States with AFDC "Fill-the-Gap" Policies.

*   Federal Poverty Income Guideline for a family of 3 (1994): $12,320.

**   In Hawaii: $14,170.

***   In Alaska: $15,400.

Source: CRS.

MOTHERS WITH CHILD CARE EXPENSES

Child care and other work-related expenses can have a significant impact on the financial returns to a mother taking a job. Under current law, States must guarantee child care to AFDC families to the extent that such care is necessary for an individual in the family to accept employment, remain employed, or participated in the AFDC Job Opportunities and Basic Skills (JOBS) program. States must also guarantee "transitional" child care (TCC) for a period of 12 months after a family leaves AFDC because of increased income from employment but must require families to pay a share of the costs under a sliding fee schedule.[9] States may use a variety of methods for providing child care for families on AFDC. For example, States may provide care directly, purchase care, provide child care vouchers, pay cash reimbursements, or disregard a portion of child care expenses from income in computing the AFDC grant.

At this time, we know very little about how States provide child care for families on AFDC or under the transitional child care provisions. We are exploring these issues further.[10] In these examples, *it is assumed that States use the AFDC child care disregard approach to providing child care.* The examples assume that working mothers' child care costs are equal to the maximum AFDC child care expense disregard ($175 per month per child), reduced pro-rata for mothers working less than full-time.

---

[9] Additional sources of child care subsidies are available. In terms of Total dollars, the largest child care subsidies are from the Dependent Care Tax Credit (DCTC), which is a nonrefundable credit against income taxes for child care expenses. However, DCTC is available only for families with positive Federal income tax liability, and in none of the illustrations shown in this report do families earn enough to pay income taxes. Low-income families may also receive child care subsidies through the "at-risk" child care program. This program, authorized by the Omnibus Budget Reconciliation Act of 1990 (P.L. 101-508), provides matching funds to States that child care to families *not* receiving AFDC but which are at "risk" of going on welfare if their employment is hindered by lack of child care. States may also assist families with child care expenses through programs using Federal funds from the child care development block grant, child and adult care food program, and the title XX social services block grant (SSBG), or with their own funds. However, the illustrations assume that none of these subsidies are received by families whose earnings are above AFDC income-eligibility thresholds.

[10] Data from a Congressional Research Service (CRS) survey of States is being analyzed to determine how they provide assistance for work-related child care expenses under AFDC-related programs, including Transitional Child Care (TCC) and At-Risk Child Care, and under programs funded by Child Care and Development Block Grants (CCDBG) or title XX SSBG.

These expenses are disregarded from earnings for purposes of calculating the AFDC grant, and a portion (up to $160 per month per child) is disregarded for purposes of calculating food stamp benefits. Because little is known about how States operate TCC programs, the figures assume that ex-AFDC families receive *no* transitional child care assistance (even though the law requires it for them). Thus, the figures actually depict the situation that ex-AFDC families with child care costs are expected to face *after being off AFDC for 1 year.*

The "series-b" figures show that working AFDC mothers who purchase child care remain eligible for AFDC at higher earnings levels than AFDC mothers with other "non-paid" arrangements (i.e., those in the "series-a" figures). A mother working three-fourths time at the minimum wage who purchases child care (figure 4b) would lose AFDC eligibility in only one State (Alabama). In comparison, if the mother had other "non-paid" arrangements, she would be ineligible for AFDC in 31 States (figure 4a). Figure 5b shows that, even if they worked full-time at the minimum wage, working mothers would continue to receive AFDC in all but six States (Alabama, Texas, Louisiana, South Carolina, Arkansas, West Virginia) if they paid for child care. Families that remain on AFDC would continue to be categorically eligible for Medicaid, whereas families that leave AFDC risk losing Medicaid coverage (or other medical insurance) after 1 year (18 months at State option).

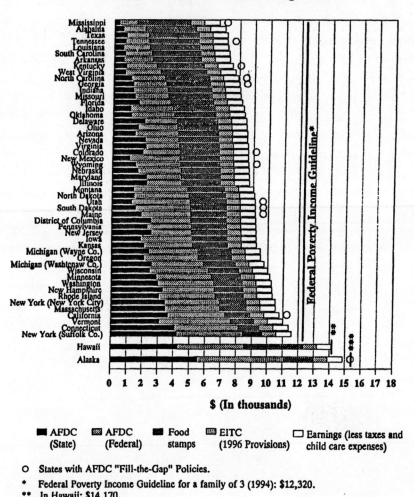

Figure 2b. Sources of Income After Child Care Expenses and Taxes for a Single Mother with 2 Children Working 1/4-time at the Minimum Wage--1994

| ■ AFDC (State) | ▨ AFDC (Federal) | ■ Food stamps | ▨ EITC (1996 Provisions) | ▢ Earnings (less taxes and child care expenses) |

O   States with AFDC "Fill-the-Gap" Policies.

*   Federal Poverty Income Guideline for a family of 3 (1994): $12,320.
**   In Hawaii: $14,170.
***   In Alaska: $15,400.

Source: CRS.

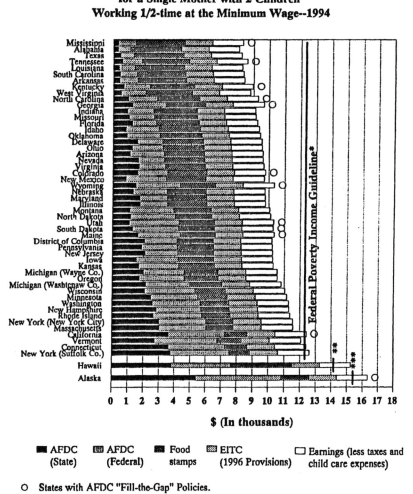

Figure 3b. Sources of Income After Child Care Expenses and Taxes
for a Single Mother with 2 Children
Working 1/2-time at the Minimum Wage--1994

$ (In thousands)

| ■ AFDC (State) | ▓ AFDC (Federal) | ▒ Food stamps | ▓ EITC (1996 Provisions) | □ Earnings (less taxes and child care expenses) |

O   States with AFDC "Fill-the-Gap" Policies.

*   Federal Poverty Income Guideline for a family of 3 (1994): $12,320.

** In Hawaii: $14,170.

*** In Alaska: $15,400.

Source: CRS.

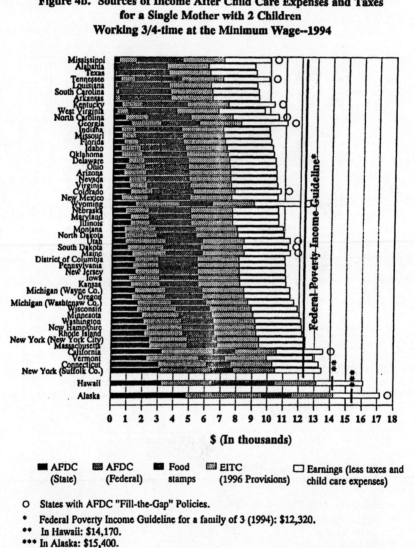

Figure 4b. Sources of Income After Child Care Expenses and Taxes for a Single Mother with 2 Children Working 3/4-time at the Minimum Wage--1994

$ (In thousands)

■ AFDC   ▨ AFDC   ■ Food   ▨ EITC   □ Earnings (less taxes and
  (State)   (Federal)   stamps   (1996 Provisions)   child care expenses)

O   States with AFDC "Fill-the-Gap" Policies.
*   Federal Poverty Income Guideline for a family of 3 (1994): $12,320.
** In Hawaii: $14,170.
*** In Alaska: $15,400.

Source: CRS.

**Figure 5b. Sources of Income After Child Care Expenses and Taxes
for a Single Mother with 2 Children
Working Full Time at the Minimum Wage--1994**

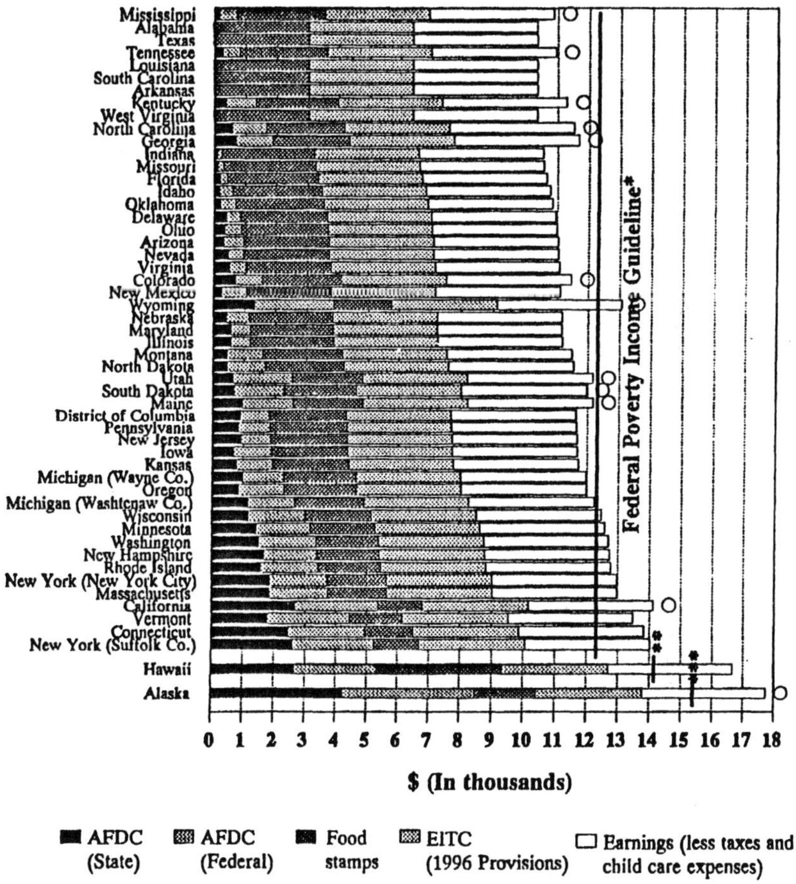

$ (In thousands)

| ■ AFDC (State) | ▨ AFDC (Federal) | ■ Food stamps | ▨ EITC (1996 Provisions) | ☐ Earnings (less taxes and child care expenses) |

O   States with AFDC "Fill-the-Gap" Policies.

*   Federal Poverty Income Guideline for a family of 3 (1994): $12,320.

**   In Hawaii: $14,170.

*** In Alaska: $15,400.

Source: CRS.

Aid To Families With Dependent Children (AFDC) In "Fill-The-Gap" States

Several States use a method of paying AFDC that allows working families to retain a greater portion of their AFDC grant as earnings increase. This method of payment, commonly referred to as "fill-the-gap," provides greater financial incentives for families to work than the standard payment method., Under the standard method, the AFDC grant is determined by subtracting countable income (e.g., earnings less disregards) from the State's payment standard and paying the "deficit." (A State's AFDC "payment standard" may be less than its "need standard" -- the amount a State recognizes as essential for a family to meet basic and special needs.) Some States having AFDC payment standards below their need standard allow families to fill part or all of the gap between the payment and need standards with earnings, before reducing the AFDC grant. Other States set a maximum payment below the payment standard, allowing families to "fill-the-gap" only up to the payment standard. Most States having AFDC payment standards below their need standards do not use a "fill-the-gap" policy -- they begin to reduce the AFDC grant dollar for dollar, for earnings in excess of the standard earnings disregards.

In January 1994, 12 States were using some form of "fill-the-gap": Mississippi, Tennessee, Kentucky, North Carolina, Georgia, Utah, South Dakota, Colorado, Wyoming, Maine, California, and Alaska. These States stand out among the neighboring States (as they are ranked by AFDC payment levels) in the figures as a mother works her way off AFDC. As shown in many of the figures, working mothers in these States have higher net income at equivalent earnings than mothers living in States with similar AFDC payment levels that do not use a "fill-the-gap" payment method.

Change In Income From Increased Earnings

The previous section showed the income and benefits for a mother working at various annual earnings levels. However, the *changes* in net income (net of taxes and work expenses) at various earnings levels are also important in determining a mother's work decisions. This section provides a look at the financial rewards to increasing work effort: how much net income rises as a mother chooses to work or *increases* the number of hours she works.[11]

Two major features of need-tested programs interact to determine how income changes when a mother chooses work over nonwork or increases her work effort: the income guarantee and the benefit reduction rate. The income *guarantee*, discussed in the previous section as the AFDC-food stamp guarantee, provides a level of well-being attainable with no work. The welfare guarantee, thus, is the level to be compared with income attainable only with work.

The second program feature affecting the financial gain of recipients who choose work is the *benefit reduction rate:* the rate at which need-tested benefits are phased out as income such as earnings increases. In most States, AFDC benefits are reduced dollar for dollar after the first $120 in monthly earnings. If a mother uses paid child care, it is assumed here that States reimburse her by deducting expenses, up to the specified amount, from earnings when computing the AFDC grant. For a mother without child care expenses, the AFDC benefit reduction rate is 100% above the first $120 in monthly earnings. AFDC benefit reduction rates are lover in "fill-the-gap" States (discussed above).

The illustrations in this report take into account AFDC, food stamps, the EITC, Federal income and payroll taxes, and where applicable, child care expenses. Thus, they show the combined effect of the AFDC and food stamp benefit reduction rates as well as Federal tax rules on net income. The Food Stamp program has a lower benefit reduction rate (25%) than AFDC (100%) for increased earnings, and also disregards certain child care expenses.[12] The EITC supplements earnings at a rate of 40% for a

---

[11] As in the previous section, the illustrations for a working mother assume AFDC program rules that apply after having worked 4 months while on AFDC. Under these rules, AFDC benefits are reduced by $1 for every $1 in earnings, after standard earnings disregards (and if applicable, child care expense disregards) have been applied. AFDC rules are different in the first 4 months on a job and after 1 year on the job.

[12] The Food Stamp program disregards 20% of earnings from mothers' "countable income," in addition to a standard deduction ($131 in 1994) and deductions for child care expenses (up to $160 per child). Food stamp benefits are reduced by 30 cents for each additional dollar of countable income.

parent with more than one child, up to a certain amount. (The EITC shown in this report reflects 1996 program rules, represented in 1994 dollars.) The EITC is also phased out above a certain income threshold, though the phase-out begins at earnings higher than those of a full-time worker earning the minimum wage.

CHANGE IN NET INCOME FROM GOING FROM NONWORK TO WORK

Most AFDC recipients report that they are not working nor actively seeking work in a given month in which they are on the program. On a purely financial basis, a woman would rationally only choose work over welfare if she were at least as well off working as she is on welfare. Her wage rate would have to be high enough for her to be willing to forgo other uses of her time, such as work at home or leisure. For work to be financially attractive, she would also have to work a sufficient number of hours to cover certain employment-related costs (such as transportation and clothing).[13]

Mothers who go to work also face the potential loss of Medicaid, particularly if they take a job that lacks health insurance benefits. Potential loss of Medicaid is thought to present a large disincentive for AFDC recipients to accept jobs that offer no health insurance. Few studies have examined the issue. Simulations from one study[14] suggest that extension of

---

Consequently, after the standard deduction is taken into account, the effective benefit reduction rate for $1 increase in earnings under the Food Stamp program is: $(.3 \times (1-.2)) = .24$.

[13] Economists call the wage rate that would attract a person to participate in the labor force the *reservation wage*. The reservation wage is determined by a person's tastes for market work (in a job) versus nonmarket work (housework) and leisure, as well as be unearned income, including the availability of income transfers such as AFDC. If the wage offered by an employer is higher than the reservation wage, the person would choose to work. If not, the person would choose not to work. Additionally, *fixed costs* of employment could affect the labor force participation decision. A fixed cost is one that does not vary by hours of work (e.g., commuting costs may be fixed at a certain amount per day regardless of the number of hours worked during a day). In such cases, a person must work a certain number of hours just to cover such fixed costs. Fixed costs may discourage part-time work or raise a person's reservation wage for part-time work. There is some evidence that fixed costs are important in women's labor force participation decisions. See: Hausman, Jerry A. The Effects of Wages, Taxes, and Fixed Costs on Women's Labor Force Participation. Journal of Public Economics, v. 14, 1980. P. 161-194.

[14] Moffit, Robert, and Barbara Wolfe. *The Effect of the Medicaid Program on Welfare Participation and Labor Supply.* NBER, working paper no. 3286, Mar. 1990.

health insurance coverage to all working female family heads could lower AFDC caseload by 210% and increase the chance that a female family head will be employed by almost 8 percentage points; if private health insurance plans were as generous as the Medicaid package, the AFDC caseload reduction could be as much as 25% and the probability of employment almost 18 percentage points higher.

Economic theory predicts that the income guarantee discourages labor force participation because it provides a level of consumption possible without work. The welfare system's high benefit reduction rates also discourage labor force participation, since they "tax" away a substantial part of a woman's gain in income from working, which lowers the effective wage rate.

Table 1a shows the net income gain in going from nonwork to work at various hours per week. That is, it measures the *change* in net income when working at 10, 20, 30, or 40 hours per week compared with the income guarantee in the State. Two measures are provided: (1) the effective average wage rate' and (2) the increase in weekly net income. The average wage rate shown is the change in net income divided by the number of hours. Worked. The nominal hourly wage rate for all workers is $4.25, but State variation in AFDC guarantee levels and benefit reduction rates produces differences in the effective wage rates.

In most states and for most work schedules, the effective wage rate is below $4.25. In a few states that employ 'fill-the-gap' rules, the EITC supplement more than offsets the effect of the AFDC and food stamp benefit reduction rates, and the effective wage rate is higher. However, this occurs only under work schedules of 10 or 20 hours per week. Effective wage rates are lowest at 20-hour and 30-hour work schedules, because AFDC's high benefit reduction rates 'tax-away' a substantial amount of earnings at these earnings levels. At full-time work, wage rates increase in many states because such a full-time schedule yields earnings well above AFDC AFDC income eligibility thresholds in most states. It is only earnings above $120 and below AFDC income eligibility thresholds that are 'taxed away' at a relatively high rate.

TABLE 1a. Increase in Weekly Net Income for a Mother on Welfare going to Work for a Specified Number of Hours Per Week at the Federal Minimum Wage
Assuming No Paid Child Care Expenses

| | 10 hours per week | | 20 hours per week | | 30 hours per week | | 40 hours per week | |
	Average wage rate	Increase in weekly net income	Average wage rate	Increase in weekly net income	Average wage rate	Increase in weekly net income	Average wage rate	Increase in weekly net income
Mississippi	$4.68	$46.79	$4.25	$84.99	$3.98	$119.36	$4.06	$162.26
Alabama	3.57	35.67	3.27	65.42	3.72	111.52	3.86	154.42
Texas	3.57	35.67	3.11	62.19	3.61	108.28	3.78	151.19
Tennessee	4.15	41.51	3.73	74.69	3.61	108.28	3.78	151.19
Louisiana	3.57	35.67	3.06	61.27	3.58	107.36	3.76	150.26
South Carolina	3.57	35.67	2.98	59.65	3.52	105.75	3.72	148.65
Arkansas	3.57	35.67	2.95	58.96	3.50	105.05	3.70	147.96
Kentucky	4.18	41.75	3.74	74.73	3.60	107.95	3.61	144.26
West Virginia	3.57	35.67	2.59	51.81	3.26	97.90	3.52	140.80
North Carolina	4.10	41.00	3.60	72.07	3.44	103.15	3.43	137.11
Georgia	4.61	46.09	3.76	75.27	3.09	92.82	3.39	135.73
Indiana	3.57	35.67	2.61	52.19	3.06	91.67	3.36	134.57
Missouri	3.57	35.67	2.60	51.96	3.03	90.98	3.35	133.88
Florida	3.57	35.67	2.60	51.96	2.97	89.13	3.30	132.03
Idaho	3.57	35.67	2.60	51.96	2.89	86.82	3.24	129.73
Oklahoma	3.57	35.67	2.60	51.96	2.86	85.67	3.21	128.57
Delaware	3.57	35.67	2.61	52.19	2.79	83.59	3.16	126.50
Ohio	3.57	35.67	2.60	51.96	2.76	82.90	3.15	125.80
Arizona	3.57	35.67	2.60	51.96	2.73	81.98	3.12	124.88
Nevada	3.57	35.67	2.61	52.19	2.73	81.98	3.12	124.88
Virginia	3.57	35.67	2.60	51.96	2.69	80.82	3.09	123.73
Colorado	3.73	37.27	2.91	58.27	2.69	80.59	3.09	123.50
New Mexico	3.57	35.67	2.60	51.96	2.68	80.36	3.08	123.26
Wyoming	4.61	46.09	4.46	89.11	3.51	105.40	3.07	122.80
Nebraska	3.57	35.67	2.60	51.96	2.64	79.21	3.05	122.11
Maryland	3.57	35.67	2.60	51.96	2.63	78.98	3.05	121.88
Illinois	3.57	35.67	2.60	51.96	2.62	78.75	3.04	121.65
Montana	3.57	35.67	2.60	51.96	2.44	73.21	2.90	116.11
North Dakota	3.57	35.67	2.60	51.96	2.40	72.05	2.87	114.96
Utah	3.82	38.22	3.10	61.90	2.85	85.58	2.85	114.03
South Dakota	3.73	37.28	2.90	58.10	2.62	78.68	2.84	113.57
Maine	3.84	38.36	3.09	61.80	2.85	85.46	2.84	113.57
District of Columbia	3.57	35.67	2.60	51.96	2.34	70.21	2.83	113.11
Pennsylvania	3.57	35.67	2.60	51.96	2.33	69.98	2.82	112.88
New Jersey	3.57	35.67	2.60	51.96	2.32	69.52	2.81	112.42
Iowa	3.57	35.67	2.60	51.96	2.31	69.28	2.80	112.19
Kansas	3.57	35.67	2.60	51.96	2.29	68.82	2.79	111.73
Michigan (Wayne Co.)	3.57	35.67	2.60	51.96	2.27	68.25	2.67	106.88
Oregon	3.57	35.67	2.60	51.96	2.27	68.25	2.67	106.65
Michigan (Washtenaw Co.)	3.57	35.67	2.60	51.96	2.27	68.25	2.55	102.03
Wisconsin	3.57	35.67	2.60	51.96	2.27	68.25	2.44	97.42
Minnesota	3.57	35.67	2.60	51.96	2.27	68.25	2.38	95.11
Washington	3.57	35.67	2.60	51.96	2.27	68.25	2.32	92.80
New Hampshire	3.57	35.67	2.60	51.96	2.27	68.25	2.30	92.11
Rhode Island	3.57	35.67	2.60	51.96	2.27	68.25	2.29	91.42
New York (New York City)	3.57	35.67	2.60	51.96	2.27	68.25	2.19	87.73
Massachusetts	3.57	35.67	2.60	51.96	2.27	68.25	2.19	87.50
California	4.61	46.09	3.46	69.27	2.85	85.55	2.47	98.88
Vermont	3.57	35.67	2.61	52.19	2.28	68.48	2.04	81.57
Connecticut	3.57	35.67	2.60	51.96	2.27	68.25	2.03	81.34
New York (Suffolk Co.)	3.57	35.67	2.60	51.96	2.27	68.25	2.03	81.34
Hawaii	3.57	35.67	2.61	52.19	2.28	68.48	2.04	81.57
Alaska	4.40	43.98	3.01	60.27	2.55	76.55	2.24	89.65

NOTE: Net income is gross income (including EITC) less Federal income and payroll taxes.
SOURCE: Estimates prepared by CRS.

TABLE 1b. Increase in Weekly Net Income for a Mother on Welfare going to Work for a Specified Number of Hours Per Week at the Federal Minimum Wage Assuming Paid Child Care Expenses

	10 hours per week		20 hours per week		30 hours per week		40 hours per week	
	Average wage rate	Increase in weekly net income	Average wage rate	Increase in weekly net income	Average wage rate	Increase in weekly net income	Average wage rate	Increase in weekly net income
Mississippi	$3.26	$32.59	$3.22	$64.50	$3.20	$96.12	$2.84	$113.53
Alabama	3.19	31.90	2.60	51.96	2.31	69.17	2.40	95.80
Texas	3.19	31.90	2.60	51.96	2.27	68.25	2.31	92.57
Tennessee	3.19	31.90	2.94	58.76	2.80	83.98	2.59	103.69
Louisiana	3.19	31.90	2.60	51.96	2.27	68.25	2.29	91.65
South Carolina	3.19	31.90	2.60	51.96	2.27	68.25	2.25	90.03
Arkansas	3.19	31.90	2.60	51.96	2.27	68.25	2.23	89.34
Kentucky	3.19	31.90	2.94	58.78	2.80	84.01	2.59	103.74
West Virginia	3.19	31.90	2.60	51.96	2.27	68.25	2.05	82.19
North Carolina	3.19	31.90	2.89	57.88	2.74	82.09	2.52	100.80
Georgia	3.19	31.90	3.19	63.81	3.05	91.55	2.56	102.57
Indiana	3.19	31.90	2.61	52.19	2.28	68.48	1.99	79.50
Missouri	3.19	31.90	2.60	51.96	2.27	68.25	1.98	79.26
Florida	3.19	31.90	2.60	51.96	2.27	68.25	1.98	79.26
Idaho	3.19	31.90	2.60	51.96	2.27	68.25	1.98	79.26
Oklahoma	3.19	31.90	2.60	51.96	2.27	68.25	1.98	79.26
Delaware	3.19	31.90	2.61	52.19	2.28	68.48	1.99	79.50
Ohio	3.19	31.90	2.60	51.96	2.27	68.25	1.98	79.26
Arizona	3.19	31.90	2.60	51.96	2.27	68.25	1.98	79.26
Nevada	3.19	31.90	2.61	52.19	2.28	68.48	1.99	79.50
Virginia	3.19	31.90	2.60	51.96	2.27	68.25	1.98	79.26
Colorado	3.19	31.90	2.69	53.88	2.42	72.46	2.15	86.00
New Mexico	3.19	31.90	2.60	51.96	2.27	68.25	1.98	79.26
Wyoming	3.19	31.90	3.19	63.81	3.19	95.71	2.91	116.42
Nebraska	3.19	31.90	2.60	51.96	2.27	68.25	1.98	79.26
Maryland	3.19	31.90	2.60	51.96	2.27	68.25	1.98	79.26
Illinois	3.19	31.90	2.60	51.96	2.27	68.25	1.98	79.26
Montana	3.19	31.90	2.60	51.96	2.27	68.25	1.98	79.26
North Dakota	3.19	31.90	2.60	51.96	2.27	68.25	1.98	79.26
Utah	3.19	31.90	2.74	54.81	2.50	75.05	2.25	90.03
South Dakota	3.19	31.90	2.68	53.66	2.41	72.37	2.15	85.81
Maine	3.19	31.90	2.75	54.94	2.50	75.05	2.25	89.90
District of Columbia	3.19	31.90	2.60	51.96	2.27	68.25	1.98	79.26
Pennsylvania	3.19	31.90	2.60	51.96	2.27	68.25	1.98	79.26
New Jersey	3.19	31.90	2.60	51.96	2.27	68.25	1.98	79.26
Iowa	3.19	31.90	2.60	51.96	2.27	68.25	1.98	79.26
Kansas	3.19	31.90	2.60	51.96	2.27	68.25	1.98	79.26
Michigan (Wayne Co.)	3.19	31.90	2.60	51.96	2.27	68.25	1.98	79.26
Oregon	3.19	31.90	2.60	51.96	2.27	68.25	1.98	79.26
Michigan (Washtenaw Co.)	3.19	31.90	2.60	51.96	2.27	68.25	1.98	79.26
Wisconsin	3.19	31.90	2.60	51.96	2.27	68.25	1.98	79.26
Minnesota	3.19	31.90	2.60	51.96	2.27	68.25	1.98	79.26
Washington	3.19	31.90	2.60	51.96	2.27	68.25	1.98	79.26
New Hampshire	3.19	31.90	2.60	51.96	2.27	68.25	1.98	79.26
Rhode Island	3.19	31.90	2.60	51.96	2.27	68.25	1.98	79.26
New York (New York City)	3.19	31.90	2.60	51.96	2.27	68.25	1.98	79.26
Massachusetts	3.19	31.90	2.60	51.96	2.27	68.25	1.98	79.26
California	3.19	31.90	3.19	63.81	2.85	85.55	2.42	96.80
Vermont	3.19	31.90	2.61	52.19	2.28	68.48	1.99	79.50
Connecticut	3.19	31.90	2.60	51.96	2.27	68.25	1.98	79.26
New York (Suffolk Co.)	3.19	31.90	2.60	51.96	2.27	68.25	1.98	79.26
Hawaii	3.19	31.90	2.61	52.19	2.28	68.48	1.99	79.49
Alaska	3.19	31.90	3.01	60.27	2.55	76.55	2.19	87.57

NOTE: Net income is gross income (including EITC) less Federal income and payroll taxes and unreimbursed child care expenses.

SOURCE: Estimates prepared by CRS.

Table 2a and 2b show the income gain from increasing work effort, expressed as the income gain per hour of *additional* work over the 10-hour increments. The Income change per hour could also be thought of as an hourly wage rate but, for all increments, except the first (0-10 hours), it differs from the hourly wage rates shown in tables 1a and 1b. That is, the rates in tables 2a and 2b represent the income gain per hour of *additional* work. The wage rates in tables 1a and 1b showed income change from the AFDC-food stamp guarantee level. These hourly wage rates (in tables 2a and 2b) show income change over each 10-hour increment.

Additionally, the tables show *implicit marginal tax rates*. These rates represent the share of the earnings gain "taxed away" over the increment. For example, in most States AFDC mothers keep $1.63 out of $4.25 per hour when they increase their work effort from 10 to 20 hours per week. They keep 38% of their earnings gain; the remaining 62% is "Taxed away," mostly by the dollar-for-dollar reduction in AFDC benefits for an earnings increase. Table 2a assumes a mother does not have paid child care expenses; table 2b assumes a mother pays for child care expenses and that those expenses are disregarded, to the extent allowed, by AFDC and the food Stamp program.

CHANGES IN NET INCOME FROM INCREASING HOURS WORKED

In addition to discouraging labor force participation and job taking, AFDC's guarantee and high benefit reduction rate may discourage those who work and receive AFDC from increasing their work effort. However, such disincentives affect few welfare recipients because simultaneous receipt o AFDC and earned income is rare.

Tables 2a and 2b show the income gain from increasing work effort, expressed as the income gain per hour of additional work over the 10-hour increments. The income change per hour could also be thought of as an hourly wage rate but, for all increments, except the first (0-10 hours), it differs from the hourly wage rates shown in tables 1a and 1b. That is, the rates in tables 2a and 2b represent the income gain per hour of *additional* work. The wage rates in tables 1a and 1b showed income change from the AFDC-foot stamp guarantee level. These hourly wage rates (in tables 2a and 2b) show income change over each 10-hour increment.

Additionally, the tables show *implicit marginal tax rates*. These rates represent the share of the earnings gain "taxed away" over the increment. For example, in most States AFDC mothers keep $1.63 out of $4.25 per hour when they increase their work effort from 10 to 20 hours per week. They keep 38% of their earnings gain; the remaining 62% is "taxed away," mostly by the dollar-for-dollar reduction in AFDC benefits for an earnings increase. Table 2a assumes a mother does not have paid child care expenses; table 2b assumes a mother pays for child care expenses and that those expenses are disregarded, to the extent allowed, by AFDC and the Food Stamp program.

TABLE 2a. Financial Reward for Increasing Work Effort for a Minimum Wage Worker, Assuming No Paid Child Care Expenses

	0 to 10 hours		10 to 20 hours		20 to 30 hours		30 to 40 hours	
	Total change in net income per hour ($)	Implicit marginal tax rate (%)	Total change in net income per hour ($)	Implicit marginal tax rate (%)	Total change in net income per hour ($)	Implicit marginal tax rate (%)	Total change in net income per hour ($)	Implicit marginal tax rate (%)
Mississippi	$4.68	-10.1	$3.82	10.1	$3.44	19.13	$4.29	-0.9
Alabama	3.57	16.1	2.97	30.0	4.61	-8.46	4.29	-0.9
Texas	3.57	16.1	2.65	37.6	4.61	-8.46	4.29	-0.9
Tennessee	4.15	2.3	3.32	21.9	3.36	20.95	4.29	-0.9
Louisiana	3.57	16.1	2.56	39.8	4.61	-8.46	4.29	-0.9
South Carolina	3.57	16.1	2.40	43.6	4.61	-8.46	4.29	-0.9
Arkansas	3.57	16.1	2.33	45.2	4.61	-8.46	4.29	-0.9
Kentucky	4.18	1.8	3.30	22.4	3.32	21.86	3.63	14.5
West Virginia	3.57	16.1	1.61	62.0	4.61	-8.46	4.29	-0.9
North Carolina	4.10	3.5	3.11	26.9	3.11	26.88	3.40	20.1
Georgia	4.61	-8.5	2.92	31.4	1.76	58.69	4.29	-0.9
Indiana	3.57	16.1	1.65	61.1	3.95	7.11	4.29	-0.9
Missouri	3.57	16.1	1.63	61.7	3.90	8.19	4.29	-0.9
Florida	3.57	16.1	1.63	61.7	3.72	12.54	4.29	-0.9
Idaho	3.57	16.1	1.63	61.7	3.49	17.97	4.29	-0.9
Oklahoma	3.57	16.1	1.63	61.7	3.37	20.68	4.29	-0.9
Delaware	3.57	16.1	1.65	61.1	3.14	26.11	4.29	-0.9
Ohio	3.57	16.1	1.63	61.7	3.09	27.20	4.29	-0.9
Arizona	3.57	16.1	1.63	61.7	3.00	29.37	4.29	-0.9
Nevada	3.57	16.1	1.65	61.1	2.98	29.91	4.29	-0.9
Virginia	3.57	16.1	1.63	61.7	2.89	32.08	4.29	-0.9
Colorado	3.73	12.3	2.10	50.6	2.23	47.47	4.29	-0.9
New Mexico	3.57	16.1	1.63	61.7	2.84	33.17	4.29	-0.9
Wyoming	4.61	-8.5	4.30	-1.2	1.63	61.68	1.74	59.1
Nebraska	3.57	16.1	1.63	61.7	2.72	35.89	4.29	-0.9
Maryland	3.57	16.1	1.63	61.7	2.70	36.43	4.29	-0.9
Illinois	3.57	16.1	1.63	61.7	2.68	36.97	4.29	-0.9
Montana	3.57	16.1	1.63	61.7	2.12	50.00	4.29	-0.9
North Dakota	3.57	16.1	1.63	61.7	2.01	52.72	4.29	-0.9
Utah	3.82	10.1	2.37	44.3	2.37	44.28	2.85	33.1
South Dakota	3.73	12.3	2.08	51.0	2.06	51.56	3.49	17.9
Maine	3.84	9.7	2.34	44.9	2.37	44.32	2.81	33.8
District of Columbia	3.57	16.1	1.63	61.7	1.82	57.06	4.29	-0.9
Pennsylvania	3.57	16.1	1.63	61.7	1.80	57.60	4.29	-0.9
New Jersey	3.57	16.1	1.63	61.7	1.76	58.69	4.29	-0.9
Iowa	3.57	16.1	1.63	61.7	1.73	59.23	4.29	-0.9
Kansas	3.57	16.1	1.63	61.7	1.69	60.32	4.29	-0.9
Michigan (Wayne Co.)	3.57	16.1	1.63	61.7	1.63	61.68	3.86	9.1
Oregon	3.57	16.1	1.63	61.7	1.63	61.68	3.84	9.6
Michigan (Washtenaw Co.)	3.57	16.1	1.63	61.7	1.63	61.68	3.38	20.5
Wisconsin	3.57	16.1	1.63	61.7	1.63	61.68	2.92	31.4
Minnesota	3.57	16.1	1.63	61.7	1.63	61.68	2.69	36.8
Washington	3.57	16.1	1.63	61.7	1.63	61.68	2.46	42.2
New Hampshire	3.57	16.1	1.63	61.7	1.63	61.68	2.39	43.8
Rhode Island	3.57	16.1	1.63	61.7	1.63	61.68	2.32	45.5
New York (New York City)	3.57	16.1	1.63	61.7	1.63	61.68	1.95	54.2
Massachusetts	3.57	16.1	1.63	61.7	1.63	61.68	1.92	54.7
California	4.61	-8.5	2.32	45.5	1.63	61.68	1.33	68.6
Vermont	3.57	16.1	1.65	61.1	1.63	61.68	1.31	69.2
Connecticut	3.57	16.1	1.63	61.7	1.63	61.68	1.31	69.2
New York (Suffolk Co.)	3.57	16.1	1.63	61.7	1.63	61.68	1.31	69.2
Hawaii	3.57	16.1	1.65	61.1	1.63	61.68	1.31	69.2
Alaska	4.40	-3.5	1.63	61.7	1.63	61.68	1.31	69.2

NOTE: Net income is gross income (including EITC) less Federal income and payroll taxes.
Negative implicit tax rates denote a net earnings "subsidy".
SOURCE: Estimates prepared by CRS.

TABLE 2b. Financial Reward for Increasing Work Effort for a Minimum Wage Worker, Assuming Paid Child Care Expenses

	0 to 10 hours		10 to 20 hours		20 to 30 hours		30 to 40 hours	
	Total change in net income per hour ($)	Implicit marginal tax rate (%)	Total change in net income per hour ($)	Implicit marginal tax rate (%)	Total change in net income per hour ($)	Implicit marginal tax rate (%)	Total change in net income per hour ($)	Implicit marginal tax rate (%)
Mississippi	$3.26	23.3	$3.19	24.9	$3.16	25.59	$1.74	59.1
Alabama	3.19	24.9	2.01	52.8	1.72	59.51	2.66	37.3
Texas	3.19	24.9	2.01	52.8	1.63	61.68	2.43	42.8
Tennessee	3.19	24.9	2.69	36.8	2.52	40.67	1.97	53.6
Louisiana	3.19	24.9	2.01	52.8	1.63	61.68	2.34	44.9
South Carolina	3.19	24.9	2.01	52.8	1.63	61.68	2.18	48.7
Arkansas	3.19	24.9	2.01	52.8	1.63	61.68	2.11	50.4
Kentucky	3.19	24.9	2.69	36.8	2.52	40.63	1.97	53.6
West Virginia	3.19	24.9	2.01	52.8	1.63	61.68	1.39	67.2
North Carolina	3.19	24.9	2.60	38.9	2.42	43.03	1.87	56.0
Georgia	3.19	24.9	3.19	24.9	2.77	34.71	1.10	74.1
Indiana	3.19	24.9	2.03	52.3	1.63	61.68	1.10	74.1
Missouri	3.19	24.9	2.01	52.8	1.63	61.68	1.10	74.1
Florida	3.19	24.9	2.01	52.8	1.63	61.68	1.10	74.1
Idaho	3.19	24.9	2.01	52.8	1.63	61.68	1.10	74.1
Oklahoma	3.19	24.9	2.01	52.8	1.63	61.68	1.10	74.1
Delaware	3.19	24.9	2.03	52.3	1.63	61.68	1.10	74.1
Ohio	3.19	24.9	2.01	52.8	1.63	61.68	1.10	74.1
Arizona	3.19	24.9	2.01	52.8	1.63	61.68	1.10	74.1
Nevada	3.19	24.9	2.03	52.3	1.63	61.68	1.10	74.1
Virginia	3.19	24.9	2.01	52.8	1.63	61.68	1.10	74.1
Colorado	3.19	24.9	2.20	48.3	1.86	56.29	1.35	68.1
New Mexico	3.19	24.9	2.01	52.8	1.63	61.68	1.10	74.1
Wyoming	3.19	24.9	3.19	24.9	3.19	24.94	2.07	51.3
Nebraska	3.19	24.9	2.01	52.8	1.63	61.68	1.10	74.1
Maryland	3.19	24.9	2.01	52.8	1.63	61.68	1.10	74.1
Illinois	3.19	24.9	2.01	52.8	1.63	61.68	1.10	74.1
Montana	3.19	24.9	2.01	52.8	1.63	61.68	1.10	74.1
North Dakota	3.19	24.9	2.01	52.8	1.63	61.68	1.10	74.1
Utah	3.19	24.9	2.29	46.1	2.02	52.36	1.50	64.8
South Dakota	3.19	24.9	2.18	48.8	1.87	55.98	1.34	68.4
Maine	3.19	24.9	2.30	45.8	2.01	52.66	1.48	65.1
District of Columbia	3.19	24.9	2.01	52.8	1.63	61.68	1.10	74.1
Pennsylvania	3.19	24.9	2.01	52.8	1.63	61.68	1.10	74.1
New Jersey	3.19	24.9	2.01	52.8	1.63	61.68	1.10	74.1
Iowa	3.19	24.9	2.01	52.8	1.63	61.68	1.10	74.1
Kansas	3.19	24.9	2.01	52.8	1.63	61.68	1.10	74.1
Michigan (Wayne Co.)	3.19	24.9	2.01	52.8	1.63	61.68	1.10	74.1
Oregon	3.19	24.9	2.01	52.8	1.63	61.68	1.10	74.1
Michigan (Washtenaw Co.)	3.19	24.9	2.01	52.8	1.63	61.68	1.10	74.1
Wisconsin	3.19	24.9	2.01	52.8	1.63	61.68	1.10	74.1
Minnesota	3.19	24.9	2.01	52.8	1.63	61.68	1.10	74.1
Washington	3.19	24.9	2.01	52.8	1.63	61.68	1.10	74.1
New Hampshire	3.19	24.9	2.01	52.8	1.63	61.68	1.10	74.1
Rhode Island	3.19	24.9	2.01	52.8	1.63	61.68	1.10	74.1
New York (New York City)	3.19	24.9	2.01	52.8	1.63	61.68	1.10	74.1
Massachusetts	3.19	24.9	2.01	52.8	1.63	61.68	1.10	74.1
California	3.19	24.9	3.19	24.9	2.17	48.83	1.12	73.5
Vermont	3.19	24.9	2.03	52.3	1.63	61.68	1.10	74.1
Connecticut	3.19	24.9	2.01	52.8	1.63	61.68	1.10	74.1
New York (Suffolk Co.)	3.19	24.9	2.01	52.8	1.63	61.68	1.10	74.1
Hawaii	3.19	24.9	2.03	52.3	1.63	61.68	1.10	74.1
Alaska	3.19	24.9	2.84	33.3	1.63	61.68	1.10	74.1

NOTE: Net income is gross income (including EITC) less Federal income and payroll taxes and unreimbursed child care expenses.

SOURCE: Estimates prepared by CRS.

The tables illustrate the high marginal tax rates faced by AFDC recipients. For mothers without child care expenses who are income-eligible for AFDC, 61.7% of their increase in earnings is "taxed" away in most States, chiefly by benefit reductions, as they increase work effort from 10 to 20 hours per week or 20 to 30 hours per week. Tax rates in the "fill-the-gap" States are lower. Additionally, women who are income-ineligible for AFDC (have worked their way off the program) face lower marginal tax rates than those in States where they retain AFDC eligibility.

Mothers without paid child care expenses lose AFDC eligibility in most States when working somewhere between 20 and 30 hours per week at the minimum wage. Once off AFDC, the implicit marginal tax rate becomes *negative* when increasing work hours up to 40 per week. That is, net income increases *faster* than earnings because of the EITC earnings supplement, and the absence of any AFDC benefit reductions.

Table 2b shows the income gain for a mother who pays for child care. She too faces relatively high marginal tax rates when increasing work from 10 to 20 or 20 to 30 hours per week. However, because she remains income-eligible for AFDC in many States at 40 hours per week, the high marginal tax rates extend to full-time work. For a mother without child care, who is income-ineligible for AFDC in most States at 40 hours of work per week, marginal tax rates at full-time work tend to be lower than for a mother who pays for child care.

Figures 6a and 6b display the incremental gains from work graphically. The first segment of each bar show the income gain from nonwork to working 10 hours per week; the second segment shows the gains from increasing work effort from 10 to 20 hours per week, and so on.

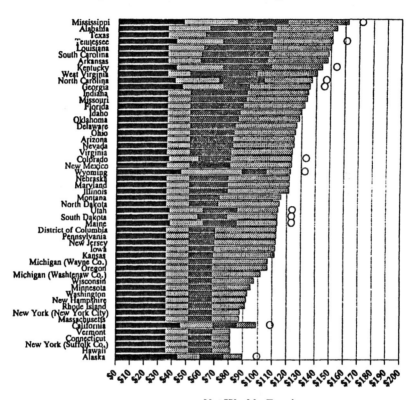

**Figure 6a. Returns from Work for a Single Mother with 2 Children
Earning the Federal Minimum Wage ($4.25/hr.)
by Number of Hours Worked During the Week**

Net Weekly Earnings

Hours Worked Per Week:

■ 10 hrs/week   ▨ 20 hrs/week   ■ 30 hrs/week   ▨ 40 hrs/week

O   States with AFDC "Fill-the-Gap" Policies.

Source: CRS.

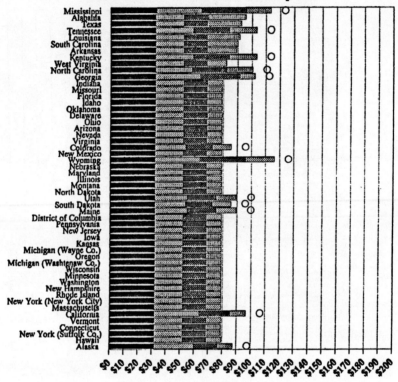

**Figure 6b. Returns from Work for a Single Mother with 2 Children
Earning the Federal Minimum Wage ($4.25/hr.)
by Number of Hours Worked During the Week
For a Mother with Paid Child Care Expenses**

Net Weekly Earnings

Hours Worked Per Week:

■ 10 hrs/week   ▨ 20 hrs/week   ■ 30 hrs/week   ▨ 40 hrs/week

O   States with AFDC "Fill-the-Gap" Policies.

Source: CRS.

STUDIES OF WELFARE WORK DISINCENTIVES

Numerous studies have estimated AFDC's effect on the work effort of women. (Though not all AFDC adults are women, most are.) These studies were reviewed by Sheldon Danziger, Robert Haveman, and Robert Plotnick in 1981[15] and Robert Moffitt in 1992.[16] Both reviews noted that studies tend to show that AFDC has a nontrivial work disincentive, but there are widely varying estimates of the magnitude of the effect . Danzinger, Haveman, and Plotnick conclude that AFDC reduces the work effort of the average recipient about 11.5 hours per week.[17] Moffitt makes some different assumptions and concludes that a midpoint estimate of the AFDC work disincentive is a reduction of about 5.4 hours of work per week.

Many studies of AFDC work disincentives have examined the effects of differences or changes in the AFDC guarantee or the AFDC benefit reduction rate.[18] Most studies find that higher guarantees reduce work effort.

---

[15] Danzinger, Sheldon, Robert Haveman, and Robert Plotnick. How Transfers Affect Work, Savings, and the Income Distribution. *Journal of Economic Literature,* v. 19, no. 3, Sept. 1981. P. 975-1028

[16] Moffitt, Robert. Incentive Effects of the U.S. Welfare System: A Review. *Journal of Economic Literature, v. 30, no. 1, Mar. 1992. P. 1-61.*

[17] In their review, the authors report that the work effort of the average AFDC recipient is reduced by an estimated 600 hours per year. This 600-hour estimate is converted into a weekly estimate of lost hours of work by dividing it by 52.

[18] Economic theory predicts that an increase in the AFDC guarantee would reduce work effort. A rise in the guarantee (holding the benefit reduction rate constant) would give all those eligible more income. Leisure is believed to be a "normal good." That is, with a rise in income, people will "purchase" more leisure by reducing their work effort. The literature refers to this as in *income effect.* Thus, the increase in the AFDC guarantee is expected to cause people to reduce work hours. On the other hand, economic theory does not unambiguously predict that a fall in the benefit reduction rate (and hence a decrease in the implicit marginal tax rate) would increase work effort. Theory predicts that a change in the *price* of work relative to nonwork that makes work more attractive (for example, lowering benefit reduction rates and implicit marginal taxes on earnings) increases the amount of hours worked. The literature labels this effect of a price change a *substitution* effect. However, this effect may be tempered by the income effect: an increase in the relative price of work causes the income of those working to increase without their having to increase work effort; as a result of their greater income, they might buy more leisure (that is, reduce their hours of work). Whether a policy change such as a decrease in the benefit reduction rate increases or decreases work effort is theoretically indeterminate and

This occurs both because people reduce their work behavior in response to higher guarantees and because a higher guarantee raises the AFDC-income eligibility threshold, making more people eligible for benefits and subject to the work disincentive effects. Federal policy has changed the AFDC benefit reduction rate several times (see next section). Moffitt concludes that the evidence also argues that women's labor supply behavior has not been strongly affected by changes in the AFDC benefit reduction rate.

POLICY CHOICES

Policy makers consistently face dilemmas when changing welfare policy. Proposals to increase the income of the poor by raising guarantees encounter the well-known work disincentives entailed by such a policy change. Essentially, raising the guarantee trades off the goal of promoting work for income adequacy. Raising the guarantee increases recipients' income, but lowers their rewards from work. A consequence of the work disincentive is that all the money spent to raise the guarantee does not raise the incomes of the poor. The late economist Arthur Okun described the welfare system as a "leaky bucket," because some of each dollar transferred to recipients does not reduce poverty, but is lost to a reduction of earnings.

Similarly, when pursuing the goal of promoting work, policy makers face certain dilemmas. The Federal Government and States have experimented with changes in welfare programs to attempt to provide greater incentives for recipients to work. AFDC benefit reduction rates were changed from 100% to 60% in 1967, and back again to 100% in 1981.[19] As

---

depends on whether the income or substitution effect dominates the behavioral response to such a change.

[19] The treatment of earnings in computing AFDC benefits and eligibility has undergone numerous changes. Before 1967, AFDC benefits were reduced $1 for each $1 in "net" earnings. Legislation in 19967 required States to disregard the first $30, and one-third of remaining earnings and "reasonable" work expenses when computing AFDC benefits. The Omnibus Budget Reconciliation Act of 1981 (P.L. 97-35) restricted the "30 and

discussed in the previous section, some conclude that women did not change their reported work effort in response to either the fall in benefit reduction rates after the 1967 legislation or the increase in benefit reduction rates after the 1981 legislation.

The presence of offsetting forces may partly explain why changes in AFDC benefit reduction rates may have little effect on overall work effort. As discussed by Moffitt, changing the AFDC benefit reduction rate has both *mechanical* and *behavioral* effects. The mechanical effect occurs because changing the AFDC benefit reduction rate changes the program's income-eligibility threshold. Lowering the AFDC benefit reduction rate expands AFDC eligibility, by extending the earnings level at which families qualify. The behavioral effect has two components. Newly eligible persons may reduce their work effort because they are subject to higher marginal tax rates. Those who received AFDC before the change may either increase or decrease their work effort. Though the incentive effects of such a decrease are theoretically ambiguous, studies have found that a fall in the marginal tax rate increases the work effort of those who were eligible for AFDC. Moffitt concludes that the evidence on changes in benefit reduction rates suggests that the increased work effort of current recipients essentially cancels out the decreased work effort of those who become eligible for AFDC.

---

one-third" disregard to the first 4 months on a job. After 4 months on a job, the AFDC benefit reduction rate reverted to 100% after $75 in monthly earnings (a standard deduction for work expenses) and child care expenses. It also established a *gross income limit* -- a second income eligibility threshold above the need standard applied to income *before* deductions and disregards -- at 150% of the State's need standard.. The Deficit Reduction Act (P.L. 98-369) extended the $30 disregard in earnings for those who remained on AFDC after 4 months on a job. It also raised the AFDC gross income limit to 185% of the State's need standard. The Family Support Act of 1988 (P.L. 100-485) raised the standard work expense deduction to $90 a month and modified the deduction for child care expenses.

Trade-offs may also occur between the goals of encouraging working recipients to increase their hours or wages and encouraging those not participating at all to take a job. For example, increasing the generosity of work expense deductions (e.g., child care) could encourage nonworkers to accept work (even part-time work). However, such an increase would also raise the AFDC income eligibility threshold, and thus subject workers at higher earnings levels to higher marginal tax rates. This in turn could discourage increased work effort. This is illustrated by comparing the gains from work for a mother with nonpaid child care arrangements (table 2a) and a mother with paid child care who takes the AFDC child care disregard (table 2b). The marginal tax rates for women who do not pay for child care (table 2a) and work between 30 and 40 hours per week are *negative* in most States, because mothers in most States lose AFDC eligibility and receive and EITC earnings supplement. (A "negative tax" implies that net income rises faster than earnings). However, mothers who pay for child care and take the disregard (table 2b) remain eligible for AFDC in most States even with 40-hour a week schedules. Marginal tax rates for these women in most States run at 74.1%.

Increasingly, Congress and the President have attempted to encourage work for low-income persons through programs other than AFDC. Large expansions of the EITC were legislated in 1986, 1990, and 1993, that reduced the high implicit tax rates among AFDC recipients. The food stamp earnings disregard, which was cut from 20% to 18% of earnings in 1981 was restored to 20% of earnings by legislation enacted in 1985.

THE CURRENT DEBATE

President Clinton's call to "end welfare as we know it" and make AFDC a transitional program to work has renewed the debate about how to promote work for those on welfare. Some proposals seek to promote work by reducing benefit reduction rates. The 1993 expansion of the EITC, which lowered benefit reduction rates for many, was praised by the Administration as the first step toward welfare reform. Through the beginning of

1994, 11 States had received "waivers" from the Federal Government to treat earnings more liberally than the disregards provided in Federal law.[20]

However, many current proposals depart from using financial incentives to *encourage* work; they instead would *require* work or education and job training as a condition of eligibility. Work requirements impose a cost (a time cost) to receiving AFDC, making welfare receipt less attractive compared to finding a job. The Administration's proposed conditional 2-year time-limit on welfare receipt (which would include education, training, and job search over the period), young mothers who had not found a job would be required to take a subsidized job (at 15 to 35 hours per week) or lose AFDC benefits. Subsidized jobs would pay the minimum wage. However, subsidized workers would be ineligible for the EITC.

The House Republican Majority's proposed "Personal Responsibility Act" would impose absolute time-limits on AFDC receipt. Under the proposal, recipients would be required to work 35 hours per week in exchange for the welfare grant. States would have the option to end cash welfare for recipients who had spent 2 years on AFDC, of which at least 1 year was spent in a work program. The proposal would prohibit AFDC for persons who had received it for 5 years.

APPENDIX A: METHODS AND ASSUMPTIONS

The figures and tables presented in this report are based on results from a CRS computer model of selected welfare programs and Federal tax provisions. The model computes income and benefits for defined "case" scenarios. The examples shown here are for a mother with two children. The figures and tables show the level of income this family would receive based on the family's earnings and benefits under selected programs in each State. The programs included in this report are AFDC, food stamps (January 1994 provisions), and the EITC (1996 provisions stated in 1994 dollars). In addition, Federal social security and income taxes (1994 provisions) are modeled. Family income and benefits are calculated based on

---

[20] U.S. Library of Congress. Congressional Research Service. *State Welfare Initiatives.* CRS Report for Congress No. 94-183 EPW, by Jennifer A. Neisner. Washington, Feb. 22, 1994. P. 10.

assumptions about the number of hours the family head works, her hourly wage rate, and work-related expenses (e.g., child care). The examples assume that all family heads who work earn at least the minimum wage ($4.25 per hour).

EARNINGS

The figures and tables in the body of the report depict annual income based on assumed hourly wage rates and annual hours worked. Workers are assumed to earn the Federal minimum wage ($4.25 per hour). Full-time full-year work is considered to be 2,080 hours per year (52 weeks at 40 hours per week). Consequently, a full-time worker would have $8,840 in gross earnings. Part-time workers are assumed to work full-year schedules of 10, 20, or 30 hours per week.

CHILD CARE EXPENSES

Some examples presented in this report assume that a single working parent incurs child care expenses. *No other work-related expenses have been considered in these examples.* The expense assumptions affect eligibility and benefit levels in AFDC and food stamps, because these programs disregard certain expenses when counting income. This analysis assumes that a working mother who purchases child care pays the maximum amount disregarded by the AFDC program ($175 per month per child ages 2 through 12, and $200 per month per child under the age of 2). The examples presented in this report assumes that both children are between the ages of 2 and 12. Child care expenses were reduced pro-rata for mothers who work less than full time.

EARNED INCOME TAX CREDIT (EITC)

The examples shown here depict the EITC provisions scheduled to take effect in 1996. Under the 1996 provisions, a family with more than one child will be eligible for as much as a 40% credit on earnings up to $8,425 (in 1994 dollars), or a maximum credit of $3,370 dollars. Families with earnings between $8,425 and $11,000 (1994 dollars) will be eligible for the maximum ($3,370) credit. In 1996, the credit will begin to phase out when earnings exceed $11,000 and will completely phase out at $27,000 (in 1994 dollars) (about the level of a full-time, full-year worker earning $13 per hour). Under current law, the EITC is reduced by about 21 cents for each additional dollar earned over the credit phaseout range.[21] Because the EITC is reduced as earnings increase, the EITC benefit reduction rate reflects an implicit 21% tax on earnings over the phaseout range. Although the EITC phaseout is based on adjustable gross income (AGI), not just earnings, the example calculations are for a family whose AGI consists solely of wage income.

AID TO FAMILIES WITH DEPENDENT CHILDREN (AFDC)

AFDC benefits shown in this analysis reflect January 1994 benefit levels and program rules based on a CRS telephone survey of the States. For a family of three, maximum monthly AFDC benefits provided to families with no other cash income are shown in the support table for figure 1 (see appendix B).

In general, States calculate AFDC benefits by subtracting income from a payment standard, after taking into account certain income disregards.[22] AFDC law treats families differently depending on how long they have been working while on the program. During the first 4 months of work, the program disregards the first $90 in monthly earnings (as a standard disregard for work-related expenses) and an additional $30 plus one-third of the remainder of earnings (as a work-incentive bonus). After 4 months, the one-third of the disregard is eliminated, which causes the AFDC benefit to be reduced $1 for each $1 in earnings (an implicit tax rate of 100 percent) after the first $120 per month. After a year, the $30 work incentive bonus

---

[21] The phaseout rate is calculated by dividing the maximum benefit by the phaseout range: $3,370/($27,000-$11,000) = .2106.

[22] Some States use somewhat different methods for calculating the AFDC grant. For example, some States calculate AFDC by the method described above, and then "ratably reduce" it by some fraction. Other States allow a family to retain a greater share of earnings than the amounts under the standard disregards before reducing the AFDC grant amount, a policy commonly referred to as "fill-the-gap."

is also eliminated. *Assumed in this analysis are the AFDC rules for a period of work exceeding 4 months but less than a year.* In addition, AFDC disregards child care expenses (up to as much as $175 per child, $200 per child under age 2).

FOOD STAMPS

Federal food stamp benefits shown in this analysis are based on January 1994 benefit levels. Food stamp benefits are calculated by first subtracting certain deductions from a household's gross monthly income (which in these examples includes earnings and AFDC). Deductions include a standard deduction of $131 per month, a 20% earnings deduction, and child care expenses (up to a maximum of $160 per month per child). These deductions are subtracted from gross income to arrive at net countable income. The food stamp benefit is computed by subtracting from a household's maximum monthly food stamp benefit 30% of *net countable income*. Consequently, after the standard deduction and child care expenses are taken into account, the effective benefit reduction rate for a $1 increase in earnings under the Food Stamp program is 24% (i.e., (0.3 x (1-0.2)) = .24). In January 1994, the maximum food stamp benefit for a family of three living in the States shown in this report was $295 per month. The 30% benefit-reduction rate on net countable income effectively represents a 30% implicit tax rate on countable income (after deductions). Because the Food Stamp program counts AFDC payments as income, AFDC families receiving the maximum AFDC grant in low-paying AFDC states receive more in food stamps than do AFDC families receiving the maximum AFDC grant in high-paying States.

GROSS AND NET INCOME

The figures and tables include gross and net income estimates. In these examples, gross income includes: earnings, AFDC, food stamps, and the EITC. Tow net-income measures are shown. The first measure, net after-tax income, represents gross income less Federal payroll taxes (employee share of FICA and HI taxes) and Federal income taxes (taking into account the Dependent Care Tax Credit (DCTC)). (The DCTC is a non-refundable credit that may amount to as much as 30% of a family's expenses for child care, up to the limits of the family's Federal income tax liability.) The second net-income measure subtracts child care expenses from net after-tax income.

MARGINAL TAX RATES

The marginal tax rates depicted in the figures and tables in this report measure changes in net income (after taxes and child care expenses) relative to changes in earnings. Marginal tax rates reflect both explicit taxes on earnings, such as Federal payroll and income taxes, and implicit taxes on earnings associated with reductions in benefits that accompany increased earnings over a specified range. Positive marginal tax rates of less than 100% mean that net income increases over the range, but at a lesser rate than the increase in earnings. For example, a marginal tax rate of 50% means that net-income increases only half as much as the increase in earnings over the specified range. Marginal tax rates over 100% imply that net income actually drops with an increase in earnings (often referred to as a "notch" in net income, depicted in some of the figures). Negative marginal tax rates imply that net income is increasing at a faster rate than the increase in earnings over a specified range (an earnings subsidy).

Marginal tax rates are sensitive to the interval over which the marginal change in income is measured. For example, tables 2a and 2b, in the body of this report, show marginal tax rates based on a change in income (after taxes and child care expenses) associated with a change in earnings attributable to working an additional 10 hours per week.

EXAMPLE OF INCOME, BENEFITS AND MARGINAL TAX RATES IN PENNSYLVANIA

The following figures and tables provide details of income, benefits, and marginal tax rates for a mother with two children at various earnings levels living in Pennsylvania. Pennsylvania was chosen for purposes of illustration, because its AFDC payment level is near that of the median State. The income and benefit amounts and marginal tax rates shown in this appendix are based on $520 per year increments in annual earnings (the change in annual income associated with a 25 cent per hour change in the hourly wage rate for a full-time, full year worker (i.e., 25 cents per hour x 40 hours per week x 52 weeks per year). Workers with hourly earnings less than a full-time, full-year worker $8,840 per year, are assumed to work less than full-time, full-year at the minimum wage ($4.25 per hour). Workers earning more, are assumed to work full-time full-year, at higher hourly earnings.

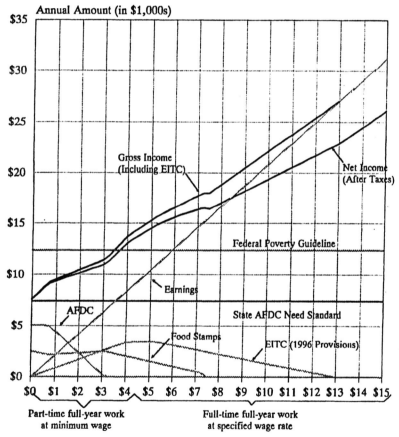

PENNSYLVANIA:
Selected Income/Benefits for a Mother with 2 Children
by Full-time Full-Year Hourly Wage Equivalent

Source: CRS.
Note: See accompanying text for discussion of methods and assumptions.

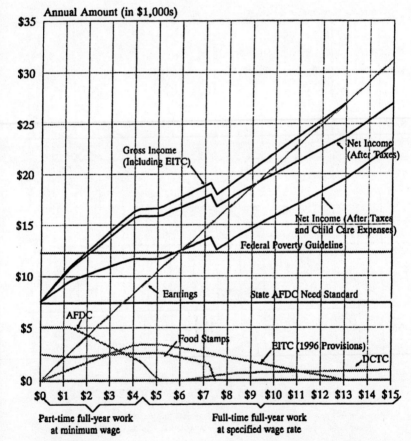

PENNSYLVANIA:
Selected Income/Benefits for a Mother with 2 Children
(assuming the mother has child care expenses)
by Full-time Full-Year Hourly Wage Equivalent

Source: CRS.
Note: See accompanying text for discussion of methods and assumptions.

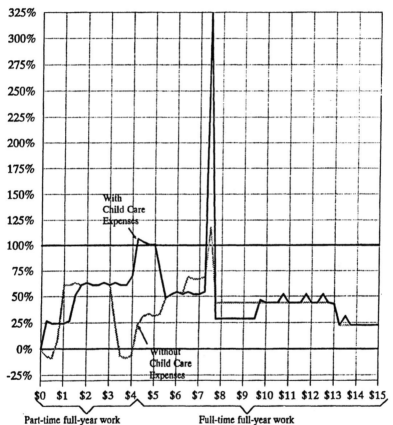

PENNSYLVANIA:
Implicit Marginal Tax Rates
(Net After-Taxes and Child Care Expenses)
for a Mother with 2 Children
by Full-Time Hourly Wage Equivalent

Source: CRS.
Note: See accompanying text for discussion of methods and assumptions.

PENNSYLVANIA: Benefits and Income for a Mother with 2 Children
(Assuming Child Care Expenses)
Based on January 1994 Benefit Levels and 1996 EITC Provisions

Full-time hourly wage equivalent	Earnings	Public Assistance		Tax Credits		Expenses	Taxes		Total Income			As a % of poverty		Implicit marginal tax rate
		AFDC	Food Stamps	EITC	DCTC	Child care	Federal income taxes (before DCTC)	Social security taxes	Gross (includes EITC) (excludes DCTC)	Net after taxes	Net after taxes and work related expenses	Gross (including tax credits)	Net after taxes	
$0.00	$0	$5,052	$2,496	$0	$0	$0	$0	$0	$7,548	$7,548	$7,548	61	61	0
0.25	520	5,052	2,436	208	0	247	0	40	8,216	8,176	7,929	67	64	27
0.50	1,040	5,052	2,388	416	0	494	0	80	8,896	8,816	8,322	72	68	24
0.75	1,560	5,052	2,340	624	0	741	0	119	9,576	9,457	8,715	78	71	24
1.00	2,080	5,052	2,292	832	0	988	0	159	10,256	10,097	9,109	83	74	24
1.25	2,600	5,052	2,232	1,040	0	1,235	0	199	10,924	10,725	9,490	89	77	27
1.50	3,120	4,854	2,244	1,248	0	1,482	0	239	11,466	11,228	9,745	93	79	51
1.75	3,640	4,581	2,280	1,456	0	1,729	0	278	11,957	11,679	9,950	97	81	61
2.00	4,160	4,308	2,304	1,664	0	1,976	0	318	12,436	12,118	10,142	101	82	63
2.25	4,680	4,036	2,340	1,872	0	2,224	0	358	12,928	12,570	10,346	105	84	61
2.50	5,200	3,763	2,376	2,080	0	2,471	0	398	13,419	13,021	10,550	109	86	61
2.75	5,720	3,490	2,400	2,288	0	2,718	0	438	13,898	13,460	10,742	113	87	63
3.00	6,240	3,217	2,436	2,496	0	2,965	0	477	14,389	13,911	10,947	117	89	61
3.25	6,760	2,944	2,460	2,704	0	3,212	0	517	14,868	14,351	11,139	121	90	63
3.50	7,280	2,671	2,496	2,912	0	3,459	0	557	15,359	14,802	11,343	125	92	61
3.75	7,800	2,398	2,532	3,120	0	3,706	0	597	15,850	15,253	11,547	129	94	61
4.00	8,320	2,125	2,520	3,328	0	3,953	0	636	16,293	15,656	11,704	132	95	70
4.25	8,840	1,852	2,484	3,370	0	4,200	0	676	16,546	15,870	11,670	134	95	106
4.50	9,360	1,332	2,508	3,370	0	4,200	0	716	16,570	15,854	11,654	134	95	103
4.75	9,880	812	2,544	3,370	0	4,200	0	756	16,606	15,850	11,650	135	95	101
5.00	10,400	292	2,580	3,370	0	4,200	0	796	16,642	15,846	11,646	135	95	101
5.25	10,920	0	2,532	3,370	0	4,200	0	835	16,822	15,987	11,787	137	96	73
5.50	11,440	0	2,412	3,277	0	4,200	0	875	17,129	16,254	12,054	139	98	49
5.75	11,960	0	2,292	3,168	0	4,200	0	915	17,420	16,505	12,305	141	100	52
6.00	12,480	0	2,160	3,058	0	4,200	0	955	17,698	16,744	12,544	144	102	54
6.25	13,000	0	2,040	2,949	8	4,200	8	995	17,989	16,994	12,794	146	104	52
6.50	13,520	0	1,908	2,839	86	4,200	86	1,034	18,267	17,233	13,033	148	106	54
6.75	14,040	0	1,788	2,730	164	4,200	164	1,074	18,558	17,484	13,284	151	108	52
7.00	14,560	0	1,668	2,620	242	4,200	242	1,114	18,848	17,734	13,534	153	110	52
7.25	15,080	0	1,536	2,511	320	4,200	320	1,154	19,127	17,973	13,773	155	112	54
7.50	15,600	0	0	2,401	398	4,200	398	1,193	18,001	16,808	12,608	146	102	324
7.75	16,120	0	0	2,292	476	4,200	476	1,233	18,412	17,179	12,979	149	105	29
8.00	16,640	0	0	2,182	554	4,200	554	1,273	18,822	17,549	13,349	153	108	29
8.25	17,160	0	0	2,073	632	4,200	632	1,313	19,233	17,920	13,720	156	111	29
8.50	17,680	0	0	1,963	710	4,200	710	1,353	19,643	18,291	14,091	159	114	29
8.75	18,200	0	0	1,854	788	4,200	788	1,392	20,054	18,661	14,461	163	117	29
9.00	18,720	0	0	1,744	866	4,200	866	1,432	20,464	19,032	14,832	166	120	29
9.25	19,240	0	0	1,635	944	4,200	944	1,472	20,875	19,403	15,203	169	123	29
9.50	19,760	0	0	1,525	1,022	4,200	1,022	1,512	21,285	19,774	15,574	173	126	29
9.75	20,280	0	0	1,416	1,008	4,200	1,100	1,551	21,696	20,053	15,853	176	129	46
10.00	20,800	0	0	1,306	1,008	4,200	1,178	1,591	22,106	20,345	16,145	179	131	44
11.00	22,880	0	0	868	966	4,200	1,490	1,750	23,748	21,474	17,274	193	140	44
12.00	24,960	0	0	430	924	4,200	1,802	1,909	25,390	22,603	18,403	206	149	44
13.00	27,040	0	0	0	882	4,200	2,114	2,069	27,040	23,740	19,540	219	159	42
14.00	29,120	0	0	0	840	4,200	2,426	2,228	29,120	25,307	21,107	236	171	23
15.00	31,200	0	0	0	840	4,200	2,738	2,387	31,200	26,916	22,716	253	184	23

NOTE: See appendix A for a discussion of methods and assumptions.
Source: Table prepared by CRS.

PENNSYLVANIA: Benefits and Income for a Mother with 2 Children
Based on January 1994 Benefit Levels and 1996 EITC Provisions

Full-time hourly wage equivalent	Earnings	Public Assistance		Tax Credits		Expenses	Taxes		Total Income					Implicit marginal tax rate
									Amount			As a % of poverty		
		AFDC	Food Stamps	EITC	DCTC	Child care	Federal income taxes (before DCTC)	Social security taxes	Gross (includes EITC) (excludes DCTC)	Net after taxes	Net after taxes and work related expenses	Gross (including tax credits)	Net after taxes	
$0.00	$0	$5,052	$2,496	$0	$0	$0	$0	$0	$7,548	$7,548	$7,548	61	61	0
$0.25	520	5,052	2,364	208	0	0	0	40	8,144	8,104	8,104	66	66	-7
$0.50	1,040	5,052	2,244	416	0	0	0	80	8,752	8,672	8,672	71	70	-9
$0.75	1,560	4,932	2,148	624	0	0	0	119	9,264	9,145	9,145	75	74	9
$1.00	2,080	4,412	2,184	832	0	0	0	159	9,508	9,349	9,349	77	76	61
$1.25	2,600	3,892	2,220	1,040	0	0	0	199	9,752	9,553	9,553	79	78	61
$1.50	3,120	3,372	2,244	1,248	0	0	0	239	9,984	9,745	9,745	81	79	63
$1.75	3,640	2,852	2,280	1,456	0	0	0	278	10,228	9,950	9,950	83	81	61
$2.00	4,160	2,332	2,304	1,664	0	0	0	318	10,460	10,142	10,142	85	82	63
$2.25	4,680	1,812	2,340	1,872	0	0	0	358	10,704	10,346	10,346	87	84	61
$2.50	5,200	1,292	2,376	2,080	0	0	0	398	10,948	10,550	10,550	89	86	61
$2.75	5,720	772	2,400	2,288	0	0	0	438	11,180	10,742	10,742	91	87	63
$3.00	6,240	252	2,436	2,496	0	0	0	477	11,424	10,947	10,947	93	89	61
$3.25	6,760	0	2,388	2,704	0	0	0	517	11,852	11,335	11,335	96	92	25
$3.50	7,280	0	2,256	2,912	0	0	0	557	12,448	11,891	11,891	101	97	-7
$3.75	7,800	0	2,136	3,170	0	0	0	597	13,056	12,459	12,459	106	101	-9
$4.00	8,320	0	2,004	3,328	0	0	0	636	13,652	13,016	13,016	111	106	-7
$4.25	8,840	0	1,884	3,370	0	0	0	676	14,094	13,418	13,418	114	109	23
$4.50	9,360	0	1,764	3,370	0	0	0	716	14,494	13,778	13,778	118	112	31
$4.75	9,880	0	1,632	3,370	0	0	0	756	14,882	14,126	14,126	121	115	33
$5.00	10,400	0	1,512	3,370	0	0	0	796	15,282	14,486	14,486	124	118	31
$5.25	10,920	0	1,380	3,370	0	0	0	835	15,670	14,835	14,835	127	120	33
$5.50	11,440	0	1,260	3,277	0	0	0	875	15,977	15,102	15,102	130	123	49
$5.75	11,960	0	1,140	3,168	0	0	0	915	16,268	15,353	15,353	132	125	52
$6.00	12,480	0	1,008	3,058	0	0	0	955	16,546	15,592	15,592	134	127	54
$6.25	13,000	0	888	2,949	0	0	8	995	16,837	15,835	15,835	137	129	53
$6.50	13,520	0	756	2,839	0	0	86	1,034	17,115	15,996	15,996	139	130	69
$6.75	14,040	0	636	2,730	0	0	164	1,074	17,406	16,168	16,168	141	131	67
$7.00	14,560	0	516	2,620	0	0	242	1,114	17,696	16,341	16,341	144	133	67
$7.25	15,080	0	384	2,511	0	0	320	1,154	17,975	16,502	16,502	146	134	69
$7.50	15,600	0	0	2,401	0	0	398	1,193	18,001	16,410	16,410	146	133	118
$7.75	16,120	0	0	2,292	0	0	476	1,233	18,412	16,703	16,703	149	136	44
$8.00	16,640	0	0	2,182	0	0	554	1,273	18,996	16,996	16,996	153	138	44
$8.25	17,160	0	0	2,073	0	0	632	1,313	19,233	17,288	17,288	156	140	44
$8.50	17,680	0	0	1,963	0	0	710	1,353	19,643	17,581	17,581	159	143	44
$8.75	18,200	0	0	1,854	0	0	788	1,392	20,054	17,874	17,874	163	145	44
$9.00	18,720	0	0	1,744	0	0	866	1,432	20,464	18,167	18,167	166	147	44
$9.25	19,240	0	0	1,635	0	0	944	1,472	20,875	18,459	18,459	169	150	44
$9.50	19,760	0	0	1,525	0	0	1,022	1,512	21,285	18,752	18,752	173	152	44
$9.75	20,280	0	0	1,416	0	0	1,100	1,551	21,696	19,045	19,045	176	155	44
$10.00	20,800	0	0	1,306	0	0	1,178	1,591	22,106	19,337	19,337	179	157	44
$11.00	22,880	0	0	868	0	0	1,490	1,750	23,748	20,508	20,508	193	166	44
$12.00	24,960	0	0	430	0	0	1,802	1,909	25,390	21,679	21,679	206	176	44
$13.00	27,040	0	0	0	0	0	2,114	2,069	27,040	22,858	22,858	219	186	42
$14.00	29,120	0	0	0	0	0	2,426	2,228	29,120	24,467	24,467	236	199	23
$15.00	31,200	0	0	0	0	0	2,738	2,387	31,200	26,076	26,076	253	212	23

NOTE: See appendix A for a discussion of methods and assumptions.
Source: Table prepared by CRS.

SUPPORT TABLE: FIGURE 1. Sources of Annual Income for a Single Mother with 2 Children and Not Working: 1994

State	AFDC			Food stamps	EITC (1996 provisions)	Earnings (after taxes)	Total income (after taxes)	Net income to poverty ratio *
	Total	State share	Federal share					
Mississippi	$1,440	$305	$1,135	$3,540	$0	$0	$4,980	0.40
Alabama	1,968	566	1,402	3,420	0	0	5,388	0.44
Texas	2,208	791	1,417	3,348	0	0	5,556	0.45
Tennessee	2,220	729	1,491	3,336	0	0	5,556	0.45
Louisiana	2,280	604	1,676	3,324	0	0	5,604	0.45
South Carolina	2,400	694	1,706	3,288	0	0	5,688	0.46
Arkansas	2,448	625	1,823	3,276	0	0	5,724	0.46
Kentucky	2,736	796	1,940	3,180	0	0	5,916	0.48
West Virginia	2,988	725	2,263	3,108	0	0	6,096	0.49
North Carolina	3,264	1,138	2,126	3,024	0	0	6,288	0.51
Georgia	3,360	1,261	2,099	3,000	0	0	6,360	0.52
Indiana	3,456	1,262	2,194	2,964	0	0	6,420	0.52
Missouri	3,504	1,379	2,125	2,952	0	0	6,456	0.52
Florida	3,636	1,644	1,992	2,916	0	0	6,552	0.53
Idaho	3,804	1,106	2,698	2,868	0	0	6,672	0.54
Oklahoma	3,888	1,151	2,737	2,844	0	0	6,732	0.55
Delaware	4,056	2,028	2,028	2,784	0	0	6,840	0.56
Ohio	4,092	1,603	2,489	2,784	0	0	6,876	0.56
Arizona	4,164	1,420	2,744	2,760	0	0	6,924	0.56
Nevada	4,176	2,075	2,101	2,748	0	0	6,924	0.56
Virginia	4,248	2,124	2,124	2,736	0	0	6,984	0.57
Colorado	4,272	1,952	2,320	2,724	0	0	6,996	0.57
New Mexico	4,284	1,107	3,177	2,724	0	0	7,008	0.57
Wyoming	4,320	1,485	2,835	2,712	0	0	7,032	0.57
Nebraska	4,368	1,661	2,707	2,700	0	0	7,068	0.57
Maryland	4,392	2,196	2,196	2,688	0	0	7,080	0.57
Illinois	4,404	2,202	2,202	2,688	0	0	7,092	0.58
Montana	4,812	1,393	3,419	2,568	0	0	7,380	0.60
North Dakota	4,908	1,417	3,491	2,532	0	0	7,440	0.60
Utah	4,968	1,274	3,694	2,520	0	0	7,488	0.61
South Dakota	5,004	1,526	3,478	2,508	0	0	7,512	0.61
Maine	5,016	1,908	3,108	2,496	0	0	7,512	0.61
District of Columbia	5,040	2,520	2,520	2,496	0	0	7,536	0.61
Pennsylvania	5,052	2,293	2,759	2,496	0	0	7,548	0.61
New Jersey	5,088	2,544	2,544	2,484	0	0	7,572	0.61
Iowa	5,112	1,875	3,237	2,472	0	0	7,584	0.62
Kansas	5,148	2,084	3,064	2,460	0	0	7,608	0.62
Michigan (Wayne Co.)	5,508	2,403	3,105	2,352	0	0	7,860	0.64
Oregon	5,520	2,091	3,429	2,352	0	0	7,872	0.64
Michigan (Washtenaw Co.)	5,868	2,560	3,308	2,244	0	0	8,112	0.66
Wisconsin	6,204	2,452	3,752	2,148	0	0	8,352	0.68
Minnesota	6,384	2,895	3,489	2,088	0	0	8,472	0.69
Washington	6,552	2,998	3,554	2,040	0	0	8,592	0.70
New Hampshire	6,600	3,300	3,300	2,028	0	0	8,628	0.70
Rhode Island	6,648	3,067	3,581	2,016	0	0	8,664	0.70
New York (New York City)	6,924	3,462	3,462	1,932	0	0	8,856	0.72
Massachusetts	6,948	3,474	3,474	1,920	0	0	8,868	0.72
California	7,284	3,642	3,642	1,824	0	0	9,108	0.74
Vermont	7,656	3,097	4,559	1,704	0	0	9,360	0.76
Connecticut	8,160	4,080	4,080	1,560	0	0	9,720	0.79
New York (Suffolk Co.)	8,436	4,218	4,218	1,476	0	0	9,912	0.80
Hawaii	8,544	4,272	4,272	3,996	0	0	12,540	0.88
Alaska	11,076	5,538	5,538	2,136	0	0	13,212	0.86

* Federal poverty income guidelines in 1994 for a family of 3: $12,320, Hawaii: $14,170, Alaska: $15,400.

NOTE: Details may not sum to totals because of rounding.

SOURCE: Congressional Research Service.

SUPPORT TABLE: FIGURE 2a. Sources of Annual Income for a Single Mother with 2 Children Working 1/4 time at the Minimum Wage: 1994

State	AFDC			Food stamps	EITC (1996 provisions)	Earnings (after taxes)	Total Income (after taxes)	Net income to poverty ratio *
	Total	State share	Federal share					
Mississippi	$1,440	$305	$1,135	$3,048	$884	$2,041	$7,413	0.60
Alabama	1,198	345	853	3,120	884	2,041	7,243	0.59
Texas	1,438	515	923	3,048	884	2,041	7,411	0.60
Tennessee	1,886	619	1,266	2,904	884	2,041	7,715	0.63
Louisiana	1,510	400	1,110	3,024	884	2,041	7,459	0.61
South Carolina	1,630	471	1,159	2,988	884	2,041	7,543	0.61
Arkansas	1,678	429	1,249	2,976	884	2,041	7,579	0.62
Kentucky	2,402	699	1,703	2,760	884	2,041	8,087	0.66
West Virginia	2,218	539	1,679	2,808	884	2,041	7,951	0.65
North Carolina	2,879	1,004	1,875	2,616	884	2,041	8,420	0.68
Georgia	3,360	1,261	2,099	2,472	884	2,041	8,757	0.71
Indiana	2,686	981	1,705	2,664	884	2,041	8,275	0.67
Missouri	2,734	1,076	1,658	2,652	884	2,041	8,311	0.67
Florida	2,866	1,296	1,570	2,616	884	2,041	8,407	0.68
Idaho	3,034	882	2,152	2,568	884	2,041	8,527	0.69
Oklahoma	3,118	923	2,195	2,544	884	2,041	8,587	0.70
Delaware	3,286	1,643	1,643	2,484	884	2,041	8,695	0.71
Ohio	3,322	1,301	2,021	2,484	884	2,041	8,731	0.71
Arizona	3,394	1,157	2,237	2,460	884	2,041	8,779	0.71
Nevada	3,406	1,692	1,714	2,448	884	2,041	8,779	0.71
Virginia	3,478	1,739	1,739	2,436	884	2,041	8,839	0.72
Colorado	3,621	1,655	1,966	2,388	884	2,041	8,934	0.73
New Mexico	3,514	908	2,606	2,424	884	2,041	8,863	0.72
Wyoming	4,320	1,485	2,835	2,184	884	2,041	9,429	0.77
Nebraska	3,598	1,368	2,230	2,400	884	2,041	8,923	0.72
Maryland	3,622	1,811	1,811	2,388	884	2,041	8,935	0.73
Illinois	3,634	1,817	1,817	2,388	884	2,041	8,947	0.73
Montana	4,042	1,170	2,872	2,268	884	2,041	9,235	0.75
North Dakota	4,138	1,195	2,943	2,232	884	2,041	9,295	0.75
Utah	4,391	1,126	3,264	2,160	884	2,041	9,475	0.77
South Dakota	4,354	1,328	3,026	2,172	884	2,041	9,451	0.77
Maine	4,434	1,687	2,747	2,148	884	2,041	9,507	0.77
District of Columbia	4,270	2,135	2,135	2,196	884	2,041	9,391	0.76
Pennsylvania	4,282	1,944	2,338	2,196	884	2,041	9,403	0.76
New Jersey	4,318	2,159	2,159	2,184	884	2,041	9,427	0.77
Iowa	4,342	1,592	2,750	2,172	884	2,041	9,439	0.77
Kansas	4,378	1,772	2,606	2,160	884	2,041	9,463	0.77
Michigan (Wayne Co.)	4,738	2,067	2,671	2,052	884	2,041	9,715	0.79
Oregon	4,750	1,799	2,951	2,052	884	2,041	9,727	0.79
Michigan (Washtenaw Co.)	5,098	2,224	2,874	1,944	884	2,041	9,967	0.81
Wisconsin	5,434	2,148	3,286	1,848	884	2,041	10,207	0.83
Minnesota	5,614	2,546	3,068	1,788	884	2,041	10,327	0.84
Washington	5,782	2,646	3,136	1,740	884	2,041	10,447	0.85
New Hampshire	5,830	2,915	2,915	1,728	884	2,041	10,483	0.85
Rhode Island	5,878	2,712	3,166	1,716	884	2,041	10,519	0.85
New York (New York City)	6,154	3,077	3,077	1,632	884	2,041	10,711	0.87
Massachusetts	6,178	3,089	3,089	1,620	884	2,041	10,723	0.87
California	7,284	3,642	3,642	1,296	884	2,041	11,505	0.93
Vermont	6,886	2,785	4,101	1,404	884	2,041	11,215	0.91
Connecticut	7,390	3,695	3,695	1,260	884	2,041	11,575	0.94
New York (Suffolk Co.)	7,666	3,833	3,833	1,176	884	2,041	11,767	0.96
Hawaii	7,774	3,887	3,887	3,696	884	2,041	14,395	1.02
Alaska	10,930	5,465	5,465	1,644	884	2,041	15,499	1.01

* Federal poverty income guidelines in 1994 for a family of 3: $12,320, Hawaii: $14,170, Alaska: $15,400.
NOTE: Details may not sum to totals because of rounding.
SOURCE: Congressional Research Service.

| | AFDC | | | | | | | |
State	Total	State share	Federal share	Food stamps	EITC (1996 provisions)	Earnings (after taxes)	Total income (after taxes)	Net income to poverty ratio [a]
Mississippi	$862	$182	$679	$2,688	$1,768	$4,082	$9,399	0.76
Alabama	0	0	0	2,940	1,768	4,082	8,790	0.71
Texas	0	0	0	2,940	1,768	4,082	8,790	0.71
Tennessee	926	304	622	2,664	1,768	4,082	9,440	0.77
Louisiana	0	0	0	2,940	1,768	4,082	8,790	0.71
South Carolina	0	0	0	2,940	1,768	4,082	8,790	0.71
Arkansas	0	0	0	2,940	1,768	4,082	8,790	0.71
Kentucky	1,444	420	1,024	2,508	1,768	4,082	9,802	0.80
West Virginia	0	0	0	2,940	1,768	4,082	8,790	0.71
North Carolina	1,774	618	1,156	2,412	1,768	4,082	10,036	0.81
Georgia	2,108	791	1,317	2,316	1,768	4,082	10,274	0.83
Indiana	476	174	302	2,808	1,768	4,082	9,134	0.74
Missouri	524	206	318	2,784	1,768	4,082	9,158	0.74
Florida	656	297	359	2,748	1,768	4,082	9,254	0.75
Idaho	824	240	584	2,700	1,768	4,082	9,374	0.76
Oklahoma	908	269	639	2,676	1,768	4,082	9,434	0.77
Delaware	1,076	538	538	2,628	1,768	4,082	9,554	0.78
Ohio	1,112	436	676	2,616	1,768	4,082	9,578	0.78
Arizona	1,184	404	780	2,592	1,768	4,082	9,626	0.78
Nevada	1,196	594	602	2,592	1,768	4,082	9,638	0.78
Virginia	1,268	634	634	2,568	1,768	4,082	9,686	0.79
Colorado	1,752	801	951	2,424	1,768	4,082	10,026	0.81
New Mexico	1,304	337	967	2,556	1,768	4,082	9,710	0.79
Wyoming	4,100	1,409	2,691	1,716	1,768	4,082	11,666	0.95
Nebraska	1,388	528	860	2,532	1,768	4,082	9,770	0.79
Maryland	1,412	706	706	2,520	1,768	4,082	9,782	0.79
Illinois	1,424	712	712	2,520	1,768	4,082	9,794	0.79
Montana	1,832	530	1,302	2,400	1,768	4,082	10,082	0.82
North Dakota	1,928	557	1,371	2,364	1,768	4,082	10,142	0.82
Utah	2,733	701	2,032	2,124	1,768	4,082	10,707	0.87
South Dakota	2,475	755	1,720	2,208	1,768	4,082	10,533	0.85
Maine	2,763	1,051	1,712	2,112	1,768	4,082	10,725	0.87
District of Columbia	2,060	1,030	1,030	2,328	1,768	4,082	10,238	0.83
Pennsylvania	2,072	940	1,132	2,328	1,768	4,082	10,250	0.83
New Jersey	2,108	1,054	1,054	2,316	1,768	4,082	10,274	0.83
Iowa	2,132	782	1,350	2,304	1,768	4,082	10,286	0.83
Kansas	2,168	878	1,290	2,292	1,768	4,082	10,310	0.84
Michigan (Wayne Co.)	2,528	1,103	1,425	2,184	1,768	4,082	10,562	0.86
Oregon	2,540	962	1,578	2,184	1,768	4,082	10,574	0.86
Michigan (Washtenaw Co.)	2,888	1,260	1,628	2,076	1,768	4,082	10,814	0.88
Wisconsin	3,224	1,274	1,950	1,980	1,768	4,082	11,054	0.90
Minnesota	3,404	1,544	1,860	1,920	1,768	4,082	11,174	0.91
Washington	3,572	1,635	1,937	1,872	1,768	4,082	11,294	0.92
New Hampshire	3,620	1,810	1,810	1,860	1,768	4,082	11,330	0.92
Rhode Island	3,668	1,692	1,976	1,848	1,768	4,082	11,366	0.92
New York (New York City)	3,944	1,972	1,972	1,764	1,768	4,082	11,558	0.94
Massachusetts	3,968	1,984	1,984	1,752	1,768	4,082	11,570	0.94
California	5,600	2,800	2,800	1,260	1,768	4,082	12,710	1.03
Vermont	4,676	1,891	2,785	1,548	1,768	4,082	12,074	0.98
Connecticut	5,180	2,590	2,590	1,392	1,768	4,082	12,422	1.01
New York (Suffolk Co.)	5,456	2,728	2,728	1,308	1,768	4,082	12,614	1.02
Hawaii	5,564	2,782	2,782	3,840	1,768	4,082	15,254	1.08
Alaska	8,720	4,360	4,360	1,776	1,768	4,082	16,346	1.06

SUPPORT TABLE: FIGURE 3a. Sources of Annual Income for a Single Mother with 2 Children Working 1/2 time at the Minimum Wage: 1994

[a] Federal poverty income guidelines in 1994 for a family of 3: $12,320, Hawaii: $14,170, Alaska: $15,400.

NOTE: Details may not sum to totals because of rounding.

SOURCE: Congressional Research Service.

	AFDC						Total	
State	Total	State share	Federal share	Food stamps	EITC (1996 provisions)	Earnings (after taxes)	Total Income (after taxes)	Net income to poverty ratio *
Mississippi	$0	$0	$0	$2,412	$2,652	$6,123	$11,187	0.91
Alabama	0	0	0	2,412	2,652	6,123	11,187	0.91
Texas	0	0	0	2,412	2,652	6,123	11,187	0.91
Tennessee	0	0	0	2,412	2,652	6,123	11,187	0.91
Louisiana	0	0	0	2,412	2,652	6,123	11,187	0.91
South Carolina	0	0	0	2,412	2,652	6,123	11,187	0.91
Arkansas	0	0	0	2,412	2,652	6,123	11,187	0.91
Kentucky	486	141	345	2,268	2,652	6,123	11,529	0.94
West Virginia	0	0	0	2,412	2,652	6,123	11,187	0.91
North Carolina	669	233	436	2,208	2,652	6,123	11,652	0.95
Georgia	0	0	0	2,412	2,652	6,123	11,187	0.91
Indiana	0	0	0	2,412	2,652	6,123	11,187	0.91
Missouri	0	0	0	2,412	2,652	6,123	11,187	0.91
Florida	0	0	0	2,412	2,652	6,123	11,187	0.91
Idaho	0	0	0	2,412	2,652	6,123	11,187	0.91
Oklahoma	0	0	0	2,412	2,652	6,123	11,187	0.91
Delaware	0	0	0	2,412	2,652	6,123	11,187	0.91
Ohio	0	0	0	2,412	2,652	6,123	11,187	0.91
Arizona	0	0	0	2,412	2,652	6,123	11,187	0.91
Nevada	0	0	0	2,412	2,652	6,123	11,187	0.91
Virginia	0	0	0	2,412	2,652	6,123	11,187	0.91
Colorado	0	0	0	2,412	2,652	6,123	11,187	0.91
New Mexico	0	0	0	2,412	2,652	6,123	11,187	0.91
Wyoming	1,890	650	1,240	1,848	2,652	6,123	12,513	1.02
Nebraska	0	0	0	2,412	2,652	6,123	11,187	0.91
Maryland	0	0	0	2,412	2,652	6,123	11,187	0.91
Illinois	0	0	0	2,412	2,652	6,123	11,187	0.91
Montana	0	0	0	2,412	2,652	6,123	11,187	0.91
North Dakota	0	0	0	2,412	2,652	6,123	11,187	0.91
Utah	1,076	276	800	2,088	2,652	6,123	11,938	0.97
South Dakota	597	182	415	2,232	2,652	6,123	11,604	0.94
Maine	1,093	416	677	2,088	2,652	6,123	11,956	0.97
District of Columbia	0	0	0	2,412	2,652	6,123	11,187	0.91
Pennsylvania	0	0	0	2,412	2,652	6,123	11,187	0.91
New Jersey	0	0	0	2,412	2,652	6,123	11,187	0.91
Iowa	0	0	0	2,412	2,652	6,123	11,187	0.91
Kansas	0	0	0	2,412	2,652	6,123	11,187	0.91
Michigan (Wayne Co.)	318	139	179	2,316	2,652	6,123	11,409	0.93
Oregon	330	125	205	2,316	2,652	6,123	11,421	0.93
Michigan (Washtenaw Co.)	678	296	382	2,208	2,652	6,123	11,661	0.95
Wisconsin	1,014	401	613	2,112	2,652	6,123	11,901	0.97
Minnesota	1,194	541	653	2,052	2,652	6,123	12,021	0.98
Washington	1,362	623	739	2,004	2,652	6,123	12,141	0.99
New Hampshire	1,410	705	705	1,992	2,652	6,123	12,177	0.99
Rhode Island	1,458	673	785	1,980	2,652	6,123	12,213	0.99
New York (New York City)	1,734	867	867	1,896	2,652	6,123	12,405	1.01
Massachusetts	1,758	879	879	1,884	2,652	6,123	12,417	1.01
California	3,390	1,695	1,695	1,392	2,652	6,123	13,557	1.10
Vermont	2,466	997	1,469	1,680	2,652	6,123	12,921	1.05
Connecticut	2,970	1,485	1,485	1,524	2,652	6,123	13,269	1.08
New York (Suffolk Co.)	3,246	1,623	1,623	1,440	2,652	6,123	13,461	1.09
Hawaii	3,354	1,677	1,677	3,972	2,652	6,123	16,101	1.14
Alaska	6,510	3,255	3,255	1,908	2,652	6,123	17,193	1.12

SUPPORT TABLE: FIGURE 4a. Sources of Annual Income for a Single Mother with 2 Children Working 3/4 time at the Minimum Wage: 1994

* Federal poverty income guidelines in 1994 for a family of 3: $12,320, Hawaii: $14,170, Alaska: $15,400.

NOTE: Details may not sum to totals because of rounding.

SOURCE: Congressional Research Service.

	AFDC							
State	Total	State share	Federal share	Food stamps	EITC (1996 provisions)	Earnings (after taxes)	Total Income (after taxes)	Net income to poverty ratio *
Mississippi	$0	$0	$0	$1,884	$3,370	$8,164	$13,418	1.09
Alabama	0	0	0	1,884	3,370	8,164	13,418	1.09
Texas	0	0	0	1,884	3,370	8,164	13,418	1.09
Tennessee	0	0	0	1,884	3,370	8,164	13,418	1.09
Louisiana	0	0	0	1,884	3,370	8,164	13,418	1.09
South Carolina	0	0	0	1,884	3,370	8,164	13,418	1.09
Arkansas	0	0	0	1,884	3,370	8,164	13,418	1.09
Kentucky	0	0	0	1,884	3,370	8,164	13,418	1.09
West Virginia	0	0	0	1,884	3,370	8,164	13,418	1.09
North Carolina	0	0	0	1,884	3,370	8,164	13,418	1.09
Georgia	0	0	0	1,884	3,370	8,164	13,418	1.09
Indiana	0	0	0	1,884	3,370	8,164	13,418	1.09
Missouri	0	0	0	1,884	3,370	8,164	13,418	1.09
Florida	0	0	0	1,884	3,370	8,164	13,418	1.09
Idaho	0	0	0	1,884	3,370	8,164	13,418	1.09
Oklahoma	0	0	0	1,884	3,370	8,164	13,418	1.09
Delaware	0	0	0	1,884	3,370	8,164	13,418	1.09
Ohio	0	0	0	1,884	3,370	8,164	13,418	1.09
Arizona	0	0	0	1,884	3,370	8,164	13,418	1.09
Nevada	0	0	0	1,884	3,370	8,164	13,418	1.09
Virginia	0	0	0	1,884	3,370	8,164	13,418	1.09
Colorado	0	0	0	1,884	3,370	8,164	13,418	1.09
New Mexico	0	0	0	1,884	3,370	8,164	13,418	1.09
Wyoming	0	0	0	1,884	3,370	8,164	13,418	1.09
Nebraska	0	0	0	1,884	3,370	8,164	13,418	1.09
Maryland	0	0	0	1,884	3,370	8,164	13,418	1.09
Illinois	0	0	0	1,884	3,370	8,164	13,418	1.09
Montana	0	0	0	1,884	3,370	8,164	13,418	1.09
North Dakota	0	0	0	1,884	3,370	8,164	13,418	1.09
Utah	0	0	0	1,884	3,370	8,164	13,418	1.09
South Dakota	0	0	0	1,884	3,370	8,164	13,418	1.09
Maine	0	0	0	1,884	3,370	8,164	13,418	1.09
District of Columbia	0	0	0	1,884	3,370	8,164	13,418	1.09
Pennsylvania	0	0	0	1,884	3,370	8,164	13,418	1.09
New Jersey	0	0	0	1,884	3,370	8,164	13,418	1.09
Iowa	0	0	0	1,884	3,370	8,164	13,418	1.09
Kansas	0	0	0	1,884	3,370	8,164	13,418	1.09
Michigan (Wayne Co.)	0	0	0	1,884	3,370	8,164	13,418	1.09
Oregon	0	0	0	1,884	3,370	8,164	13,418	1.09
Michigan (Washtenaw Co.)	0	0	0	1,884	3,370	8,164	13,418	1.09
Wisconsin	0	0	0	1,884	3,370	8,164	13,418	1.09
Minnesota	0	0	0	1,884	3,370	8,164	13,418	1.09
Washington	0	0	0	1,884	3,370	8,164	13,418	1.09
New Hampshire	0	0	0	1,884	3,370	8,164	13,418	1.09
Rhode Island	0	0	0	1,884	3,370	8,164	13,418	1.09
New York (New York City)	0	0	0	1,884	3,370	8,164	13,418	1.09
Massachusetts	0	0	0	1,884	3,370	8,164	13,418	1.09
California	1,180	590	590	1,536	3,370	8,164	14,250	1.16
Vermont	256	104	152	1,812	3,370	8,164	13,602	1.10
Connecticut	760	380	380	1,656	3,370	8,164	13,950	1.13
New York (Suffolk Co.)	1,036	518	518	1,572	3,370	8,164	14,142	1.15
Hawaii	1,144	572	572	4,104	3,370	8,164	16,782	1.18
Alaska	4,300	2,150	2,150	2,040	3,370	8,164	17,874	1.16

SUPPORT TABLE: FIGURE 5a. Sources of Annual Income for a Single Mother with 2 Children Working Full-time at the Minimum Wage: 1994

* Federal poverty income guidelines in 1994 for a family of 3: $12,320, Hawaii: $14,170, Alaska: $15,400.

NOTE: Details may not sum to totals because of rounding.

SOURCE: Congressional Research Service.

SUPPORT TABLE: FIGURE 2b. Sources of Annual Income After Child Care Expenses and Taxes for a Single Mother with 2 Children Working 1/4 time at the Minimum Wage: 1994

State	Total	AFDC State share	AFDC Federal share	Food stamps	EITC (1996 provisions)	Earnings (after child care expenses and taxes)	Total income (after child care expenses and taxes)	Net income to poverty ratio *
Mississippi	$1,440	$305	$1,135	$3,360	$884	$991	$6,675	0.54
Alabama	1,968	566	1,402	3,204	884	991	7,047	0.57
Texas	2,208	791	1,417	3,132	884	991	7,215	0.59
Tennessee	2,220	729	1,491	3,120	884	991	7,215	0.59
Louisiana	2,280	604	1,676	3,108	884	991	7,263	0.59
South Carolina	2,400	694	1,706	3,072	884	991	7,347	0.60
Arkansas	2,448	625	1,823	3,060	884	991	7,383	0.60
Kentucky	2,736	796	1,940	2,964	884	991	7,575	0.61
West Virginia	2,988	725	2,263	2,892	884	991	7,755	0.63
North Carolina	3,264	1,138	2,126	2,808	884	991	7,947	0.65
Georgia	3,360	1,261	2,099	2,784	884	991	8,019	0.65
Indiana	3,456	1,262	2,194	2,748	884	991	8,079	0.66
Missouri	3,504	1,379	2,125	2,736	884	991	8,115	0.66
Florida	3,636	1,644	1,992	2,700	884	991	8,211	0.67
Idaho	3,804	1,106	2,698	2,652	884	991	8,331	0.68
Oklahoma	3,888	1,151	2,737	2,628	884	991	8,391	0.68
Delaware	4,056	2,028	2,028	2,568	884	991	8,499	0.69
Ohio	4,092	1,603	2,489	2,568	884	991	8,535	0.69
Arizona	4,164	1,420	2,744	2,544	884	991	8,583	0.70
Nevada	4,176	2,075	2,101	2,532	884	991	8,583	0.70
Virginia	4,248	2,124	2,124	2,520	884	991	8,643	0.70
Colorado	4,272	1,952	2,320	2,508	884	991	8,655	0.70
New Mexico	4,284	1,107	3,177	2,508	884	991	8,667	0.70
Wyoming	4,320	1,485	2,835	2,496	884	991	8,691	0.71
Nebraska	4,368	1,661	2,707	2,484	884	991	8,727	0.71
Maryland	4,392	2,196	2,196	2,472	884	991	8,739	0.71
Illinois	4,404	2,202	2,202	2,472	884	991	8,751	0.71
Montana	4,812	1,393	3,419	2,352	884	991	9,039	0.73
North Dakota	4,908	1,417	3,491	2,316	884	991	9,099	0.74
Utah	4,968	1,274	3,694	2,304	884	991	9,147	0.74
South Dakota	5,004	1,526	3,478	2,292	884	991	9,171	0.74
Maine	5,016	1,908	3,108	2,280	884	991	9,171	0.74
District of Columbia	5,040	2,520	2,520	2,280	884	991	9,195	0.75
Pennsylvania	5,052	2,293	2,759	2,280	884	991	9,207	0.75
New Jersey	5,088	2,544	2,544	2,268	884	991	9,231	0.75
Iowa	5,112	1,875	3,237	2,256	884	991	9,243	0.75
Kansas	5,148	2,084	3,064	2,244	884	991	9,267	0.75
Michigan (Wayne Co.)	5,508	2,403	3,105	2,136	884	991	9,519	0.77
Oregon	5,520	2,091	3,429	2,136	884	991	9,531	0.77
Michigan (Washtenaw Co.)	5,868	2,560	3,308	2,028	884	991	9,771	0.79
Wisconsin	6,204	2,452	3,752	1,932	884	991	10,011	0.81
Minnesota	6,384	2,895	3,489	1,872	884	991	10,131	0.82
Washington	6,552	2,998	3,554	1,824	884	991	10,251	0.83
New Hampshire	6,600	3,300	3,300	1,812	884	991	10,287	0.83
Rhode Island	6,648	3,067	3,581	1,800	884	991	10,323	0.84
New York (New York City)	6,924	3,462	3,462	1,716	884	991	10,515	0.85
Massachusetts	6,948	3,474	3,474	1,704	884	991	10,527	0.85
California	7,284	3,642	3,642	1,608	884	991	10,767	0.87
Vermont	7,656	3,097	4,559	1,488	884	991	11,019	0.89
Connecticut	8,160	4,080	4,080	1,344	884	991	11,379	0.92
New York (Suffolk Co.)	8,436	4,218	4,218	1,260	884	991	11,571	0.94
Hawaii	8,544	4,272	4,272	3,780	884	991	14,199	1.00
Alaska	11,076	5,538	5,538	1,920	884	991	14,871	0.97

* Federal poverty income guidelines in 1994 for a family of 3: $12,320, Hawaii: $14,170, Alaska: $15,400.

NOTE: Details may not sum to totals because of rounding.

SOURCE: Congressional Research Service.

State	AFDC Total	State share	Federal share	Food stamps	EITC (1996 provisions)	Earnings (after child care expenses and taxes)	Total income (after child care expenses and taxes)	Net income to poverty ratio *
		AFDC						
Mississippi	$1,440	$305	$1,135	$3,144	$1,768	$1,982	$8,334	0.68
Alabama	1,088	313	775	3,252	1,768	1,982	8,090	0.66
Texas	1,328	476	852	3,180	1,768	1,982	8,258	0.67
Tennessee	1,838	604	1,234	3,024	1,768	1,982	8,612	0.70
Louisiana	1,400	371	1,029	3,156	1,768	1,982	8,306	0.67
South Carolina	1,520	440	1,080	3,120	1,768	1,982	8,390	0.68
Arkansas	1,568	400	1,168	3,108	1,768	1,982	8,426	0.68
Kentucky	2,355	685	1,670	2,868	1,768	1,982	8,972	0.73
West Virginia	2,108	512	1,596	2,940	1,768	1,982	8,798	0.71
North Carolina	2,824	984	1,840	2,724	1,768	1,982	9,298	0.75
Georgia	3,360	1,261	2,099	2,568	1,768	1,982	9,678	0.79
Indiana	2,576	940	1,636	2,808	1,768	1,982	9,134	0.74
Missouri	2,624	1,033	1,591	2,784	1,768	1,982	9,158	0.74
Florida	2,756	1,246	1,510	2,748	1,768	1,982	9,254	0.75
Idaho	2,924	850	2,074	2,700	1,768	1,982	9,374	0.76
Oklahoma	3,008	891	2,117	2,676	1,768	1,982	9,434	0.77
Delaware	3,176	1,588	1,588	2,628	1,768	1,982	9,554	0.78
Ohio	3,212	1,258	1,954	2,616	1,768	1,982	9,578	0.78
Arizona	3,284	1,120	2,164	2,592	1,768	1,982	9,626	0.78
Nevada	3,296	1,638	1,658	2,592	1,768	1,982	9,638	0.78
Virginia	3,368	1,684	1,684	2,568	1,768	1,982	9,686	0.79
Colorado	3,528	1,612	1,916	2,520	1,768	1,982	9,798	0.80
New Mexico	3,404	879	2,525	2,556	1,768	1,982	9,710	0.79
Wyoming	4,320	1,485	2,835	2,280	1,768	1,982	10,350	0.84
Nebraska	3,488	1,326	2,162	2,532	1,768	1,982	9,770	0.79
Maryland	3,512	1,756	1,756	2,520	1,768	1,982	9,782	0.79
Illinois	3,524	1,762	1,762	2,520	1,768	1,982	9,794	0.79
Montana	3,932	1,138	2,794	2,400	1,768	1,982	10,082	0.82
North Dakota	4,028	1,163	2,865	2,364	1,768	1,982	10,142	0.82
Utah	4,308	1,105	3,203	2,280	1,768	1,982	10,338	0.84
South Dakota	4,260	1,299	2,961	2,292	1,768	1,982	10,302	0.84
Maine	4,351	1,655	2,696	2,268	1,768	1,982	10,369	0.84
District of Columbia	4,160	2,080	2,080	2,328	1,768	1,982	10,238	0.83
Pennsylvania	4,172	1,894	2,278	2,328	1,768	1,982	10,250	0.83
New Jersey	4,208	2,104	2,104	2,316	1,768	1,982	10,274	0.83
Iowa	4,232	1,552	2,680	2,304	1,768	1,982	10,286	0.83
Kansas	4,268	1,728	2,540	2,292	1,768	1,982	10,310	0.84
Michigan (Wayne Co.)	4,628	2,019	2,609	2,184	1,768	1,982	10,562	0.86
Oregon	4,640	1,758	2,882	2,184	1,768	1,982	10,574	0.86
Michigan (Washtenaw Co.)	4,988	2,176	2,812	2,076	1,768	1,982	10,814	0.88
Wisconsin	5,324	2,105	3,219	1,980	1,768	1,982	11,054	0.90
Minnesota	5,504	2,496	3,008	1,920	1,768	1,982	11,174	0.91
Washington	5,672	2,596	3,076	1,872	1,768	1,982	11,294	0.92
New Hampshire	5,720	2,860	2,860	1,860	1,768	1,982	11,330	0.92
Rhode Island	5,768	2,661	3,107	1,848	1,768	1,982	11,366	0.92
New York (New York City)	6,044	3,022	3,022	1,764	1,768	1,982	11,558	0.94
Massachusetts	6,068	3,034	3,034	1,752	1,768	1,982	11,570	0.94
California	7,284	3,642	3,642	1,392	1,768	1,982	12,426	1.01
Vermont	6,776	2,741	4,035	1,548	1,768	1,982	12,074	0.98
Connecticut	7,280	3,640	3,640	1,392	1,768	1,982	12,422	1.01
New York (Suffolk Co.)	7,556	3,778	3,778	1,308	1,768	1,982	12,614	1.02
Hawaii	7,664	3,832	3,832	3,840	1,768	1,982	15,254	1.08
Alaska	10,820	5,410	5,410	1,776	1,768	1,982	16,346	1.06

SUPPORT TABLE: FIGURE 3b. Sources of Annual Income After Child Care Expenses and Taxes for a Single Mother with 2 Children Working 1/2 time at the Minimum Wage: 1994

* Federal poverty income guidelines in 1994 for a family of 3: $12,320, Hawaii: $14,170, Alaska: $15,400.
NOTE: Details may not sum to totals because of rounding.
SOURCE: Congressional Research Service.

SUPPORT TABLE: FIGURE 4b. Sources of Annual Income After Child Care Expenses and Taxes for a Single Mother with 2 Children Working 3/4 time at the Minimum Wage: 1994

State	AFDC Total	AFDC State share	AFDC Federal share	Food stamps	EITC (1996 provisions)	Earnings (after child care expenses and taxes)	Total income (after child care expenses and taxes)	Net income to poverty ratio *
Mississippi	$1,426	$302	$1,124	$2,928	$2,652	$2,973	$9,978	0.81
Alabama	0	0	0	3,360	2,652	2,973	8,985	0.73
Texas	168	60	108	3,312	2,652	2,973	9,105	0.74
Tennessee	1,334	438	896	2,964	2,652	2,973	9,923	0.81
Louisiana	240	64	176	3,288	2,652	2,973	9,153	0.74
South Carolina	360	104	256	3,252	2,652	2,973	9,237	0.75
Arkansas	408	104	304	3,240	2,652	2,973	9,273	0.75
Kentucky	1,852	539	1,313	2,808	2,652	2,973	10,285	0.83
West Virginia	948	230	718	3,072	2,652	2,973	9,645	0.78
North Carolina	2,244	782	1,462	2,688	2,652	2,973	10,557	0.86
Georgia	3,048	1,144	1,904	2,448	2,652	2,973	11,121	0.90
Indiana	1,416	517	899	2,940	2,652	2,973	9,981	0.81
Missouri	1,464	576	888	2,916	2,652	2,973	10,005	0.81
Florida	1,596	722	874	2,880	2,652	2,973	10,101	0.82
Idaho	1,764	513	1,251	2,832	2,652	2,973	10,221	0.83
Oklahoma	1,848	547	1,301	2,808	2,652	2,973	10,281	0.83
Delaware	2,016	1,008	1,008	2,760	2,652	2,973	10,401	0.84
Ohio	2,052	804	1,248	2,748	2,652	2,973	10,425	0.85
Arizona	2,124	724	1,400	2,724	2,652	2,973	10,473	0.85
Nevada	2,136	1,061	1,075	2,724	2,652	2,973	10,485	0.85
Virginia	2,208	1,104	1,104	2,700	2,652	2,973	10,533	0.85
Colorado	2,547	1,164	1,383	2,592	2,652	2,973	10,764	0.87
New Mexico	2,244	580	1,664	2,688	2,652	2,973	10,557	0.86
Wyoming	4,320	1,485	2,835	2,064	2,652	2,973	12,009	0.97
Nebraska	2,328	885	1,443	2,664	2,652	2,973	10,617	0.86
Maryland	2,352	1,176	1,176	2,652	2,652	2,973	10,629	0.86
Illinois	2,364	1,182	1,182	2,652	2,652	2,973	10,641	0.86
Montana	2,772	802	1,970	2,532	2,652	2,973	10,929	0.89
North Dakota	2,868	828	2,040	2,496	2,652	2,973	10,989	0.89
Utah	3,438	882	2,556	2,328	2,652	2,973	11,391	0.92
South Dakota	3,274	999	2,276	2,376	2,652	2,973	11,275	0.92
Maine	3,474	1,322	2,152	2,316	2,652	2,973	11,415	0.93
District of Columbia	3,000	1,500	1,500	2,460	2,652	2,973	11,085	0.90
Pennsylvania	3,012	1,367	1,645	2,460	2,652	2,973	11,097	0.90
New Jersey	3,048	1,524	1,524	2,448	2,652	2,973	11,121	0.90
Iowa	3,072	1,127	1,945	2,436	2,652	2,973	11,133	0.90
Kansas	3,108	1,258	1,850	2,424	2,652	2,973	11,157	0.91
Michigan (Wayne Co.)	3,468	1,513	1,955	2,316	2,652	2,973	11,409	0.93
Oregon	3,480	1,318	2,162	2,316	2,652	2,973	11,421	0.93
Michigan (Washtenaw Co.)	3,828	1,670	2,158	2,208	2,652	2,973	11,661	0.95
Wisconsin	4,164	1,646	2,518	2,112	2,652	2,973	11,901	0.97
Minnesota	4,344	1,970	2,374	2,052	2,652	2,973	12,021	0.98
Washington	4,512	2,065	2,447	2,004	2,652	2,973	12,141	0.99
New Hampshire	4,560	2,280	2,280	1,992	2,652	2,973	12,177	0.99
Rhode Island	4,608	2,126	2,482	1,980	2,652	2,973	12,213	0.99
New York (New York City)	4,884	2,442	2,442	1,896	2,652	2,973	12,405	1.01
Massachusetts	4,908	2,454	2,454	1,884	2,652	2,973	12,417	1.01
California	6,540	3,270	3,270	1,392	2,652	2,973	13,557	1.10
Vermont	5,616	2,272	3,344	1,680	2,652	2,973	12,921	1.05
Connecticut	6,120	3,060	3,060	1,524	2,652	2,973	13,269	1.08
New York (Suffolk Co.)	6,396	3,198	3,198	1,440	2,652	2,973	13,461	1.09
Hawaii	6,504	3,252	3,252	3,972	2,652	2,973	16,101	1.14
Alaska	9,660	4,830	4,830	1,908	2,652	2,973	17,193	1.12

* Federal poverty income guidelines in 1994 for a family of 3: $12,320, Hawaii: $14,170, Alaska: $15,400.
NOTE: Details may not sum to totals because of rounding.
SOURCE: Congressional Research Service.

SUPPORT TABLE: FIGURE 5b. Sources of Annual Income After Child Care Expenses and Taxes for a Single Mother with 2 Children Working Full-time at the Minimum Wage: 1994

State	AFDC Total	State share	Federal share	Food stamps	EITC (1996 provisions)	Earnings (after child care expenses and taxes)	Total income (after child care expenses and taxes)	Net income to poverty ratio *
Mississippi	$730	$154	$575	$2,820	$3,370	$3,964	$10,883	0.88
Alabama	0	0	0	3,036	3,370	3,964	10,370	0.84
Texas	0	0	0	3,036	3,370	3,964	10,370	0.84
Tennessee	830	273	558	2,784	3,370	3,964	10,948	0.89
Louisiana	0	0	0	3,036	3,370	3,964	10,370	0.84
South Carolina	0	0	0	3,036	3,370	3,964	10,370	0.84
Arkansas	0	0	0	3,036	3,370	3,964	10,370	0.84
Kentucky	1,349	392	957	2,628	3,370	3,964	11,311	0.92
West Virginia	0	0	0	3,036	3,370	3,964	10,370	0.84
North Carolina	1,664	580	1,084	2,532	3,370	3,964	11,530	0.94
Georgia	1,888	709	1,179	2,472	3,370	3,964	11,694	0.95
Indiana	256	93	163	2,964	3,370	3,964	10,554	0.86
Missouri	304	120	184	2,940	3,370	3,964	10,578	0.86
Florida	436	197	239	2,904	3,370	3,964	10,674	0.87
Idaho	604	176	428	2,856	3,370	3,964	10,794	0.88
Oklahoma	688	204	484	2,832	3,370	3,964	10,854	0.88
Delaware	856	428	428	2,784	3,370	3,964	10,974	0.89
Ohio	892	349	543	2,772	3,370	3,964	10,998	0.89
Arizona	964	329	635	2,748	3,370	3,964	11,046	0.90
Nevada	976	485	491	2,748	3,370	3,964	11,058	0.90
Virginia	1,048	524	524	2,724	3,370	3,964	11,106	0.90
Colorado	1,566	716	850	2,568	3,370	3,964	11,468	0.93
New Mexico	1,084	280	804	2,712	3,370	3,964	11,130	0.90
Wyoming	3,880	1,334	2,546	1,872	3,370	3,964	13,086	1.06
Nebraska	1,168	444	724	2,688	3,370	3,964	11,190	0.91
Maryland	1,192	596	596	2,676	3,370	3,964	11,202	0.91
Illinois	1,204	602	602	2,676	3,370	3,964	11,214	0.91
Montana	1,612	467	1,145	2,556	3,370	3,964	11,502	0.93
North Dakota	1,708	493	1,215	2,520	3,370	3,964	11,562	0.94
Utah	2,568	659	1,909	2,268	3,370	3,964	12,170	0.99
South Dakota	2,288	698	1,590	2,352	3,370	3,964	11,974	0.97
Maine	2,597	988	1,609	2,256	3,370	3,964	12,187	0.99
District of Columbia	1,840	920	920	2,484	3,370	3,964	11,658	0.95
Pennsylvania	1,852	841	1,011	2,484	3,370	3,964	11,670	0.95
New Jersey	1,888	944	944	2,472	3,370	3,964	11,694	0.95
Iowa	1,912	701	1,211	2,460	3,370	3,964	11,706	0.95
Kansas	1,948	789	1,159	2,448	3,370	3,964	11,730	0.95
Michigan (Wayne Co.)	2,308	1,007	1,301	2,340	3,370	3,964	11,982	0.97
Oregon	2,320	879	1,441	2,340	3,370	3,964	11,994	0.97
Michigan (Washtenaw Co.)	2,668	1,164	1,504	2,232	3,370	3,964	12,234	0.99
Wisconsin	3,004	1,187	1,817	2,136	3,370	3,964	12,474	1.01
Minnesota	3,184	1,444	1,740	2,076	3,370	3,964	12,594	1.02
Washington	3,352	1,534	1,818	2,028	3,370	3,964	12,714	1.03
New Hampshire	3,400	1,700	1,700	2,016	3,370	3,964	12,750	1.03
Rhode Island	3,448	1,591	1,857	2,004	3,370	3,964	12,786	1.04
New York (New York City)	3,724	1,862	1,862	1,920	3,370	3,964	12,978	1.05
Massachusetts	3,748	1,874	1,874	1,908	3,370	3,964	12,990	1.05
California	5,380	2,690	2,690	1,428	3,370	3,964	14,142	1.15
Vermont	4,456	1,802	2,654	1,704	3,370	3,964	13,494	1.10
Connecticut	4,960	2,480	2,480	1,548	3,370	3,964	13,842	1.12
New York (Suffolk Co.)	5,236	2,618	2,618	1,464	3,370	3,964	14,034	1.14
Hawaii	5,344	2,672	2,672	3,996	3,370	3,964	16,674	1.18
Alaska	8,500	4,250	4,250	1,932	3,370	3,964	17,766	1.15

* Federal poverty income guidelines in 1994 for a family of 3: $12,320, Hawaii: $14,170, Alaska: $15,400.
NOTE: Details may not sum to totals because of rounding.
SOURCE: Congressional Research Service.

WELFARE REFORM: THE FAMILY CAP*

Carmen D. Solomon

BACKGROUND

In general, "family cap" proposals, sometimes referred to as child exclusions, eliminate or limit the increase in Aid to Families with Dependent Children (AFDC) benefits upon the birth of an additional child for which the family would otherwise be eligible. In other words, full AFDC benefits for a baby born to a person already receiving AFDC would be prohibited. Several States have implemented a "family cap," or are attempting to do so. A number of Governors, legislators, and State budget welfare officials favor the limits. Proponents argue that it is irresponsible for a woman already on AFDC to have additional children and expect taxpayers to provide increased AFDC benefits to support those children. They maintain that a cap will eliminate any financial incentive for an AFDC recipient to have another child. They contend that a family cap would have the dual benefit of saving the States money and promoting parental responsibility. At the end of 1994, more than 30 family cap bills had been introduced in 17 States.

---

* Excerpted from *CRS Report* 95-503 EPW

Opponents say that if a family cap deters childbearing, it is likely to do so by increasing the rate of abortion. Some groups view it as opening the door to potentially coercive policies affecting fertility behavior of women. Concern about these possibilities has resulted in an alliance of pro-choice and pro-life groups, along with civil rights organizations and religious groups. A couple of these groups have challenged the family cap policies in court. Some say that the policy will serve only to harm children. They argue that the welfare system currently provides less than adequate financial support to children, and little incentive for women to bear children. They contend that capping benefits to women who bear additional children while on AFDC is likely to have little impact on women's behavior, but a significant impact on the lives of poor children.

FAMILY MAXIMUMS VERSUS FAMILY CAPS/CHILD EXCLUSIONS

Although all States, the District of Columbia, Guam, Puerto Rico, and the Virgin Islands have an AFDC program, Federal law does not mandate that States operate an AFDC program. State participation is voluntary. While participating States and jurisdictions must comply with the terms of Federal AFDC law, States traditionally have been at liberty to pay as little or as much as they choose. To determine eligibility and benefit amounts, each State decides what a family's "need"" is and what it is willing and able to pay to meet that need. The need standard is the amount of money a State determines essential to meet a minimal standard of living in the State for a family of a specified size. *Current law requires States to take account of family size as an element of need in setting AFDC benefit levels.* The payment standard represents the extent to which the State will meet the needs of a specified size family. The maximum benefit is the amount of money a State pays to an AFDC family with no countable income. Although Federal law has no requirement that a State pay the full amount of its need standard, and only 11 States (jurisdictions) do so, Federal regulations provide that if full individual payments are precluded by maximum or insufficient funds, adjustment must be made by methods applied uniformly statewide.

Several States have an AFDC family maximum amount that may not be exceeded for any family, regardless of size. That is, eight States do not make incremental AFDC benefit increases for families over a certain size.[1] For example, Virginia does not make incremental AFDC benefit increases for AFDC families of more than six. In Virginia, the maximum amount of AFDC benefits that can be paid to a 6-person family is $518 per month. A 9-person Virginia family also would receive $518 monthly if it had no countable income, as would a 7-person family and a 12-person family.

Family maximums are substantively different from family cap policies, which limit the amount of AFDC benefits to the family size at the time of enrollment. While Federal law currently permits States to freeze the maximum level of AFDC benefits at a particular family size, generally families of the same size are required to be treated equally. Family cap provisions, sometimes referred to as child exclusions, treat families of the same size differently if one or more of the births occur after the mother enrolls in the AFDC program. The needs of any child born after enrollment in AFDC, are reduced or not considered when determining the family's AFDC benefit amount.

EFFECT OF FAMILY CAPS ON AFDC BENEFITS

Generally under the family cap proposals, the family's AFDC benefit would not be increased with the birth of a new baby, but the newborn would be considered part of the AFDC unit. This means that the AFDC benefit for the family would remain the same (assuming other things are unchanged). Thus, the unchanged AFDC cash income would have to cover the support and care of a larger family.

---

[1] The following States do not incrementally increase AFDC benefits for families larger than the size indicated: Georgia (11), California (10), Arkansas and Oklahoma (9), Washington and West Virginia (8), Kentucky (7), Virginia (6). (January 1994 telephone survey data).

Table 1 of appendix B show the maximum monthly amount a 3-person family would receive under current law and under the family cap. It shows that implementation of the cap would result in a reduction of the AFDC benefit (as compared to current law) of a mother with two children, one of whom was born after she began receiving AFDC, by between 11% and 27%, depending on the State in which she lives. In combination with Food Stamps, the AFDC family cap could result in between a 4% and 12% decline in combined AFDC and Food Stamp benefits, depending on the State. An AFDC mother living in the median State ranked by benefit level, whose second child was born while she was receiving AFDC, would have combined AFDC and Food Stamp income equal to 57.5% of the Federal poverty guideline (12,320 for a family of 3 in 1994) under current law, versus 53.2% under a family cap proposal.

The reader should note the following. There are no comprehensive national data on the number of children women bear after they enroll in the AFDC program. The research on the relationship between AFDC benefits and having additional children is inconclusive. However, a few studies (California and Wisconsin) have traced the subsequent fertility of women receiving AFDC and a few studies (Urban Institute and Department of Health and Human Services (DHHS) have analyzed AFDC Quality Control (QC) data to estimate impacts of a family cap. Nonetheless, these studies do not address causality. The evaluation of New Jersey's family cap demonstration will provide the first scientific data on behavioral responses to a cap (i.e., whether the "freezing" of the AFDC benefit causes women to not have additional children while on AFDC).

CALIFORNIA SURVEY

A California survey of characteristics of AFDC families found that during July 1992, 38.4% of AFDC families contained at least one child born after the family was first approved for aid (24.9% had one subsequent child, 9.4% two subsequent children, and 4.1%, three or more subsequent children). (AFDC Characteristics Study, State of California, Program Information Series Report 1993-03)

WISCONSIN STUDY

A study of welfare recipients in Wisconsin, by Mark Rank, found that 11.5% of women receiving welfare had a subsequent birth within 3 years of coming on the program.[2] Rank compared the fertility rates (number of births per 1, 000 women) between women on welfare to all women. He found the fertility rate of women on welfare to be less (45.8 births per 1,000 women), than that of women of childbearing age in the national population (71.1 births per 1,000 women). After statistically controlling for background factors that might account for differences in fertility between women on welfare and all women (e.g., age, marital status, etc.), Rank found the fertility rate of women on welfare to be lower, and the probability of their having an additional child to decline, the longer a woman was on welfare.

URBAN INSTITUTE STUDY

The Urban Institute has estimated that 3.9% of the AFDC caseload would be affected by a family cap after the first year of implementation, and 10.8% of the caseload after 3 years. The unpublished 1993 study, which used an AFDC QC simulation model, estimated that the caseload's average monthly benefit would fall by 0.9% after the first year, and by 3.3% after 3 years. The study's estimated effect on the caseload and average monthly benefits does not account for behavioral changes in childbearing or marriage that might result from the implementation of a family cap. The Urban Institute study of AFDC QC survey data also found that 18% of AFDC mothers in FY1991 appeared to have conceived a child after enrolling the program.

DHHS STUDY

As part of its study of the impacts of H>R> 4 (as passed by the House) on States and caseloads, DHHS has estimated that upon full implementation

---

[2] See: Rank, Mark Robert. *Living on the Edge: The Realities of Welfare in America.* New York, Columbia University Press, 1994. P.71-79.

of the bill 2.2 million children would be denied cash benefits because they were born to women already receiving Federal cash welfare payments. The DHHS estimate is based on the 1993 AFDC caseload using the 1993 AFDC QC data. According to the DHHS report, because the research on the relationship between AFDC benefits and having additional children is inconclusive, its projections of the impact of the family cap provision do not assume changes in behavior such as the decision to have children.[3]

RUTGERS STUDY

In accordance with DHHS guidelines, all demonstrations under the Section 1115 waiver authority must be rigorously evaluated. Usually this means that individuals must be assigned at random into experimental and control groups, and it always entails that an entity independent of the agency conducting the demonstration perform the evaluation. Rutgers University is doing the evaluation of New Jersey's (the first State to implement a cap) family cap demonstration. Under the demonstration, AFDC recipients were randomly assigned to two different groups: an "experimental" group, which was subject to the family cap, and a "control" group, which was exempt from the cap. This procedure will provide scientific results of the behavioral effects of the family cap by comparing the experimental group with the control group.[4]

THE AFDC "FAMILY CAP" -- STATE INITIATIVES

Many AFDC changes are occurring at the State level. Both the Reagan and Bush Administrations encouraged State experiments in welfare, granting waivers from Federal rules to test program changes, and the Clinton Administration has continued the process. Section 1115 of the Social Security Act authorizes the DHHS Secretary to waive specific Federal AFDC requirements to allow States to conduct an "experiment, pilot, or demonstra-

---

[3] U.S. Dept. of Health and Human Services and U.S. Dept. of Agriculture. H.R. 4, *the Personal Responsibility Act of 1995--Preliminary Impacts, Summary and State-by-State Analysis.* Apr. 7, 1995.

[4] A report by Rutgers University evaluating New Jersey's family cap provisions is expected to be available in April 1995.

tion project which, in the judgment of the Secretary is likely to assist in promoting the objectives" of the Social Security Act. Under current Federal law, States must obtain section 1115 waivers to implement AFDC family cap policies. Most waivers reflect at least one of the following assumptions about AFDC: *that program rules serve as a disincentive t work and therefore encourage long-term dependency; that they discourage marriage and encourage illegitimacy; and that welfare dependence is a cycle of hopelessness passed on from one generation to the next.*

Through implementation of demonstration projects and experiments, approved by the Secretary under section 1115 waiver authority, States are exploring a variety of approaches to reduce welfare costs, and to assist AFDC recipients in making the transition to self-sufficiency,[5] including eliminating the increment in AFDC benefits for which the family would otherwise be eligible as a result of the birth of an additional child.

As of Apr. 7, 1995, four States (New Jersey, Georgia, Wisconsin, and Nebraska) had enacted AFDC family cap measures and obtained the necessary Federal waivers to implement them. The family cap provision in New Jersey is currently being challenged in court. Four States (Arizona, California, Kansas, and Virginia) enacted similar measures, but as of Apr. 7, 1995 have not received Federal Waivers to implement them. Two States (Arkansas and Indiana) received waivers in 1994, and indicated that they did not need legislation to implement them. Arkansas' family cap provision went into effect July 1, 1994 and Indiana's is expected to go into effect in 1995. Appendix A contains descriptions of the State family cap initiatives.

---

[5] For further information about waivers generally, see: U.S. Library of Congress. Congressional Research Service. *State Welfare Initiatives.* CRS Report for Congress No. 94-183 EPW, by Jennifer A. Neisner. Washington, 1995.

THE AFDC "FAMILY CAP" -- FEDERAL LEGISLATION

104TH CONGRESS

Proposals to deny additional AFDC benefits to mothers who bear additional children while on AFDC are a response to a growing concern that welfare benefits encourage out-of-wedlock childbearing. The original Personal Responsibility Act of 1995 H.R. 4), a part of the House Republican "Contract with America," was introduced Jan. 4, 1995 and included a mandatory family cap provision. Under the original version of H.R. 4, States would have been forbidden from giving AFDC benefits to a child born to an AFDC recipient or to an individual who had received AFDC at any time during the 10-month period preceding the child's birth.

On Mar. 24, 1995, the House passed H.R. 4, as amended, by a vote of 234 to 199. The House-passed bill would convert AFDC into a State block grant program and would prohibit States from using the block grant funds to provide cash benefits for a child born to a recipient of cash welfare, or an individual who received cash benefits at any time during the 10-month period preceding the birth of the child. The bill would require States to exempt children born as a result of rape or incest. In response to concerns that the family cap might result in an economic incentive for some women to have an abortion, during the House floor debate a provision was added to explicitly allow States to provide noncash assistance to AFDC families denied additional cash benefits upon the birth of a child.

103RD CONGRESS

The Clinton Administration's 1994 welfare reform bill, the Work and Responsibility Act (H.R. 4605/S. 2224), would have given States the option of denying or reducing AFDC benefits to a baby conceived by a woman already receiving AFDC or born to an AFDC child in the same family. (However, States would have been prohibited from denying AFDC benefits to a child born as a result of a rape or in "other cases that the State agency found would have violated standards of fairness and good conscience.") States would have had to assure access to family planning services and permit the family to offset the loss of the newborn's benefit by disregarding as income counted against the benefit, a sum equal to that loss in child support for the new baby, earned income, or other income of a family member.

The Clinton Administration has not resubmitted its welfare reform bill in the 104th Congress. During House consideration of H.R. 4, the Administration indicated that it favored giving States the option of implementing a family cap.

Many of the bills that included a mandatory family cap provision also included provisions that allowed an AFDC recipient/family to earn what otherwise would have been paid in AFDC benefits generally through more liberal earned income disregard rules.

APPENDIX A: STATE FAMILY CAP STATUTES

ENACTED -- WAIVER APPROVED

NEW JERSEY

New Jersey prohibits AFDC benefit increases for otherwise eligible families as a result of the birth of a child to an AFDC adult recipient, or to a parent/family who is temporarily ineligible for AFDC benefits because of failure to comply with eligibility requirements. New Jersey law requires that AFDC families affected by the family cap provision be given an enhanced (higher) disregard of earned income. The Legislature approved the family cap provision in January 1992. New Jersey's waiver was approved in June 1992, and the State began implementing the family cap provision in October 1992. The statute was drafted to be gender neutral. N. J. Stat. Ann. § 44:10-3.5.

GEORGIA

Georgia prohibits AFDC benefit increases for additional children born to an AFDC mother who has received cash benefits for a period of a total of 24 months after Jan. 1, 1994, or who is temporarily ineligible for AFDC because of failure to comply with eligibility requirements, except in cases in which the birth is the result of a verifiable rape or incest. The Legislature approved the family cap provision in 1993. Georgia's waiver was approved in November 1993, and the State began implementing the family cap provision in January 1994. GA. Code Ann. § 49-4-115.

WISCONSIN

Wisconsin's "parental responsibility" pilot program applies to AFDC applicants and recipients under age 10 who have only one child when they enter the program. Wisconsin reduces and/or eliminates the AFDC benefit increase for AFDC parents who bear additional children. The family receives an additional $38 monthly for a child born after the family begins participating in the parental responsibility program. In the case of a multiple birth, $38 monthly for one of the children and a full benefit increased for the additional children. The State prohibits AFDC benefit increases for any subsequent children. The State is to provide education on parenting, human growth and development, family planning and independent living skills, and employment-related training to pilot program participants. The Legislature approved this family cap provision in July 1991. The waiver application was approved in April 1992, with the program scheduled to go into effect in several counties in July 1994. Wis. Stat. Ann. § 49.25(4).

Wisconsin's "work not welfare" program prohibits AFDC benefit increases for additional children born into a family participating in the work not welfare program if the birth occurs after the family has been receiving AFDC for more than 10 months. The Legislature approved this family cap provision in October 1993. The waiver application also was approved in October 1993, and the demonstration program is scheduled to go into effect in two counties in January 1995. Wis. Stat. Ann. § 49.2 7 (c).

The Wisconsin "AFDC Benefit Cap" (ABC) Demonstration Project, scheduled to be implemented statewide, will eliminate AFDC benefit increases for additional children born more than 10 months after the family has initially applied for benefits, except for verified cases of rape or incest, or if the child has been placed in the care of a legally responsible relative. The prohibition does not apply to children who are the firstborn (including all children in the case of a multiple birth) or minors in the AFDC family who become first-time minor mothers. The State would provide access to family planning services and parenting classes. Wisconsin's waiver request for this family cap provision was approved in June 1994.

NEBRASKA

Nebraska prohibits AFDC benefit increases for additional children born more than 10 months after the family began receiving AFDC benefits, except that any child support or other income received on behalf of such child(ren) is not to be counted as income in determining the family's AFDC benefit. The Legislature approved the family cap provision in April 1994. The required waiver has not yet been obtained. 1994 Neb. Laws LB 1224 § 24(2) (b).

ENACTED -- WAIVER NOT YET APPROVED (AS OF APR. 7, 1995)

ARIZONA

Arizona prohibits AFDC benefit increases for additional children born more than 10 months after a parent or relative enrolls in the AFDC program, or born to a parent or relative who is temporarily ineligible for AFDC because of failure to comply with eligibility requirements, except in cases in which the birth is the result of rape or incest. The prohibition is effective for a child born during any period following waiver approval that is less than 5 years after the family was previously enrolled in the AFDC program. Arizona's statute would permit the parents or relatives of the "additional" child to earn income in an amount equal to the disallowed benefit payment without affecting the AFDC eligibility. That statute requires the welfare agency to inform the parents and other relatives receiving AFDC benefits of the family planning services available. The Legislature approved the family cap provision in April 1994. The required waiver has not yet been obtained. The family cap is to be effective within 180 days after waiver approval. 1994 Ariz. Sess. Laws ch. 319, to be codified at Ariz. Rev. Stat. Ann. § 46-292.

VIRGINIA

Virginia's "Independence Program" (VIP) prohibits AFDC benefit increases for additional children born more than 10 months after an AFDC recipient enters the program. The prohibition continues during participation in the program, for the 12-month period following program participation, or during a temporary period in which the recipient/family is ineligible for AFDC benefits because of failure to comply with AFDC or child support requirements. The prohibition is scheduled to expire 2 years after waiver approval. The Legislature approved the family cap provision in April 1994. The required waiver has not yet been obtained. Va. Code Ann.§ 63.1-133.48.

KANSAS

Kansas prohibits AFDC benefit increases for the fourth or subsequent child born to a family receiving AFDC, or during a temporary period in which the recipient/family is ineligible for AFDC benefits because of failure to comply with AFDC program requirements. In the case of a third child born to an AFDC family, the AFDC benefit increase would be limited to 50% of what it otherwise would have been. In the case of an AFDC family with fewer than three children, the family cap does not apply. Kansas's statute provides that the monthly earned income disregard for each employed person in the family shall increase by an amount equal to that which the family would have otherwise received by parenting an additional child. Moreover, in the case of a family in which only one adult recipient is employed, the monthly earned income disregard shall increase by an amount not more than 100% of that which the family would have otherwise received by parenting an additional child The Kansas law provides that each child in a multiple birth shall be entitled to receive the same incremental increase in benefits as the first child in such birth. The Legislature approved the family cap provision in May 1994. The family cap provisions were scheduled to take effect on July 1, 1994; however, the required waiver has not yet been obtained. 1994 Kan. ALS 359.

CALIFORNIA

California prohibits AFDC benefit increases for additional children born into a family that received AFDC continuously for the 10 months before the child's birth. The prohibition does not apply in cases where the child was conceived as (1) a result of a reported rape, (2) a result of reported incest, or (3) a result of contraceptive failure from use of an intrauterine device, norplant, or sterilization. The prohibition does not apply to children born on or before Nov. 1, 1995 or to families that were not receiving AFDC for a 2-year period while the child was living with the family. This prohibition does not apply to any child conceived when either parent was a non-needy caretaker relative or to any child who is no longer living in the same home with either parent. California's family cap provision also requires that all child support payments made on behalf of the additional child must be paid to the family without affecting their AFDC benefit. The Legislature approved the family cap provision in July 1994. The required waiver has not yet been obtained. The family cap provisions are scheduled to take effect in January 1995. 1994 Cal. ALS 196, to be codified at Cal. Welf. & Inst. Code § 11450.04.

WAIVER APPROVED -- NO STATE LEGISLATION NEEDED TO IMPLEMENT

ARKANSAS

Arkansas eliminates AFDC benefit increases for additional children born into an AFDC family that was receiving AFDC benefits when the child was conceived, or born into a family that was temporarily ineligible for AFDC because of failure to comply with eligibility requirements, except in cases in which the birth is the result of a verifiable rape or incest or the birth is to a dependent child member of the AFDC unit who becomes a first-time mother. The waiver requires the State to provided access to family planning services and information about the availability of these services to recipients, including group counseling sessions for recipients aged 13-17 focusing on family planning issues and the effects of parenthood. Arkansas' waiver application was approved April 1994. Arkansas had indicated that the State does not need to enact legislation to implement the family cap provision, which went into effect in July 1994.

INDIANA

Indiana prohibits AFDC benefit increases for additional children born more than 10 months after a parent or relative enrolls in the AFDC program. The prohibition does not apply in (1) cases where the child was conceived as a result of incest or a verified sexual assault, (2) cases where the child (includes all children in a multiple birth) is born to a first-time minor mother, (3) cases where the child does not live with his or her parent, or (4) cases where the child was conceived in a month the family was not receiving AFDC benefits. The waiver requires the State to offer family planning services to all AFDC applicants and recipients. The State is required to ensure that family planning services are geographically accessible and available without delays to all AFDC recipients. Indiana's waiver application was approved December 1994. Indiana has indicated that the State does not need to enact legislation to implement the family cap provision. The family cap provision is expected to go into effect sometime during 1995.

APPENDIX B: EFFECT OF A FAMILY CAP ON COMBINED AFDC AND FOOD STAMPS BENEFITS, BY STATE[6]

Because States set their AFDC payment levels, the effect of a family cap on families' welfare income would vary from state to State. State AFDC payment levels vary markedly from State to State, and the adjustments States use for scaling benefits to various size families also differ.[7] Because most family cap proposals only limit the cash portion of the welfare grant (AFDC), the proposals' effects on total family income would be lessened somewhat by other welfare benefits that are not capped (e.g., Food Stamps). The Administration's proposal would require States adopting a family cap to allow AFDC families to make up for the reduction in their grant with other outside income, such as earnings or child support.

COMBINED AFDC/FOOD STAMP BENEFIT LEVELS

In January, 1994, State's monthly AFDC benefits for a mother with one child ranged from $96, in Mississippi, to $821 in Alaska. (See table 1). The median State AFDC benefit level for a mother with one child was $303. Federal Food Stamp benefits are higher in low- paying AFDC States than in high-paying States, because the Food Stamp program counts AFDC as income for purposes of calculating benefits. In Mississippi, a mother with one child and no other income, other than AFDC, would receive $206 per month in Food Stamps; in Alaska, she would receive $91 in Food Stamps. Measured against the Federal poverty guideline, the mother's combined AFDC and Food Stamp income in Mississippi, for a two-person family, amounts to about 37% of the poverty line, and in Alaska, to about 89% of the poverty line.[8] (See table 3). Combined AFDC and Food Stamp

---

[6] This appendix was prepared by Thomas Gabe, Specialist in Social Legislation, Education and Public Welfare Division, CRS.

[7] For a discussion of State AFDC payment standards, see: U.S. Library of Congress. Congressional Research Service. *Aid to Families with Dependent Children (AFDC): Need Standards, Payment Standards, and Maximum Benefits.* CRS Report for Congress No. 93-63 EPW. Washington, 1993.

[8] The Federal poverty guidelines vary by family size. In 1994, the Federal poverty guideline in the lower-48 States, and the District of Columbia, for a two-person family is $9,840 per year.

benefits in the median State were $457, or about 56% of the federal poverty guideline for two-person family.

EFFECTS OF A FAMILY CAP ON AFDC AND COMBINED AFDC/FOOD STAMP BENEFITS

Tables 1 and 2 show the effect of an AFDC family cap on combined AFDC and Food Stamp benefits, by State, for a mother with one child, who has a second child while on AFDC (table 1), and for a mother with two children, who has a third child while on AFDC (table 2). Table 1 shows that a family cap could result in between an 11% (Alaska) and 27% (Louisiana) decline in cash AFDC for a mother with a single child, who bears a second while AFDC, depending on the State in which she lives. However, the effect of food stamps somewhat mitigates the effect of the AFDC family cap on total family income. In combination with food stamps, the AFDC family cap could result in between a 4% (Texas) and 12% (Illinois) decline in combined AFDC and Food Stamp benefits, depending on the State in which the mother lives.

TABLE 1. Effects of a Family Cap on Combined Monthly (January 1994) AFDC and Food Stamp Benefits for a Mother Who Bears a Second Child while Receiving AFDC, by State

| | Mother with one child | | | Mother with two children (Second child born while mother is on AFDC) | | | | | | Difference — Family Cap vs. AFDC | | | | | |
| | | | | Current law | | | Family cap | | | Dollar difference | | | Percent difference | |
	AFDC	Food stamps	Total	AFDC	Food stamps	Total	AFDC	Food stamps	Total	AFDC	Food stamps	Total	Percent loss in AFDC	Percent loss combined benefits
Alabama	$137	$204	$341	$164	$285	$449	$137	$293	$430	-$27	$8	-$19	-16.5%	-4.2%
Alaska	$821	$91	$912	$923	$178	$1,101	$821	$208	$1,029	-$102	$30	-$72	-11.1%	-6.5%
Arizona	$275	$162	$437	$347	$230	$577	$275	$251	$526	-$72	$21	-$51	-20.7%	-8.8%
Arkansas	$162	$196	$358	$204	$273	$477	$162	$285	$447	-$42	$12	-$30	-20.6%	-6.3%
California	$490	$98	$588	$607	$152	$759	$490	$187	$677	-$117	$35	-$82	-19.3%	-10.8%
Colorado	$280	$161	$441	$356	$227	$583	$280	$250	$530	-$76	$23	-$53	-21.3%	-9.1%
Connecticut	$549	$80	$629	$680	$130	$810	$549	$169	$718	-$131	$39	-$92	-19.3%	-11.4%
Delaware	$270	$164	$434	$338	$232	$570	$270	$253	$523	-$68	$21	-$47	-20.1%	-8.2%
District of Columbia	$330	$146	$476	$420	$208	$628	$330	$235	$565	-$90	$27	-$63	-21.4%	-10.0%
Florida	$241	$173	$414	$303	$243	$546	$241	$262	$503	-$62	$19	-$43	-20.5%	-7.9%
Georgia	$235	$174	$409	$280	$250	$530	$235	$263	$498	-$45	$13	-$32	-16.1%	-6.0%
Hawaii	$565	$229	$794	$712	$333	$1,045	$565	$378	$943	-$147	$45	-$102	-20.6%	-9.8%
Idaho	$251	$170	$421	$317	$239	$556	$251	$259	$510	-$66	$20	-$46	-20.8%	-8.3%
Illinois	$268	$164	$432	$367	$224	$591	$268	$253	$521	-$99	$29	-$70	-27.0%	-11.8%
Indiana	$229	$176	$405	$288	$247	$535	$229	$265	$494	-$59	$18	-$41	-20.5%	-7.7%
Iowa	$361	$137	$498	$426	$206	$632	$361	$226	$587	-$65	$20	-$45	-15.3%	-7.1%
Kansas	$352	$139	$491	$429	$205	$634	$352	$228	$580	-$77	$23	-$54	-17.9%	-8.5%
Kentucky	$196	$186	$382	$228	$265	$493	$196	$275	$471	-$32	$10	-$22	-14.0%	-4.5%

TABLE 1. Effects of a Family Cap on Combined Monthly (January 1994) AFDC and Food Stamp Benefits for a Mother Who Bears a Second Child while Receiving AFDC, by State—Continued

| | Mother with one child | | | Mother with two children (Second child born while mother is on AFDC) | | | | | | Difference – Family Cap vs. AFDC | | | | |
| | | | | Current law | | | Family cap | | | Dollar difference | | | Percent difference | |
	AFDC	Food stamps	Total	AFDC	Food stamps	Total	AFDC	Food stamps	Total	AFDC	Food stamps	Total	Percent loss in AFDC	Percent loss combined benefits
Louisiana	$138	$203	$341	$190	$277	$467	$138	$292	$430	-$52	$15	-$37	-27.4%	-7.9%
Maine	$312	$151	$463	$418	$208	$626	$312	$240	$552	-$106	$32	-$74	-25.4%	-11.8%
Maryland	$286	$159	$445	$366	$224	$590	$286	$248	$534	-$80	$24	-$56	-21.9%	-9.5%
Massachusetts	$486	$99	$585	$579	$160	$739	$486	$188	$674	-$93	$28	-$65	-16.1%	-8.8%
Michigan -Washtenaw Co.	$401	$125	$526	$489	$187	$676	$401	$214	$615	-$88	$27	-$61	-18.0%	-9.0%
Michigan -Wayne Co.	$371	$134	$505	$459	$196	$655	$371	$223	$594	-$88	$27	-$61	-19.2%	-9.3%
Minnesota	$437	$114	$551	$532	$174	$706	$437	$203	$640	-$95	$29	-$66	-17.9%	-9.3%
Mississippi	$96	$206	$302	$120	$295	$415	$96	$295	$391	-$24	$0	-$24	-20.0%	-5.8%
Missouri	$234	$175	$409	$292	$246	$538	$234	$264	$498	-$58	$18	-$40	-19.9%	-7.4%
Montana	$318	$149	$467	$401	$214	$615	$318	$238	$556	-$83	$24	-$59	-20.7%	-9.6%
Nebraska	$293	$157	$450	$364	$225	$589	$293	$246	$539	-$71	$21	-$50	-19.5%	-8.5%
Nevada	$288	$158	$446	$348	$229	$577	$288	$247	$535	-$60	$18	-$42	-17.2%	-7.3%
New Hampshire	$481	$101	$582	$550	$169	$719	$481	$190	$671	-$69	$21	-$48	-12.5%	-6.7%
New Jersey	$322	$148	$470	$424	$207	$631	$322	$237	$559	-$102	$30	-$72	-24.1%	-11.4%
New Mexico	$283	$160	$443	$357	$227	$584	$283	$249	$532	-$74	$22	-$52	-20.7%	-8.9%
New York-New York City	$468	$104	$572	$577	$161	$738	$468	$193	$661	-$109	$32	-$77	-18.9%	-10.4%
New York-Suffolk Co.	$576	$72	$648	$703	$123	$826	$576	$161	$737	-$127	$38	-$89	-18.1%	-10.8%
North Carolina	$236	$174	$410	$272	$252	$524	$236	$263	$499	-$36	$11	-$25	-13.2%	-4.8%
North Dakota	$333	$145	$478	$409	$211	$620	$333	$234	$567	-$76	$23	-$53	-18.6%	-8.5%
Ohio	$279	$161	$440	$341	$232	$573	$279	$250	$529	-$62	$18	-$44	-18.2%	-7.7%

TABLE 1. Effects of a Family Cap on Combined Monthly (January 1994) AFDC and Food Stamp Benefits for a Mother Who Bears a Second Child while Receiving AFDC, by State—continued

| | Mother with one child | | | Mother with two children (Second child born while mother is on AFDC) | | | | | | Difference – Family Cap vs. AFDC | | | | |
| | | | | Current law | | | Family cap | | | Dollar difference | | | Percent difference | |
	AFDC	Food stamps	Total	AFDC	Food stamps	Total	AFDC	Food stamps	Total	AFDC	Food stamps	Total	Percent loss in AFDC	Percent loss combined benefits
Oklahoma	$251	$170	$421	$324	$237	$561	$251	$259	$510	-$73	$22	-$51	-22.5%	-9.1%
Oregon	$395	$126	$521	$460	$196	$656	$395	$215	$610	-$65	$19	-$46	-14.1%	-7.0%
Pennsylvania	$330	$146	$476	$421	$208	$629	$330	$235	$565	-$91	$27	-$64	-21.6%	-10.2%
Rhode Island	$449	$110	$559	$554	$168	$722	$449	$199	$648	-$105	$31	-$74	-19.0%	-10.2%
South Carolina	$159	$197	$356	$200	$274	$474	$159	$286	$445	-$41	$12	-$29	-20.5%	-6.1%
South Dakota	$368	$134	$502	$417	$209	$626	$368	$223	$591	-$49	$14	-$35	-11.8%	-5.6%
Tennessee	$142	$202	$344	$185	$278	$463	$142	$291	$433	-$43	$13	-$30	-23.2%	-6.5%
Texas	$158	$197	$355	$184	$279	$463	$158	$286	$444	-$26	$7	-$19	-14.1%	-4.1%
Utah	$332	$145	$477	$414	$210	$624	$332	$234	$566	-$82	$24	-$58	-19.8%	-9.3%
Vermont	$536	$84	$620	$638	$142	$780	$536	$173	$709	-$102	$31	-$71	-16.0%	-9.1%
Virginia	$294	$157	$451	$354	$228	$582	$294	$246	$540	-$60	$18	-$42	-16.9%	-7.2%
Washington	$440	$113	$553	$546	$170	$716	$440	$202	$642	-$106	$32	-$74	-19.4%	-10.3%
West Virginia	$201	$185	$386	$249	$259	$508	$201	$274	$475	-$48	$15	-$33	-19.3%	-6.5%
Wisconsin	$440	$113	$553	$517	$179	$696	$440	$202	$642	-$77	$23	-$54	-14.9%	-7.8%
Wyoming	$320	$149	$469	$360	$226	$586	$320	$238	$558	-$40	$12	-$28	-11.1%	-4.8%
Median	$303	$157	$457	$367	$225	$591	$303	$246	$546	-$73	$22	-$51	-19.3%	-8.4%
Minimum	$96	$72	$302	$120	$123	$415	$96	$161	$391	-$147	$0	-$102	-27.4%	-11.8%
Maximum	$821	$229	$912	$923	$333	$1,101	$821	$378	$1,029	-$24	$45	-$19	-11.1%	-4.1%

Source: Table prepared by the Congressional Research Service (CRS).

TABLE 2. Effects of a Family Cap on Combined Monthly (January 1994) AFDC and Food Stamp Benefits for a Mother with Two Children Who Bears an Additional Child while Receiving AFDC, by State

| | Mother with two children | | | Mother with three children (Third child born while mother is on AFDC) | | | | | | Difference – *Family Cap vs. AFDC* | | | | |
| | | | | Current law | | | Family cap | | | Dollar difference | | | Percent difference | |
	AFDC	Food stamps	Total	AFDC	Food stamps	Total	AFDC	Food stamps	Total	AFDC	Food stamps	Total	Percent loss in AFDC	Percent loss combined benefits
Alabama	$164	$285	$449	$194	$356	$550	$164	$365	$529	-$30	$9	-$21	-15.5%	-3.8%
Alaska	$923	$178	$1,101	$1,025	$251	$1,276	$923	$282	$1,205	-$102	$31	-$71	-10.0%	-5.6%
Arizona	$347	$230	$577	$418	$288	$706	$347	$310	$657	-$71	$22	-$49	-17.0%	-6.9%
Arkansas	$204	$273	$477	$247	$340	$587	$204	$353	$557	-$43	$13	-$30	-17.4%	-5.1%
California	$607	$152	$759	$723	$197	$920	$607	$232	$839	-$116	$35	-$81	-16.0%	-8.8%
Colorado	$356	$227	$583	$432	$284	$716	$356	$307	$663	-$76	$23	-$53	-17.6%	-7.4%
Connecticut	$680	$130	$810	$792	$176	$968	$680	$210	$890	-$112	$34	-$78	-14.1%	-8.1%
Delaware	$338	$232	$570	$407	$292	$699	$338	$312	$650	-$69	$20	-$49	-17.0%	-7.0%
District of Columbia	$420	$208	$628	$513	$260	$773	$420	$288	$708	-$93	$28	-$65	-18.1%	-8.4%
Florida	$303	$243	$546	$364	$305	$669	$303	$323	$626	-$61	$18	-$43	-16.8%	-6.4%
Georgia	$280	$250	$530	$330	$315	$645	$280	$330	$610	-$50	$15	-$35	-15.2%	-5.4%
Hawaii	$712	$333	$1,045	$859	$422	$1,281	$712	$466	$1,178	-$147	$44	-$103	-17.1%	-8.0%
Idaho	$317	$239	$556	$382	$299	$681	$317	$319	$636	-$65	$20	-$45	-17.0%	-6.6%
Illinois	$367	$224	$591	$414	$290	$704	$367	$304	$671	-$47	$14	-$33	-11.4%	-4.7%
Indiana	$288	$247	$535	$346	$310	$656	$288	$327	$615	-$58	$17	-$41	-16.8%	-6.3%
Iowa	$426	$206	$632	$495	$265	$760	$426	$286	$712	-$69	$21	-$48	-13.9%	-6.3%
Kansas	$429	$205	$634	$497	$265	$762	$429	$285	$714	-$68	$20	-$48	-13.7%	-6.3%
Kentucky	$228	$265	$493	$285	$328	$613	$228	$345	$573	-$57	$17	-$40	-20.0%	-6.5%

TABLE 2. Effects of a Family Cap on Combined Monthly (January 1994) AFDC and Food Stamp Benefits for a Mother with Two Children Who Bears an Additional Child while Receiving AFDC, by State—Continued

| | Mother with two children | | | Mother with three children (Third child born while mother is on AFDC) | | | | | | Difference — Family Cap vs. AFDC | | | | |
| | | | | Current law | | | Family cap | | | Dollar difference | | | Percent difference | |
	AFDC	Food stamps	Total	AFDC	Food stamps	Total	AFDC	Food stamps	Total	AFDC	Food stamps	Total	Percent loss in AFDC	Percent loss combined benefits
Louisiana	$190	$277	$467	$234	$344	$578	$190	$357	$547	-$44	$13	-$31	-18.8%	-5.4%
Maine	$418	$208	$626	$526	$256	$782	$418	$288	$706	-$108	$32	-$76	-20.5%	-9.7%
Maryland	$366	$224	$590	$441	$282	$723	$366	$304	$670	-$75	$22	-$53	-17.0%	-7.3%
Massachusetts	$579	$160	$739	$668	$213	$881	$579	$240	$819	-$89	$27	-$62	-13.3%	-7.0%
Michigan -Washtenaw Co.	$489	$187	$676	$593	$236	$829	$489	$267	$756	-$104	$31	-$73	-17.5%	-8.8%
Michigan -Wayne Co.	$459	$196	$655	$563	$245	$808	$459	$276	$735	-$104	$31	-$73	-18.5%	-9.0%
Minnesota	$532	$174	$706	$621	$228	$849	$532	$254	$786	-$89	$26	-$63	-14.3%	-7.4%
Mississippi	$120	$295	$415	$144	$371	$515	$120	$375	$495	-$24	$4	-$20	-16.7%	-3.9%
Missouri	$292	$246	$538	$342	$311	$653	$292	$326	$618	-$50	$15	-$35	-14.6%	-5.4%
Montana	$401	$214	$615	$484	$269	$753	$401	$294	$695	-$83	$25	-$58	-17.1%	-7.7%
Nebraska	$364	$225	$589	$435	$283	$718	$364	$305	$669	-$71	$22	-$49	-16.3%	-6.8%
Nevada	$348	$229	$577	$408	$291	$699	$348	$309	$657	-$60	$18	-$42	-14.7%	-6.0%
New Hampshire	$550	$169	$719	$613	$230	$843	$550	$249	$799	-$63	$19	-$44	-10.3%	-5.2%
New Jersey	$424	$207	$631	$488	$267	$755	$424	$287	$711	-$64	$20	-$44	-13.1%	-5.8%
New Mexico	$357	$227	$584	$431	$285	$716	$357	$307	$664	-$74	$22	-$52	-17.2%	-7.3%
New York -New York City	$577	$161	$738	$687	$208	$895	$577	$241	$818	-$110	$33	-$77	-16.0%	-8.6%
New York -Suffolk Co.	$703	$123	$826	$824	$167	$991	$703	$203	$906	-$121	$36	-$85	-14.7%	-8.6%
North Carolina	$272	$252	$524	$297	$325	$622	$272	$332	$604	-$25	$7	-$18	-8.4%	-2.9%
North Dakota	$409	$211	$620	$501	$264	$765	$409	$291	$700	-$92	$27	-$65	-18.4%	-8.5%
Ohio	$341	$232	$573	$421	$288	$709	$341	$312	$653	-$80	$24	-$56	-19.0%	-7.9%

TABLE 2. Effects of a Family Cap on Combined Monthly (January 1994) AFDC and Food Stamp Benefits for a Mother with Two Children Who Bears an Additional Child while Receiving AFDC, by State—Continued

| | Mother with two children | | | Mother with three children (Third child born while mother is on AFDC) | | | | | | Difference – Family Cap vs. AFDC | | | | |
| | | | | Current law | | | Family cap | | | Dollar difference | | | Percent difference | |
	AFDC	Food stamps	Total	AFDC	Food stamps	Total	AFDC	Food stamps	Total	AFDC	Food stamps	Total	Percent loss in AFDC	Percent loss combined benefits
Oklahoma	$324	$237	$561	$402	$293	$695	$324	$317	$641	-$78	$24	-$54	-19.4%	-7.8%
Oregon	$460	$196	$656	$565	$244	$809	$460	$276	$736	-$105	$32	-$73	-18.6%	-9.0%
Pennsylvania	$421	$208	$629	$514	$260	$774	$421	$288	$709	-$93	$28	-$65	-18.1%	-8.4%
Rhode Island	$554	$168	$722	$632	$224	$856	$554	$248	$802	-$78	$24	-$54	-12.3%	-6.3%
South Carolina	$200	$274	$474	$240	$342	$582	$200	$354	$554	-$40	$12	-$28	-16.7%	-4.8%
South Dakota	$417	$209	$626	$464	$275	$739	$417	$289	$706	-$47	$14	-$33	-10.1%	-4.5%
Tennessee	$185	$278	$463	$226	$346	$572	$185	$358	$543	-$41	$12	-$29	-18.1%	-5.1%
Texas	$184	$279	$463	$221	$348	$569	$184	$359	$543	-$37	$11	-$26	-16.7%	-4.6%
Utah	$414	$210	$624	$484	$269	$753	$414	$290	$704	-$70	$21	-$49	-14.5%	-6.5%
Vermont	$638	$142	$780	$717	$199	$916	$638	$222	$860	-$79	$23	-$56	-11.0%	-6.1%
Virginia	$354	$228	$582	$410	$291	$701	$354	$308	$662	-$56	$17	-$39	-13.7%	-5.6%
Washington	$546	$170	$716	$642	$221	$863	$546	$250	$796	-$96	$29	-$67	-15.0%	-7.8%
West Virginia	$249	$259	$508	$312	$320	$632	$249	$339	$588	-$63	$19	-$44	-20.2%	-7.0%
Wisconsin	$517	$179	$696	$617	$229	$846	$517	$259	$776	-$100	$30	-$70	-16.2%	-8.3%
Wyoming	$360	$226	$586	$390	$297	$687	$360	$306	$666	-$30	$9	-$21	-7.7%	-3.1%
Median	$367	$225	$591	$438	$284	$721	$367	$305	$671	-$71	$22	-$49	-16.5%	-6.6%
Minimum	$120	$123	$415	$144	$167	$515	$120	$203	$495	-$147	$4	-$103	-20.5%	-9.7%
Maximum	$923	$333	$1,101	$1,025	$422	$1,281	$923	$466	$1,205	-$24	$44	-$18	-7.7%	-2.9%

Source: Table prepared by the Congressional Research Service (CRS).

TABLE 3. Combined AFDC and Food Stamp Benefits as a Percent of Federal Poverty Guideline				
		Two children		Three children
		Second child born while mother is on AFDC		Third child born while mother is on AFDC
	One Child	Current law	Family cap	Current law	Family cap
Alabama	41.6%	43.7%	41.9%	44.6%	42.9%
Alaska	89.0%	85.8%	80.2%	82.8%	78.2%
Arizona	53.3%	56.2%	51.2%	57.2%	53.3%
Arkansas	43.7%	46.5%	43.5%	47.6%	45.2%
California	71.7%	73.9%	65.9%	74.6%	68.0%
Colorado	53.8%	56.8%	51.6%	58.1%	53.8%
Connecticut	76.7%	78.9%	69.9%	78.5%	72.2%
Delaware	52.9%	55.5%	50.9%	56.7%	52.7%
District of Columbia	58.0%	61.2%	55.0%	62.7%	57.4%
Florida	50.5%	53.2%	49.0%	54.2%	50.8%
Georgia	49.9%	51.6%	48.5%	52.3%	49.5%
Hawaii	84.2%	88.5%	79.9%	90.3%	83.1%
Idaho	51.3%	54.2%	49.7%	55.2%	51.6%
Illinois	52.7%	57.6%	50.7%	57.1%	54.4%
Indiana	49.4%	52.1%	48.1%	53.2%	49.9%
Iowa	60.7%	61.6%	57.2%	61.6%	57.7%
Kansas	59.9%	61.8%	56.5%	61.8%	57.9%
Kentucky	46.6%	48.0%	45.9%	49.7%	46.5%
Louisiana	41.6%	45.5%	41.9%	46.9%	44.4%
Maine	56.5%	61.0%	53.8%	63.4%	57.2%
Maryland	54.3%	57.5%	52.0%	58.6%	54.3%
Massachusetts	71.3%	72.0%	65.6%	71.4%	66.4%
Michigan (Washtenaw Co.)	64.1%	65.8%	59.9%	67.2%	61.3%
Michigan (Wayne Co.)	61.6%	63.8%	57.9%	65.5%	59.6%
Minnesota	67.2%	68.8%	62.3%	68.8%	63.7%
Mississippi	36.8%	40.4%	38.1%	41.8%	40.1%
Missouri	49.9%	52.4%	48.5%	52.9%	50.1%
Montana	57.0%	59.9%	54.2%	61.1%	56.4%
Nebraska	54.9%	57.4%	52.5%	58.2%	54.2%
Nevada	54.4%	56.2%	52.1%	56.7%	53.3%
New Hampshire	71.0%	70.0%	65.4%	68.4%	64.8%
New Jersey	57.3%	61.5%	54.4%	61.2%	57.6%
New Mexico	54.0%	56.9%	51.8%	58.1%	53.8%
New York (New York City)	69.8%	71.9%	64.4%	72.6%	66.3%
New York (Suffolk Co.)	79.0%	80.5%	71.8%	80.4%	73.5%
North Carolina	50.0%	51.0%	48.6%	50.4%	49.0%

See notes at end of table.

		Two children		Three children	
		Second child born while mother is on AFDC		Third child born while mother is on AFDC	
	One Child	Current law	Family cap	Current law	Family cap
TABLE 3. Combined AFDC and Food Stamp Benefits as a Percent of Federal Poverty Guideline--Continued					
North Dakota	58.3%	60.4%	55.2%	62.0%	56.8%
Ohio	53.7%	55.8%	51.5%	57.5%	52.9%
Oklahoma	51.3%	54.6%	49.7%	56.4%	52.0%
Oregon	63.5%	63.9%	59.4%	65.6%	59.7%
Pennsylvania	58.0%	61.3%	55.0%	62.8%	57.5%
Rhode Island	68.2%	70.3%	63.1%	69.4%	65.0%
South Carolina	43.4%	46.2%	43.3%	47.2%	44.9%
South Dakota	61.2%	61.0%	57.6%	59.9%	57.2%
Tennessee	42.0%	45.1%	42.2%	46.4%	44.0%
Texas	43.3%	45.1%	43.2%	46.1%	44.0%
Utah	58.2%	60.8%	55.1%	61.1%	57.1%
Vermont	75.6%	76.0%	69.1%	74.3%	69.7%
Virginia	55.0%	56.7%	52.6%	56.8%	53.7%
Washington	67.4%	69.7%	62.5%	70.0%	64.5%
West Virginia	47.1%	49.5%	46.3%	51.2%	47.7%
Wisconsin	67.4%	67.8%	62.5%	68.6%	62.9%
Wyoming	57.2%	57.1%	54.4%	55.7%	54.0%
Median	55.7%	57.5%	53.2%	58.4%	54.4%
Minimum	36.8%	40.4%	38.1%	41.8%	40.1%
Maximum	89.0%	88.5%	80.2%	90.3%	83.1%

NOTE: 1994 Federal poverty income guidelines in 1994 are:

. For a mother with one child: $9,840 in all States except Alaska ($12,300) and Hawaii ($11,320).
For a mother with two children: $12,320 in all States except Alaska ($15,400) and Hawaii ($14,170).
For a mother with three children: $14,800 in all States except Alaska ($18,500) and Hawaii ($17,020).

Source: Table prepared by the Congressional Research Service (CRS).

CHILD CARE: A COMPARISON OF WELFARE REFORM PROPOSALS[*]

Karen Spar

INTRODUCTION

Welfare reform has been a major focus of the 104th Congress, and child care has been a key component of the welfare reform debate. Congress has passed welfare reform legislation twice, as a component of omnibus budget reconciliation legislation (H.R. 2491) and as a free-standing bill (H.R. 4). Both of these bills were vetoed by President Clinton, who cited inadequate child care funding as one of his objections.

After the vetoes, the National Governors Association (NGA) recommended modifications to the congressional welfare reform package, including additional funding for child care. On May 22, identical welfare and Medicaid reform bills were introduced in the House and Senate, by Ways and Means Chairman Archer (H.R. 3507) and by Finance Chairman Roth (S. 1795). This new Republican initiative is based on the vetoed version of H.R. 4 but reflects some of the NGA recommendations, including the additional child care funding. On May 24, Senator Dole introduced S. 1823, which appears to contain identical welfare reform provisions to the

[*] Excerpted from *CRS Report* 96-511 EPW

Archer-Roth bill, but would not restructure Medicaid. In addition, a bipartisan group of House members, led by Representatives Tanner and Castle, introduced H.R. 3266 on April 17, which also reflects some of the NGA proposals but is not identical to the new Republican bill.

OVERALL CONTEXT OF WELFARE REFORM

The child care provisions described on the following pages should be analyzed in the larger context of welfare reform. Specifically, all of the pending proposals would eliminate Aid to Families with Dependent Children (AFDC) and create new cash assistance programs intended to limit duration of welfare receipt and move participants from welfare into work. Thus, these changes in cash welfare could affect the size of the population of low-income parents in need of child care assistance.

Both the republican and Administration bills would generally require parents to engage in some type of work or related activity after receiving cash assistance for a maximum of 2 years. The Administration would exempt certain categories of recipients from these work requirements, including parents of children under 1 (or 6 months at state option) or under 3 months in the case of a new baby born to a family already receiving benefits, or single parents unable to obtain child care assistance. The Republican bill would establish no federal exemptions, but would allow states to exempt single parents with children under age 1. In addition, the Republican bill would not penalize single parents with children under 6 if they refused to work because of a demonstrated inability to obtain child care.

Under current law, most AFDC parents whose youngest child is at least 3 (or 1, at state option) must participate in an education, work or training program, provided state resources permit. The law requires states to "guarantee" child care to those who need it to work or study. States also must guarantee child care for former AFDC recipients who are no longer eligible for cash benefits because of increased earnings, for up to 1 year after leaving AFDC.

While there are significant differences between the congressional and White House approaches to child care, there also are important similarities. All of the pending proposals attempt to streamline the four existing major child care programs into a single program at the state level. All of the proposals attempt to ensure that welfare recipients receive child care necessary to work or participate in school or training, while also providing substantial child care funding for low-income working families with no connection to the welfare system. The bills differ with regard to child care standards and regulation and earmarking of funds for quality and availability improvement. Overall funding levels and state matching requirements also differ.

Side-by-Side Comparison of Child Care Provisions

Item/Current Law	"Personal Responsibility and Work Opportunity Act" (H.R. 4 Conference Agreement, vetoed by President Clinton)	"Work First and Personal Responsibility Act" (Administration Draft Bill)	"Personal Responsibility and Work Opportunity Act (H.R. 3507/S. 1795/S. 1823)"[a]
Legislative Structure			
Three child care entitlement programs are permanently authorized under title IV-A of the Social Security Act, which also authorizes Aid to Families with Dependent Children (AFDC): (1) child care for AFDC recipients engaged in education, work, or training; (2) transitional child care for former AFDC recipients (up to 12 months after leaving welfare); and (3) child care for low-income families "at risk" of becoming welfare recipients. In addition, the Child Care and Development Block Grant (CCDBG) authorizes discretionary funds for child care for low-income working families. Authorization of appropriations for the CCDBG expired at the end of FY1995; however, the program continues to be funded in FY1996.	AFDC would be repealed and replaced with a Temporary Assistance for Needy Families (TANF) program, authorized under title IV-A of the Social Security Act. Capped entitlement funds for child care would be authorized through FY2002 under title IV-A. In addition, discretionary child care funds would be authorized through FY2002 under a revised CCDBG.	AFDC would be repealed and replaced with a Temporary Employment Assistance (TEA) program under title IV-A of the Social Security Act. Entitlement and discretionary funds for child care would be authorized through FY2002 under a revised CCDBG.	Same as H.R. 4.

[a]Unless otherwise noted, the child care provisions in H.R. 3266 (Castle-Tanner proposal) are the same as those described here.

Item/Current Law	"Personal Responsibility and Work Opportunity Act" (H.R. 4 Conference Agreement, vetoed by President Clinton)	"Work First and Personal Responsibility Act" (Administration Draft Bill)	"Personal Responsibility and Work Opportunity Act (H.R. 3507/S. 1795/S. 1823)"
Goals or Purpose			
No provision.	Five goals would be established: (1) to allow states maximum flexibility in developing child care programs and policies; (2) to promote parental choice; (3) to encourage states to provide consumer education information regarding child care: (4) to help states provide child care to parents trying to become independent of welfare; and (5) to help states implement health, safety, licensing and registration standards established in state regulations.	Three purposes would be established: (1) to eliminate program fragmentation and create a seamless child care system that allows continuity for children as parents move from welfare to work; (2) to provide for parental choice among high quality programs; and (3) to increase the availability of high quality affordable child care.	Same as H.R. 4.

Item/Current Law	"Personal Responsibility and Work Opportunity Act" (H.R. 4 Conference Agreement, vetoed by President Clinton)	"Work First and Personal Responsibility Act" (Administration Draft Bill)	"Personal Responsibility and Work Opportunity Act (H.R. 3507/S. 1795/S. 1823)"
Funding			
Open-ended entitlement funding is provided for child care for AFDC recipients and for transitional child care for former AFDC recipients. (The Congressional Budget Office estimates FY1996 spending for these programs at $770 million for AFDC child care, and $245 million for transitional child care.) Capped entitlement funding equal to $300 million per year is provided for "at-risk" child care. For the discretionary CCDBG, $935 million is appropriated in FY1996.	$9.85 billion in entitlement funds for child care would be provided under title IV-A during the 6-year period FY1997-FY2002. These entitlement funds would begin at $1.3 billion in FY1997 and rise to $2.05 billion in FY2002. In addition, $1 billion in discretionary funds would be authorized under the CCDBG for each year during FY1996-FY2002.	$12.2 billion in entitlement funds for child care would be provided during the 6-year period FY1997-FY2002. These entitlement funds would begin at $1.6 billion in FY1997 and rise to $2.5 billion in FY2002. In addition, the following discretionary funds would be authorized: $2 billion for FY1996 and such sums as necessary for FY1997-FY2002.	$13.9 billion in entitlement funds for child care would be provided under title IV-A during the 6-year period FY1997-FY2002. These entitlement funds would begin at $2 billion in FY1997 and rise to $2.7 billion in FY2002. In addition, $1 billion in discretionary funds would be authorized under the CCDBG for each year during FY1996-FY2002.

Item/Current Law	"Personal Responsibility and Work Opportunity Act" (H.R. 4 Conference Agreement, vetoed by President Clinton)	"Work First and Personal Responsibility Act" (Administration Draft Bill)	"Personal Responsibility and Work Opportunity Act (H.R. 3507/S. 1795/S. 1823)"
Allocations to States			
No formula applies to AFDC and transitional child care, which are funded on an open-ended entitlement basis. Allocations to states for "at-risk" child care are based on the state's population of children under age 13. State allocations under the CCDBG are determined by a formula based on states' relative population of low-income children under age 5, children receiving free or reduced-price school lunches, and state per capita income.	Of entitlement funds provided for child care under TANF, each state would first receive a "guaranteed" amount equal to its share of funds under the existing three AFDC-related child care programs in FY1994, or the average of FY1992-FY1994, whichever is greater. Remaining entitlement funds for child care would be allocated among states (subject to a nonfederal match) according to the current formula used for "at-risk" child care (population of children under age 13). Discretionary funds would be allocated to states according to the current CCDBG formula.	Entitlement funds would be allocated among states (subject to a nonfederal match) according to their percentage of funds under the three existing AFDC-related child care programs in FY1994. Discretionary funds would be allocated to states according to the current CCDBG formula.	Same as H.R. 4, except that each state's guaranteed amount would equal its share of funds under the existing three AFDC-related child care programs in FY1994 or 1995, or the average of FY1992-FY1994, whichever is greater.

Item/Current Law	"Personal Responsibility and Work Opportunity Act" (H.R. 4 Conference Agreement, vetoed by President Clinton)	"Work First and Personal Responsibility Act" (Administration Draft Bill)	"Personal Responsibility and Work Opportunity Act (H.R. 3507/S. 1795/S. 1823)"
Nonfederal Matching and Maintenance-of-Effort			
States must match their allocations under the three AFDC-related child care programs, at the matching rate used for Medicaid (which is inversely related to state per capita income). States may not use "at-risk" child care funds to supplant federal or state funds otherwise available for child care. States are not required to match CCDBG allotments. However, states may use their CCDBG allotments only to supplement, and not supplant, any federal, state or local funds otherwise available for child care.	States would not be required to match their allocations of "guaranteed" child care funds (see above). Entitlement funds remaining, after guaranteed allotments are made, would be payable to states subject to nonfederal matching at the Medicaid matching rate. States would have to maintain 100% of their FY1994 nonfederal expenditure level under AFDC-related child care programs, before receiving these remaining entitlement funds. (For states to receive their allotments for cash assistance under TANF, they would have to maintain at least 75% of nonfederal expenditures in the immediately preceding fiscal year for cash assistance and related activities, including child care.) No match would be required for discretionary CCDBG funds. The current law prohibition against supplantation of funds would be eliminated.	States would be required to match their entire allocation of entitlement funds, at the Medicaid matching rate. No match would be required for discretionary funds. The current CCDBG prohibition against supplantation of funds would continue to apply.	Same as H.R. 4.

Item/Current Law	"Personal Responsibility and Work Opportunity Act" (H.R. 4 Conference Agreement, vetoed by President Clinton)	"Work First and Personal Responsibility Act" (Administration Draft Bill)	"Personal Responsibility and Work Opportunity Act (H.R. 3507/S. 1795/S. 1823)"
Provisions for Indian Tribes			
No funds are specifically reserved for Indian tribes under the three AFDC child care programs. Under the CCDBG, 3% of appropriations are reserved for grants or contracts to Indian tribes or tribal organizations, pending the submission of applications and approval by the Secretary.	One percent of all funds provided for child care (entitlement and discretionary) would be set-aside for grants to Indian tribes and tribal organizations. In consultation with Indian tribes and tribal organizations, the Secretary would be required to develop minimum child care standards applicable to such tribes or organizations, in lieu of state licensing or regulatory requirements. In addition, the Secretary would be authorized to approve requests from Indian tribes or tribal organizations to use a portion of their funds for construction or renovation purposes, unless such use of funds would decrease the level of child care services provided.	Three percent of entitlement child care funds would be reserved for grants to Indian tribes and tribal organizations.	Same as H.R. 4.

Item/Current Law	"Personal Responsibility and Work Opportunity Act" (H.R. 4 Conference Agreement, vetoed by President Clinton)	"Work First and Personal Responsibility Act" (Administration Draft Bill)	"Personal Responsibility and Work Opportunity Act (H.R. 3507/S. 1795/S. 1823)[a]
Eligibility and Targeting			
States must guarantee child care for AFDC recipients who need such care in order to work, and for AFDC recipients engaged in state-approved education or training. States must guarantee transitional child care for former AFDC recipients who need such care to remain employed, for up to 12 months after becoming ineligible for AFDC benefits. States also may provide child care to low-income working families that are not receiving AFDC but who would be at risk of dependency in the absence of subsidized child care. Eligibility for child care funded by the CCDBG is limited to families with incomes no higher than 75% of state median, where the parents are working or attending school.	Of entitlement child care funds received by a state, no less than 70% must be used for services to families who are receiving cash assistance under TANF, or who are trying to transition off cash assistance through work activities, or who are working but at risk of becoming dependent on cash assistance. States would be required to demonstrate in their state plans how they are meeting the needs of such families. After complying with this 70% requirement, states would be required to use a substantial portion of their discretionary and remaining entitlement funds for services to low-income working families other than those described above. Eligibility for the CCDBG would be amended to 85% of state median income.	States would be required to guarantee child care for TEA recipients participating in state-approved education or training; TEA recipients who need child care in order to work, including in a community service job; or for families no longer receiving TEA because of increased earnings, for up to 12 months after last receiving TEA benefits. States would be required to use significant portions of their child care funds for the groups just described, plus families that are not current or former recipients of TEA and have annual incomes below 75% of the state median.	Same as H.R. 4.

Item/Current Law	"Personal Responsibility and Work Opportunity Act" (H.R. 4 Conference Agreement, vetoed by President Clinton)	"Work First and Personal Responsibility Act" (Administration Draft Bill)	"Personal Responsibility and Work Opportunity Act (H.R. 3507/S. 1795/S. 1823)"
State Administration			
A single state agency must administer or supervise administration of AFDC, including the related child care programs. Under the CCDBG, states must designate a lead agency to administer the program.	All child care funding, including entitlement funding, would be transferred to the lead agency under the CCDBG and spent according to the requirements and limitations of the CCDBG. States would be allowed to use no more than 3% of their total allotments (entitlement and discretionary) for administrative costs.	Same as current law under the CCDBG.	Same as H.R. 4, except that states would be allowed to use up to 5% of their total allotments for administrative costs.

Item/Current Law	"Personal Responsibility and Work Opportunity Act" (H.R. 4 Conference Agreement, vetoed by President Clinton)	"Work First and Personal Responsibility Act" (Administration Draft Bill)	"Personal Responsibility and Work Opportunity Act (H.R. 3507/S. 1795/S. 1823)"
Payment Rates and Sliding Fee Scales			
In calculating AFDC eligibility and benefit levels, states may disregard child care expenses up to specified limits. Under the AFDC-related child care programs, reimbursement for child care must equal the lesser of the actual cost of care or a statewide limit (which may be the child care disregard or a higher amount). Families receiving transitional and at-risk child care must contribute to the cost of care. Under the CCDBG, states must establish child care payment rates sufficient to ensure equal access for children receiving subsidies to comparable child care available to children who are not eligible for subsidies. States also must establish a sliding fee scale to enable cost sharing by families receiving subsidies under the CCDBG.	Current law provisions under CCDBG requiring payment rates that ensure equal access and sliding fee scales would apply.	Same as H.R. 4, except that sliding fee scales would apply only to working families that are no longer receiving cash assistance because of increased earnings, or who are not receiving cash assistance and whose income does not exceed 75% of state median.	Same as H.R. 4.

Item/Current Law	"Personal Responsibility and Work Opportunity Act" (H.R. 4 Conference Agreement, vetoed by President Clinton)	"Work First and Personal Responsibility Act" (Administration Draft Bill)	"Personal Responsibility and Work Opportunity Act (H.R. 3507/S. 1795/S. 1823)"
Standards and Regulation			
AFDC-related child care must meet applicable state and local standards. Under AFDC and transitional child care, states must ensure that center-based care is subject to state and local health and safety standards, including fire safety protections. States must try to develop guidelines for family day care. At-risk child care providers must be licensed, regulated, or registered with the state or locality (unless caring only for child relatives). Under CCDBG, providers must comply with applicable state and local licensing, regulatory, or registration requirements. Providers exempt from licensing or regulation must be registered with the state. States must assure that state or local health and safety requirements are in effect, which must include infectious disease prevention (including immunization), building and physical premises safety, and health and safety training.	States would be required to certify that they have child care licensing requirements in effect and to describe such requirements and their enforcement. This provision would not require that licensing requirements be applied to specific types of child care providers. The bill would retain the current CCDBG provision that requires states to ensure that providers receiving funds are in compliance with applicable state or local health and safety requirements.	Current law under the CCDBG would apply.	Same as H.R. 4. (NOTE: The Castle-Tanner proposal, H.R. 3266, would not delete the current CCDBG provision requiring states to assure that state or local health and safety requirements are in effect, including infectious disease prevention, building and physical premises safety, and health and safety training.)

Item/Current Law	"Personal Responsibility and Work Opportunity Act" (H.R. 4 Conference Agreement, vetoed by President Clinton)	"Work First and Personal Responsibility Act" (Administration Draft Bill)	"Personal Responsibility and Work Opportunity Act (H.R. 3507/S. 1795/S. 1823)[a]
Standards and Regulations—continued			
States must ensure that providers receiving CCDBG funds are in compliance with applicable state or local health and safety requirements. States that reduce their level of standards must inform the Secretary of Health and Human Services (HHS) of their rationale.			

Item/Current Law	"Personal Responsibility and Work Opportunity Act" (H.R. 4 Conference Agreement, vetoed by President Clinton)	"Work First and Personal Responsibility Act" (Administration Draft Bill)	"Personal Responsibility and Work Opportunity Act (H.R. 3507/S. 1795/S. 1823)"
Quality and Availability Improvement			
Under the CCDBG, states must reserve 25% of their allotments for activities to improve the quality of child care and to expand the availability of before- and after-school care and early childhood development services. Of these reserved funds, no less than 20% must be used for quality improvement activities such as resource and referral, assistance in meeting state and local standards, compliance monitoring, training, and improving compensation of child care staff. At least 75% of the reserved funds must be used to provide before- and after-school care and early childhood services.	States would be required to use no less than 3% of their total allotments (entitlement and discretionary funds) for activities designed to provide comprehensive consumer education to parents and the public, activities to increase parental choice, and activities to improve the quality and availability of child care, such as resource and referral services.	States would be required to reserve 10% of their allotments for activities to improve the quality of child care. Such activities would include those listed under current law, plus the following: before- and after-school activities, infant care, and child care during nontraditional work hours. In addition, HHS would establish a child care quality improvement incentive initiative to provide funds to states that demonstrate progress in innovative teacher training programs and enhanced child care quality standards and licensing and monitoring procedures. Of discretionary funds appropriated for the CCDBG, HHS would reserve $25 million annually for this initiative.	Same as H.R. 4. (NOTE: The Castle/Tanner proposal, H.R. 3266, would require states to certify that they would not implement any policies or practices that would significantly restrict parental choice. Further, H.R. 3266 would require states to certify that parents would be informed of their options under the program, including the option to receive a child care certificate or voucher.)

Item/Current Law	"Personal Responsibility and Work Opportunity Act" (H.R. 4 Conference Agreement, vetoed by President Clinton)	"Work First and Personal Responsibility Act" (Administration Draft Bill)	"Personal Responsibility and Work Opportunity Act (H.R. 3507/S. 1795/S. 1823)"
Reporting			
States must submit annual reports to HHS on their use of "at-risk" child care funds. States also must submit annual reports to HHS on their use of CCDBG funds, with data on the number of children served, types of child care programs and providers in the state, staff compensation, activities to promote business involvement in child care, the extent to which child care affordability and availability has increased, any relevant information on reviews of state licensing and regulatory requirements, and standards and health and safety requirements applicable to child care in the state. HHS must summarize and analyze these data in annual reports submitted to Congress.	States would be required to collect and report to HHS data on families receiving child care assistance, including family income; county of residence; gender, race and age of children; single-parent status; sources and amounts of family income; duration of benefit receipt; type of child care provided, including relative care; cost of child care; and average hours per week of child care. These data would be collected monthly and submitted to HHS quarterly: States also would submit reports every 6 months with aggregate data on number of child care providers funded; costs of child care and portion of such cost paid for with federal funds; number of payments made through vouchers, contracts, cash, or earnings disregard; consumer education information provided; and total number of children and families served. HHS would report on state data to Congress every 2 years.	Same as current law under CCDBG. States also would be required to specify the total amount spent by the state for guaranteed child care services for specified types of families, and to describe the types of child care provided, such as child care provided to families no longer eligible for cash assistance because of increased earnings or families that would be at risk of becoming eligible for cash assistance in the absence of subsidized child care.	Same as H.R. 4.

Item/Current Law	"Personal Responsibility and Work Opportunity Act" (H.R. 4 Conference Agreement, vetoed by President Clinton)	"Work First and Personal Responsibility Act" (Administration Draft Bill)	"Personal Responsibility and Work Opportunity Act (H.R. 3507/S. 1795/S. 1823)[a]
Repeals	The three AFDC-related child care programs would be repealed. In addition, the following would be repealed: child development associate scholarship assistance; state dependent care development grants; programs of national significance under title X of the Elementary and Secondary Education Act; and Native Hawaiian family-based education centers.	The three AFDC-related child care programs would be repealed. In addition, the following would be repealed: child development associate scholarship assistance; and state dependent care development grants.	Same as H.R. 4.

Item/Current Law	"Personal Responsibility and Work Opportunity Act" (H.R. 4 Conference Agreement, vetoed by President Clinton)	"Work First and Personal Responsibility Act" (Administration Draft Bill)	"Personal Responsibility and Work Opportunity Act (H.R. 3507/S. 1795/S. 1823)[a]
Related Provisions:			
Social Services Block Grants			
Social Services Block Grants to states are permanently authorized under title XX of the Social Security Act, as a capped entitlement. The permanent annual entitlement ceiling is $2.8 billion; however, this ceiling was reduced for FY1996 only to $2.38 billion.	Would reduce the SSBG entitlement ceiling to $2.52 billion for FY1996-FY2002. (NOTE: Appropriations legislation has already reduced the FY1996 ceiling to $2.38 billion.)	Would reduce the entitlement ceiling to $2.52 billion, beginning in FY1997. (NOTE: Would also reduce the FY1996 ceiling to $2.73 billion; however, appropriations legislation already has reduced the FY1996 ceiling to $2.38 billion.)	Would reduce the entitlement ceiling to $2.38 billion in FY1997, and to $2.24 in FY1998[b]-FY2002. (NOTE: Would maintain the FY1996 ceiling at $2.8 billion; however, appropriations legislation already has reduced the FY1996 ceiling to $2.38 billion.)
Transfer of Funds			
No provision.	Would allow states to transfer up to 30% of their allotments for TANF cash assistance, provided under title I of the bill, to one of three programs: the Child Care and Development Block Grant; the Social Services Block Grant; and the Child Protection Block Grant, including foster care and adoption assistance.	No provision.	Same as H.R. 4.

[a] The text of the legislation contains a typographical error, establishing two different ceiling amounts for FY1997. The bill is described here as it is intended, according to bill sponsors.

Subject Index

A

ABC, 157
Agriculture, 152
Aid to Families with Dependent
  Children, 1, 2, 3, 4, 9, 10, 11, 12, 13,
  14, 15, 16, 17, 18, 19, 20, 21, 45, 46,
  47, 49, 51, 53, 54, 58, 59, 60, 61, 62,
  63, 64, 65, 66, 67, 84, 86, 93, 94, 95,
  97, 98, 104, 105, 110, 111, 112, 113,
  116, 117, 120, 123, 124, 125, 126,
  127, 128, 129, 130, 131, 147, 148,
  149, 150, 151, 152, 153, 154, 155,
  156, 157, 158, 159, 160, 161, 162,
  172
Alabama, 3, 98, 105
Alaska, 2, 3, 9, 98, 110, 161, 162
America, 1, 2, 151, 154
Arizona, 3, 4, 10, 16, 17, 18, 20, 21,
  153, 157
Arkansas, 3, 4, 18, 20, 98, 105, 149,
  153, 160
Armed Forces, 49

B

benefit levels, 9, 20, 93, 94, 97, 98, 128,
  129, 130, 148

C

California, 3, 4, 9, 14, 16, 17, 18, 20, 21,
  110, 149, 150, 153, 159
cash aid, 1, 10, 11
cash grant, 1
child care, 2, 4, 11, 12, 13, 15, 19, 21,
  45, 61, 64, 66, 94, 97, 104, 105, 111,
116, 117, 120, 125, 126, 128, 130, 131,
  171, 172, 173
child support, 4, 21, 155, 157, 158, 159
childbearing, 148, 151, 154
Clinton, President William, 2, 3, 14, 77,
  85, 87, 90, 91, 126, 152, 154, 155,
  171
Colorado, 3, 4, 10, 12, 16, 18, 20, 110
*Colorado Personal Responsibility and
  Employment Program*, 12
community service jobs, 13
competition, 53, 66, 78
Congress, 1, 2, 10, 17, 20, 45, 46, 49,
  51, 78, 79, 80, 83, 84, 85, 87, 89, 90,
  93, 95, 98, 126, 127, 153, 154, 155,
  161, 171
Connecticut, 3, 4, 9, 10, 15, 16, 17, 18,
  98
consumption, 113

D

DHHS, 2, 3, 9, 10, 11, 14, 150, 151, 152
disabilities, 10
Disincentives, 123
District of Columbia, 2, 3, 9, 148, 161

E

Earned Income Tax Credit, 17, 94, 98,
  111, 113, 120, 126, 127, 128, 130
earnings, 5, 15, 16, 46, 57, 58, 59, 60,
  61, 62, 63, 65, 66, 67, 79, 92, 93, 94,
  98, 104, 105, 110, 111, 113, 116,
  117, 120, 123, 124, 125, 126, 127,
  128, 129, 130, 131, 132, 161, 172
economic growth, 56